Teachers of No-Thing & Nothing
Eating The "I" Parts II & III
William Patrick Patterson

Barbara Allen Patterson, Editor

Arete Communications, Publishers
Fairfax, California

Teachers of No-Thing & Nothing—
Eating The "I" Parts II & III
© 2020 by William Patrick Patterson

Design by WordPlay Consulting, Santa Rosa, California
korman@wp-consulting.com

Library of Congress Catalog Number: 2019935092
Patterson, William Patrick
Teachers of No-Thing & Nothing—
Eating the "I" Parts II & III
Includes photos, chronology, references, bibliography and index

1. Sunyata
2. Jean Klein
3. Lord Pentland
4. Advaita
5. Kashmir Shaivism
6. G. I. Gurdjieff
7. The Fourth Way

ISBN: 978-1-879514-30-0

First softcover edition 2020

This paper meets the requirements of ANSI/NISO Z39.48—1992 (Permanence of Paper for Printed Library Materials.)
All rights reserved under International and Pan-American Copyright Conventions. No part of this book may be reproduced or transmitted in any form or by any means, electronic or mechanical, including photocopying, recording, or any information storage or retrieval system, without prior permission in writing from the publisher.

Arete Communications LLC
773 Center Boulevard, #58
Fairfax, CA 94978-0058

Email: Arete@GurdjieffLegacy.Org
Website: www.GurdjieffLegacy.Org

Printed in Canada

Dedication

To my benefactors,

Sunya and Jean Klein,

and to my teacher,

Lord John Pentland

Other Works by the Author

Books

Eating The "I": A Direct Account of The Fourth Way— The Way of Transformation in Ordinary Life

Struggle of the Magicians: Exploring the Teacher-Student Relationship

Taking with the Left Hand: Enneagram Craze, People of the Bookmark & the Mouravieff 'Phenomenon'

Ladies of the Rope: Gurdjieff's Special Left Bank Women's Group

Voices in the Dark: Esoteric, Occult & Secular Voices in Nazi-Occupied Paris 1940–44

The Life & Teachings of Carlos Castaneda

Adi Da Samraj—Realized or/and Deluded?

Georgi Ivanovitch Gurdjieff: The Man, The Teaching, His Mission

Films

The Life & Significance of G. I. Gurdjieff
Vol. 1 Gurdjieff in Egypt 1872–1912
Vol. 2 Gurdjieff's Mission 1912–1924
Vol. 3 Gurdjieff's Legacy 1924–1949

Spiritual Pilgrimage: Mr. Gurdjieff's Father's Grave

Introduction to The Fourth Way
Vol. 1 From Selves to Individual Self to The Self
Vol. 2 The Movement from Sex to Love
Vol. 3 What Is the Meaning of Human Life on the Planet Earth?

Journal

The Gurdjieff Journal, est. 1992, now in its 80th edition

Contents

1980 "Nothing to teach, nothing to sell."   **3**
"The witness is a high state, but only a state." Sunyata, rare-born mystic. The music stopped. "A little death now and then is salutary." Jobless. Westward ho! Cheeke's interrogation. Kings do not hire former kings. Lord Pentland. Language of Silence. Don Hoyt. Betty Camhi. "Cut him up?" *Industry Week.* "One Great Round." "You sure you're not a drug addict, an alkie, or something?" Advaita. Mr. Nobody button. Crank's Ridge. "Nothing to teach, nothing to sell." The Roots of Consciousness. Bhagavan Sri Dollar. Sri Wuji. "This Sorensen is a hypocrite." Albert Bouwmeester. Rewrite of book. "This one's yours, Mabel."

1981 "We are always aware, Sunyata."   **35**
Mr. Gurdjieff's celebratory birthday. "Don't sit long where you shouldn't sit." No power or radiance. Lama Govinda and *I Ching*. Anger quick, big, mechanical. Gnostics, Aurobindo. Dr. Vasavada. The Prince and the frog. Lord Pentland and Sunya. Original invitation and Charles Fort's *The Book of the Damned*. Leaving the Work. Delightful uncertainty. *Neither This Nor That I Am*. History of Sunya's life. Tagore. *A Search in Secret India*. Ramana Maharshi—"We are always aware, Sunyata." Wu language bubbles up. Anandamayi. Lizelle Reymond. Sri Anirvan. *Psychology of Man's Possible Evolution*. Beethoven's last quartets.

1982 "You are tired of the phenomenal."   **66**
Nisargadatta's Dhyana Yoga. Black rabbit. "Mr. Gurdjieff called you." *Lord Have Mercy*. The Void Sisters. Nothingness. Maitreya. "I have come to God." Lunch with King Yama. Jean Klein—"You are tired of the phenomenal." Two paintings. Sunya moves in. "Eve and Adam." "So I contradict myself." Suffering is a choice. Taped darshan. Lama Govinda. *Pacific Sun* & Sunya. Alexandra, Queen of the Nile & Jesus Christ Incarnate. *Turiya*. Making new karma. Jean Klein's seminar. Sunya's Rolls Royce. Wuji Chauffeur Application.

1983   "My God. This is for *real*."   100
Rowena Pattee. Jean Klein—"All points to the Ultimate Subject." Tradition. The moment out of time. Lottie Rose. Isaac answers questions at darshan. Dream of Lord Pentland. Taped Wuti darshan. Rajneesh's disappearance. The body appears in Consciousness. *Hedda Gabler*. 2-3-1 or 3-2-1. *Innerstanding*. Shankara. Justin, an actor with a Devil mother and angel sister. "My God. This is for *real!*" Yoga with subtle body. Pure action, no time. Tradition is the living transmission of Reality. What is enlightenment? Spine ablaze. Mataji. Washing feet. Alan Watts Happening. John and Toni Lilly. Robin Wordsworth Carlsen. Albert's death letter.

1984   "Take me with you."   126
Taping Jean Klein's talks. Lord Pentland's passing. *Sword of the North*. Valhalla. Sri Wuji's Palace. Chicago letter. "Heatmare." Prince of Denmark. Shimmering light. "Take me with you." Justin—"I'm enlightened, too." Sunya hit by car. Sharon Burch. Coma. Justin threatens lawsuit. Technological crucifixion. Invisible Real. Silence is the ceremony. *The Serpent of Paradise*. "Teachers of Nothing." Jean Klein dialogue at Sri Wuji's Palace. "The 46 Commandments of Isaac Satori." Shakti's cardboard cutout of Sunya.

1985   "Absence is the greatest presence."   152
Mystery of Nature. Pungent atmosphere. Connor Barrett and Alfred. Michi, the medium. "Jacob." Unloved child. Connor's letters. Jung's home. Jean Klein in Paris. "Fuck you, Jean Klein." Café de la Paix. *Samarta*. Absence is the greatest presence. Spiritual wimpism. Advaita. Third degree initiate.

1986   The Subject-Object Relationship   166
Path of Self-knowledge. Lessening the subject-object relationship. The expanded body. Being behind. Patañjali. Knowledge. Mother moves to Pittsburgh. *Muladhara* opens. *Sri Wuji I & II*. Letters on Sunya. Indira Gandhi letter on Sunya's passing. Interview with Jean Klein. René Guénon and Tradition. Kashmir system. *Shakta* and *Shakti*. Sunya: Godhead is hermaphroditic. *Turiya*.

1987   Passing of Tradition   184
Buying Sri Wuji's Palace. Mt. Madonna seminar. Breathing. Dream of Jean and Lord Pentland. Mother moves to Petaluma. "You're selfish!"

1988 Geometric Understanding   188
All & Everything. Chess with Lord Pentland. *The Art of Asha.* A. Alekhine. Krishna Menon. "My Dear Pat." Paris again. Emma Edwards. Integrating senses. Healer. Yoga teacher. Spinal twist. Coccyx crack. Perpetuation of "I" concept. Editing *Who Am I? The Sacred Quest.* Geometric understanding. Blank state. "Don't take me for granted!" "Goodbye, you son-of-a-bitch."

1989 Huge Red Chinese Dragon   205
Wrongful Termination. Helen Palmer. Sir John Pentland. *Lord Have Mercy.* Ray Bradbury. Exploder. Leave *Industry Week.* Man in the attic. Editor, *Semiconductors Monthly.* Places on spine. "Quit your job." *Listening* published. Huge red Chinese dragon. On the street, again.

1990 Sunya's 100th Birthday   210
Cold calling. Mother moves in. Publish *Lord Have Mercy* or not? *To Live Within.* "Come to India." Sunya's 100th birthday. New Delhi. Snake charmer, begging, "shit trick." Varanasi. Burning bodies by the Ganges. Almora. Crank's Ridge. Sunya's hut. La Banda. Rishikesh. Ritual cleansing in Ganges. Greece. Jean's seminar at Delphi.

1991 *Eating The "I"*   221
Subject determines the object. Be the perceiving, not the perceiver. *Eating The "I"* born. Picasso. Self-publish. Testimonials. Miguel Serrano—"One of the more important writings." Lady Pentland—"Fresh breath of air for the Work." Jean Klein—"a panoramic vision." *Parabola* magazine—"Book not serious." Don Hoyt—"You've caught the essence of Lord Pentland." The idea for *Telos* born. First copy of book to Jean Klein.

1992 Consciousness-Without-Objects   226
Perception must be strong. Not two. Great Harmonizer. Unheard symphony. Unholy refuge. Health & Harmony Fair. Subject disappears. Consciousness-without-objects. "Don't become Shiva." "You still want experience."

1993 Thought Bullet   232
Open Secret. Thought bullet. Letter. Second letter. Book review: "Silence Was His Specialty." She "felt a resonance." Gurdjieff Study Group formed.

1994 Speaking Two Languages   235
Additional Study Groups form. Jean Klein seminar in Israel. "Unbelievable, unbelievable!" Mother passes. Speaking two languages, one the extension of the other. *ALL & Everything & No-Thing & Nothing* .

1995 Happy Birthday, The Jewish Law & Charles Fort   241
Jean's massive stroke. "Happy birthday." Final gathering. Sinning and contributing.

Appendices   243

Appreciation   265

Index   267

Bibliography   269

Acknowledgements   272

Foreword

I had died and didn't know it. I was still in the body, talking, acting like everyone else, but inside ... there was nothing. I went through paces but there was no one there. The past was too painful, the future I couldn't imagine. All my dreams exploded right in my face. All I had believed in, worked for, lived for — my whole world — all gone now. It was just another story. A slab of memory. I was one of the living dead, and too dead to know it.

That was how my first book, *Eating The "I": The Way of Transformation in Ordinary Life*, began. It was where I was before I entered Gurdjieff's teaching of The Fourth Way in 1970. Inexplicably, several years later my teacher, Lord Pentland, after I showed him an essay I wrote, said rather nonchalantly, "Someday you should write a book about the voluntary life."

I didn't take it seriously, but his words lived on and in 1979 I began to write a book about the death of my father and how the Work helped me to live that consciously and not in reaction. After many rewrites over the years, wishing and willing to get as close to the bone of the truth as possible, I changed the title from *Death of My Father* to *Lord Have Mercy* and finally *Eating The "I."*

Sunya, whom I had first met in 1980, called a "rare-born mystic" by Ramana Maharshi, told me in much the same way before he passed in 1984, "In eight or ten years you'll write a book about me." I wrote and published two editions of the *Sri Wuji* journal, but it has taken me until now to do so.

Before he "went Home," as he said, he introduced me to Jean Klein, a master of Advaita Vedanta, whom I continued to experience as he opened me to the Tradition in the pretext of yoga, meditation and direct impressions. I've added his teaching to this book which is really a continuation of *Eating The "I,"* so I added *Parts II & III*.

After so many years had gone by, I pondered whether I should write the book since though once blessed with a "Celtic memory," I had aged, endured five stents, diabetes, inflammation and a stroke. Much of the past had simply disappeared. But fortunately I had kept diaries of my time with Sunya and some of my time with Jean Klein.

Being a writer, I had written down what I thought to be important, and these helped in reliving these times. Beginning with when I first met Sunya aboard Alan Watts' houseboat, I could move through the years mostly in date form from the diaries just as they occurred. Many dreams were also written down as I felt they were message dreams and not the usual trash. Life is not a straight line. Its many jigs and jangles testing what is really our unconscious intent. Looking back now, the direction seems obvious but then

I lived and was lived in not-knowing and all the questioning and suffering that accompanies this.

Occasionally, rereading what was written at the time, it is seen that comments are called for. These are set in brackets, but all else is just as it was recorded. In mid-1986 diary-keeping stopped, but there remained troves of letters, remembrances and notes that could be drawn upon. I've also included some paintings that give a taste of the time.

This is my tenth and last book. The first, *Eating The "I"* published in 1992, now comes full circle with the completion in 2020 of *Teachers of No-Thing & Nothing*, a two-book memoir.

—William Patrick Patterson
San Anselmo, California

First painting, 1973

Man and Woman, 1974

Consorts of Cronus, 1975

The Petitioner, The End of Time, 11/1978

Taken to The Unknown, 5/1979

1980

"Nothing to teach, nothing to sell."

1 April 1980
  "The witness is a high state, but only a state," said the odd, androgynous, turbaned figure perched on a cot.
  I had been sitting in the back of the main cabin of the old houseboat and about to leave when he told me to sit closer, and when I did, he said, "The witness . . . ."
  I was here because of an ad in the local paper, the *Pacific Sun*:

Rare-Born Mystic, 90-Year-Old Sunyata Will Speak Aboard S.S. Vallejo, *Gate 5 Road, Sausalito, Tues., 7:30 P.M. Donation.*

Rare-Born Mystic, Sunyata—what did that mean? Had no idea. But I did know that the 103-year-old SS *Vallejo* was Alan Watts' old houseboat and years ago, in the late 1960s, Watts had given a talk in New York on meditation and it was the first time I had ever intentionally closed my eyes. It was my introduction to meditation. Watts had died years ago. I wanted to see the houseboat he had lived on.

The SS *Vallejo* was docked in Richardson Bay in Sausalito. It was listing in the water, its hull sunk in a sea of mud. I tramped up its gangplank and into the boat's main cabin. It was filled with flickering candles, heavy incense and a rather motley group of people, mostly young, sitting on chairs and cushions, and there on a cot in front of them was this strange slender figure dressed in a red turban, orange kurta and black slippers. Obviously he was Western, so why the Indian garb?

A slender, curly-haired fellow rose and gave his name as Bill Keeler from the Alan Watts Society. He said:

> Sunya Bhai took peasant birth in Denmark in 1890 and having little "headucation" was taken early on for a simpleton. But in India he met Ramana Maharshi who recognized him as a "rare-born mystic," an enlightened being who was born so. He has now settled here but says he has "Nothing to teach, nothing to sell." So congratulations on your good luck in being here.

With that, Keeler sat down and looked toward the enigmatic figure who, for what seemed a long time, either smiled or looked off into space. Finally, he spoke, the voice small, soft and whispery, a slight Scandinavian accent. It seemed to vibrate, but with so little force that it was hard to hear all of what he was saying.

The people looked to be mostly low-lifers to no-lifers, their questions the usual safe "spiritual" ones. This Sunya Bhai spoke simply, but didn't seem to stay on subject, often repeating himself. The words were nothing I hadn't heard before. I was about to leave when his eyes looked at me and he told me to move up and sit on the empty pillow in front of him in the first row. I moved closer and that's when he looked directly at me and spoke about the witness being a high state . . . .

"You've never said that before," someone said loudly.

He smiled impishly. "That's true," he admitted.

No one spoke.

Sunya Bhai giggled to himself and murmured, "States aren't real. They come and go. Only Being is real. *Tat Twam Asi*. Being, Consciousness, Grace. Not all these tantric tricks, ego-fuss and shakti-business."

For his first seven years he said he had no ego. He called it "pre-ego consciousness." Of course, ego was there but in a latent state, not active. He spoke of living in Silence. No duality. No becoming, only being. Later, ego-consciousness arose. A duality formed. "Both are coexisting and unclashing parts of the Whole," he said.

My heart pounding, the urge rising to speak, but I had no question. Words came finally and I told him, "I was in New York a long time. The music stopped. My energy left. I felt I should come out here. It didn't make any sense. Finally, I did. I had to give up a great deal. Now I don't know where I am. I've gone through a lot of suffering."

"A little death now and then," Sunya Bhai said softly, "is salutary."

Then he added, almost in a whisper, "Only a mature ego can surrender itself."

After a bit he continued, "The ego gets so large that one day"—he raises his hand above his head and, like a magician pulling a rabbit out of a hat, he pulls an imaginary something from the crown of his head, and says in a small voice—"*poof!*"

My first impression had been that he was just a harmless old coot on a cot who had some experience and believed he was a holy man and who now got dressed up in some Indian garb, but his saying "the witness was only a state" ... and now about death being salutary ... and surrender ... and *poof!* Well, who was he really?

Returning home, I tried to tell my wife about this Sunya Bhai but there were so many contradictions I finally just sighed and shook my head.

"Well," Barbara told me, "I think you should go back. It was good for you. You look so mellowed out."

Yes, I had been under a lot of pressure. Barbara and I had been in the Gurdjieff Work of self-transformation for nine years. My job as editor-in-chief of *Food Management* was no more. I'd been given a large severance package. I had wanted to go to California since college, so now I asked our teacher Lord Pentland about leaving the New York Foundation and joining the Foundation in San Francisco, which he regularly visited. In passing, he mentioned that "All great men spend a stint of time there." Odd comment. I wondered what he meant. Then he said he had an appointment and to call him later. Over the next days I called a number of times. He was never available, as he had always been before. Finally, it hit me—*he wants me to make the decision*. So I flew out to San Francisco, interviewed for a job, and got the promise of a position.

So on a bright day, August 24, 1979, our house rented, two cars packed up, the two kids in the blue Volkswagen Rabbit, and me in the driver's seat of the old yellow Hornet and there in the living room window holding Christmas lights in her hands was Barbara, tears streaming down her face—and just at that moment, like in a play, I hear the phone ring, Barbara puts down the lights, answers it, then raises the window telling me I have a phone call. It's from the company that had agreed to hire me.

"Sorry, there's been a hiring freeze," the company voice told me. "We're not hiring anyone now."

Good God! Nineteen years in New York, job, friends, house. We're leaving all that for California and no job? Should we stay, should we go? Are we crazy?

Barbara and I had entered the Work in 1970, me in January, she in April, and that October we married, and in 1973 had our first son, in 1975 our second. Over the years New York had lost its magic for me, and with Barbara born in California and my always thinking of living out there and knowing it would be better for the kids to grow up there.

Crazy or not, off we went. Barbara driving the Rabbit with John, 6, and Matthew, 4. I'm in the old Hornet with Thea, our calico cat. Crossing the Tappan Zee Bridge, heading West, Thea, her first time in a car, suddenly screeching like a banshee leapt onto my shoulder, digging her claws deep into my skin. Barbara had never driven a car more than fifty miles and here we were stopping in Pittsburgh, nine hours later, to see Marjorie, my older sister. She thought our plan was crazy.

Stopped in Boulder, stayed overnight with a friend, wakened to find the Hornet broken into, stripped of anything of value. Outside Lake Havasu City, Arizona, the heat 116 degrees, John collapsed with heat prostration and Matthew threw up. The next day just beyond Needles, halfway up the long slow rising hill into California, the Hornet dies. Needs a new radiator, hoses, the works. Next day, traveling at night to avoid the heat we make it.

Stop in Los Angeles to see Barbara's parents. Their faces say we're crazy, too, but no words. At dinner I sit beside her father who near the end puts a butter knife to my throat and says, laughing-but-meaning-it, "Better get a job!" Going north, we finally come to San Francisco and cross through the fog of the Golden Gate bridge and up to a long dark tunnel, its opening painted in bright circular rainbow colors, and into the sunshine of Marin County—we've made it! Now we drive up over the mountains to Stinson Beach to see the Pacific Ocean. We walk on the beach and splash water and return only to find that the roof of the Hornet which holds a spare tire is *empty*!

So there we are, September 16th, getting through all that, and now to get a job. I didn't think it would be a problem. I had a strong resume: advertising with two of the largest agencies, J. Walter Thompson and BBD&O, then IBM, then *In New York*, a consumer magazine for single people, the first of its type, selling it after several years, then on to Harcourt Brace Jovanovich to create a new trade magazine, *Food Management*, which became the leader in its field and won a number of awards.

I was so confident that I would get a job that I changed my mind and decided not to look for one until January. Instead, I began to write a book about my father's death which I had used the principles of the Work to guide me through. But then I remembered what Lord Pentland had told me soon after I entered the Work. I had given him one of my writings, *The Outlaw Christs*, and after reading it he said, "You're a serious writer." Later on, he casually mentioned, "Someday you might write a book about the voluntary life," so I decided to combine the two. I finished the first draft at the end of December and so only then began to look at where I was and only then began to realize that San Francisco was not New York City. There were only 135 magazines and a newspaper out here and that meant including San Jose. In New York at one building alone, the Harcourt Brace, we had half as many. I first tried to get a job with the local magazines, then the *San Francisco Chronicle*, then smaller papers, but nothing.

In January, at the first interview I had, a public relations outfit offered me a job as art director but I turned it down. I wanted to write for real. I had interviews with the *Berkeley Barb*, *The Daily Planet*—but no luck. Finally, at the end of February a major timber company, Potlatch, had an opening not for editing but public relations. The director, Holly Hutchins, and I hit it off immediately. The look-see interviews up the chain of command went well. The pay was even better than what I made in New York where I'd been the highest paid editor at Harcourt. My worries were over. Now just a last interview with G. M. Cheeke, the senior vice president. Holly warned me, "He's an ex-newspaper man and an intellectual. He's read just about everything. He tears people apart if he finds any discrepancies. So be sure you can back up anything you say."

I pressed the elevator button that would take me up to the top floor of the Embarcadero Center building that looked out on the pyramid of the TransAmerica building and much of San Francisco's business district.

Ushered into Cheeke's office, I saw a muscular, balding man, quite visceral, with hard challenging eyes who greeted me with a solid handshake. The initial talk was genial, he kidded a bit, then told me a little about the company. Then the grilling began, first going through my resume, then my personal life, finally he took a big inhale-exhale from his cigarette.

"Who are you reading?" he asked.

Tell him *Beelzebub's Tales to His Grandson* and I'm dead. I was reading Peter Hanke's *A Moment of True Feeling,* so I said that.

"Yeah—what's that about?"

"I'm just getting into it, but Hanke is pointing out that the feeling we have isn't true feeling. It's all conditioned, mechanical."

"What about Sartre," he asked.

Sartre was a communist. Cheeke was clever. "No, I'm more interested in Heidegger."

That was a new name to him. Cheeke didn't want to go there.

"What about best sellers?"

"Never read them." I answered too quickly.

"And why not?!"

"Too commercial, too mental." The words were out of my mouth before I could stop them. I wasn't there at all.

Cheeke ran off a list of books. I hadn't read any of them.

"Well, then—what *do* you read?"

"Jung," I told him.

"Oh, really . . . why is that?"

"His concepts of the anima and animus, archetypes and synchronicity—they're grids. You can see reality through them. Like scaffolding on an invisible building."

Cheeke crushed his cigarette in the ashtray.

That had killed it. I was probably a New Age liberal intellectual. Certainly no Republican or capitalist. As my manager at IBM once told me: "Yes, we want wild ducks, but ducks who fly in formation."

Cheeke's interrogation had knocked me out. I remember pressing "G" for the subterranean garage. But I'd forgotten what level I'd parked the Hornet on. I stumbled around level to level like a zombie. Finally, a Latino attendant took pity. He was like an angel.

I'd parked the car on B level, I'd been looking on C level. I drove out onto the street and only came to myself as the Hornet crossed the Golden Gate Bridge, a favorite of people wanting to jump.

[For the full interview, see Appendices, "Cheeke Interview."]

2 April 1980

Been here seven months sitting on orange crates in an apartment, buying day-old bread, eating peanut butter, getting only essentials at thrift stores, doing all that and still spending $1K a month. I was a witness with no future . . .

3 April 1980

Prime rate now at 20.5% and soaring. Finally, saw an ad for a job as a reporter on the local free paper, the *Pacific Sun*. I redid my resume and got an interview. Steve McNamara, the editor, takes one look at me and does all the talking, doesn't want to see my work, doesn't have a job, most people, he says, work freelance. I want to show him my work. "No, I don't have a job," he tells me "and don't want to get involved in all that." Then he lectures me about perseverance, pluck, etc. At that moment I realized the obvious: *Kings do not hire former kings.* No editor hires their potential replacement.

That very day I came home and heard John and Matthew in the garage laughing hysterically. I opened the door and saw them smashing the metal soldiers I'd been given as a kindergartner against the cement floor, knocking off their heads and arms, leaving only their bodies. My whole world died. It was only noon. I just went to bed.

5 April 1980

Notice arrived that this was the end of unemployment. Don't know what will happen now. Have tried all the obvious places of employment. Called Donna and asked if I could write some freelance for *Food Management* under another name. She agreed readily. What a blessing!

[Donna Boss was the assistant editor for *Food Management* and

I'd introduced her into the Work. She had refused to take my job unless I got the severance I wanted. Now she had become editor.]

7 April 1980
Barbara and I go to our weekly Gurdjieff meeting at "St. Elmo." [This is the Foundation's large house and grounds on St. Elmo Street in San Francisco.] Lord Pentland led the meeting. He opened with, "This time period is a new dawn after the dark tunnel of winter. The *Philokalia* fathers had said each time we awaken in the morning it is Easter. If we don't immediately know what we want, like Napoleon on holiday at Corsica, we spend our time plotting new crimes." Was he speaking to me?

8 April 1980
Darshans on Alan Watts' houseboat were on Tuesday nights and Gurdjieff meetings on Mondays, so I could attend both.
Found the same fifteen or so people, with Bill Keeler once again introducing Sunya Bhai as a simple gardener. Again, he is saying that in 1929 Sunya played Beethoven's last quartets on a gramophone by the River Dart for the world-renowned Indian poet Rabindranath Tagore who gave him a casual invitation to "come to India to teach Silence."
"Now look at that!" Sunya Bhai chuckles, bouncing a little on the cot, his long fingers fluttering like birds. "An utterly simple gardener fellow who had escaped 'headucation' asked to—come to India to teach Si-lence?!"
"Can you *teach* Silence?" Bill Keeler asks.
Sunya Bhai simply sits, deep stillness takes birth. Finally he says—
"You make me talk-talk-talk." He whispers to himself impishly, "I don't know what to do . . . and I don't care either."
He makes a mock face and shrugs his shoulders. "What can you do but play with words?" he asks.
"But Sunya Bhai . . ." someone says.
He responds, "It is not what I say but what *I am* . . . that sometimes gets across."

Again, the stillness, the space.

The tide has come in now. The houseboat rocks, the bay water slapping against its sides. The candlelight casts patterns of moving shadows on the walls and ceiling. Incense everywhere. Someone coughs. Another readjusts his chair. The stillness is making people tense.

"You are so mental here in the West," muses Sunya Bhai. "All the time thinking-thinking-thinking, wearing out the little brain. In India there is an intuitive language, the language of Silence, the language of Being."

Then he quotes from the Bhagavad Gita:
> Never the Spirit was born; the Spirit shall cease
> To be — never! Never was time it was not;
> Ends and beginnings are dreams!
> Birthless and deathless and changeless
> Remaineth the Spirit forever . . .

And with a big smile and nod to everyone Sunya Bhai gets up and leaves.

[When he writes this, he capitalizes the word *Spirit*. The *Harvard Classics* show it in lower case.]

9 April 1980

Barbara began working as a temp. She really wants to stay here. So do I, but money is running out.

13 April 1980

At the Sunday Work Day, Lord Pentland opened the day with, "Where is my place? We have lost our place. We are not even on the map. Between the two great forces of energy we will find ourselves."

He had us experience areas of the body, sensing and breathing into them, all coming together and then doing the circle exercise, and its elaboration.

"Now, just stay there in the middle between these two great forces, and you are awake."

"Nothing to teach, nothing to sell." 13

14 April 1980

Lord Pentland answered a question, saying, "You are not reborn, you have not even died yet. You are still within your own skin suffering." Sounds like he is talking to me.

There followed a reading from a Gurdjieff meeting in 1943. Gurdjieff says: "P is mad and when he is not mad he is insolent. When he comes to me and he is mad I give him everything because he is not responsible. But when he is insolent, if a policeman is not around, I will knock his teeth out of his mouth."

At this point, Lord Pentland had the reading stopped.

I wondered if he had read this with me, the "P," in mind. I do range now between mad and insolent.

[The meeting has just been published in *G. I. Gurdjieff Paris Meetings 1943* and the person referred to is not "P."]

15 April 1980

This night I had a dream with LP, Don Hoyt and myself. Don had a small mic in his left hand and the cord in the right. It reminded me of the way Frank Sinatra held it. I took the mic and showed him, accentuating the crooning posture. Everyone laughed.

LP then asked Don whether they should just give the patient a checkup or cut him up. Don wasn't sure. LP said, "Well, we already know he has a tumor." Don agreed.

LP asked if I had eaten anything. I said I had. "So be prepared to lose it. You'll throw it all up."

"Cut him up?" Don asked.

"How else can we get inside?" LP answered.

I woke up.

21 April 1980

Lord Pentland had left for New York. Don Hoyt, who was one of the first students in 1954 when Pentland opened the Foundation here, led the meeting. Hoyt said a few weeks ago someone had said they were unified, but it was only one center pretending to be so. He spoke about including resistance. The resistance was everything, all our unconscious habits—the whole ground of our being. The resistance is not an adversary.

22 April 1980
Sunya sat in a chair close to the cot where he usually sits. He was dressed in his usual red turban and kurta.

Bill Keeler opened with a question to Sunya about the guru.

Sunya said the concept of the guru was different in India. There every family had its guru, somewhat like having a family doctor.

He said he was prejudiced against tantra until he read Rajneesh's *I Am the Gate*. Now he is not. He is against kundalini as it leads to power and he who has power uses it. His friend Lama Govinda says, "It is like crossing electric wires."

A young girl asked about jealousy. Sunya said he couldn't answer because he had never been jealous. Later he talked about finding what is permanent, indestructible in the transitory nature of life, of not being ego-less but ego-free, not fearless but fear-free, not problem-less but problem-free.

His is a way of transcendence of the ego. The ego he feels is very much related to the ordinary mind. To transcend the ego, the ego has to die. To die you must surrender. Surrendering you can then be still. From one's stillness, one's wholeness, the Silence is entered—this aloneness leads to Oneness.

Sunya seems to stress stillness, silence, aloneness, a desire-free state of pure consciousness. It is a mystic path. It seems contrary to the Work or perhaps a transcendence of it.

Keeler said Sunya was making his annual journey to Chicago to speak to people there and would be back in six weeks or so.

And with a big smile and nod to everyone Sunya leaves the SS *Vallejo*.

Betty Camhi introduced herself to me. She said she had been in a Sufi group for ten years and then in 1978 met Sunya. She said she was Sunya's chauffeur and would drive him to homes and churches and bookstores. He was also very fond of coffee shops where she said "I spent many hours with him drinking up his wisdom." He wrote and received a lot of letters to which he needed to respond, so she also acted as his typist. On Friday evenings she would cook dinner and Sunya, who didn't live far away, often stopped by. Like Keeler, Betty congratulated me on my good luck on being here.

7 May 1980
   Saw an ad for a field reporter to cover Silicon Valley's hi-tech industry for *Industry Week*, a business magazine based in Cleveland. Something in me just knew I was going to get this job. If not, we're down to $3K and eating up $1K per month and we'll have to go back to New York. Fortunately, only rented our house so we'll have a place to live.

8 May 1980
   Sent resume and references for the field reporter job. They were all from presidents I either worked for or knew. Barbara thought I shouldn't do that, but I said it showed I could make top-level connections and were I hiring someone that's what I would look for.

12 May 1980
   At St. Elmo I spoke about the intractability of my mind, how I was defenseless in front of it, how it all seemed hopeless and that I was losing my belief. Hoyt reminded me that I had a very deep wish.

15 May 1980
   Met with Don Hoyt. He asked with a smile, "How's it going?" "I'm going crazy," I exclaimed, and went into what happened with Potlatch and Cheeke, the money problem, Barbara thinking this was Mecca out here, and me thinking of leaving.

16 May 1980
   I don't write poems but a poem came to me:

One Great Round

It's been a long time	But suddenly He showed
out of the sunshine	his Great Teaching—
standin' in the rain	How all things grow
I've seen the winds rise up	from the Ground
and the sun go down	How the rains, darkness
I've watched the dark clouds	and sunshine
comin' from all around	are really One Great Round
I've felt the sharp rains	Now I'm back in the sunshine
beatin' down	I hope I always remember the rain
knew they wouldn't let up	For I've known His mercy
Till they beat me right into	I've known His pain . . .
that Ground	Yes—That I wouldn't see
I prayed to my god—	His whole way—
It seemed a lie	His brightness, darkness
I thought then I was gonna die	and His Rain

27 May 1980

    Bob Gardiner, *Industry Week* managing editor, called. He said they wanted a reporter out here to cover hi-tech. A lot of questions. But his big question to me was—could I take orders?

29 May 1980

    Drove down to Burlingame, near the airport, where *Industry Week* has an advertising office, for an interview with the editor, Stan Modic.

    He was about my age, thinning hair, sharp eyes. No formalities. He looked at my resume, shook his head, in a low guttural belly voice says—

    "You sure you're not a drug addict, an alkie or something? You give up a top of the ladder job to come out to California and piss away your energy as a field reporter?"

    I told him I was looking for a better life for my family and me, and that "the music had stopped in New York, my energy had left."

    "But you know nothing about hi-tech," he said.

    I admitted I didn't know a thing about hi-tech but assured him

I would learn, as I had about food.

It's a painful conversation. Speaking to me he was doing something gut-level he thought he shouldn't do. The pauses were long, uncomfortable. I self-sensed, breathed, remembered, divided attention. Finally, he told me, "I'm hard-nosed Polack and don't take crap from anybody. You understand?"

I smiled and told him I understood.

2 June 1980

Phone rings. The low guttural voice.

"I've piddled around long enough," Modic says, "have to make a decision."

He's checked all my references, pauses, asks cryptically— "How much ya pay 'em?"

I laughed.

A long pause.

Finally— "Okay, you got the job, if you pass the physical." He said the last like I might have cancer or something.

"In six months," he continued, "there'll be a review."

The way he says it the words underneath are, "*If you last that long.*"

I was to be not a Field Reporter but a Regional Editor, work out of the Burlingame office. In good traffic it would be about an hour-and-a-half's drive away from our home in Corte Madera.

But, finally, a job!

Why had I come, really? There were of course many reasons, but in terms of the Work it was the unanswered question: what was the self in self-remembering? It was always alive in the background. Gurdjieff uses the word *self* three times in speaking about self-sensing, self-remembering and self-observations. He could have easily said sensing-remembering-observation. Everyone, he said, was an assemblage of "I"s with no real individual I. We say "I" to everything, like we were there, but it was only an "I" in quotation marks. Only with long and sincere work on oneself could one come to a "Work I," see one's rampant egotism, become a Witness and then an Individual I. Gurdjieff said the ancient, sacred, esoteric teaching he was introducing was "completely self-supporting"—that word *self* again. So his use of the word meant something definite, but what?

The day before we left New York a book from a top shelf of a bookstore fell into my hands. It was Shankara's *Crest-Jewel of Discrimination*, the primary text, as I later learned, of the ancient Hindu teaching of Advaita Vedanta, non-dualism. It holds that only the Self is real, all else is *maya*.

> I am That
> You are That
> All this is That
> That alone Is.

So here I am now with the Work and this Sunya Bhai.

3 June 1980

I'm essentially alone working at the *Industry Week* office, no one else but two salesmen, who are mostly gone, and a secretary. Everyone in Silicon Valley talks and writes in acronyms like EEPROM. Everyone assumes I know. But it's all gibberish to me. At lunchtime I just went out and laid on a bench and fell into a deep sleep. The pressure was too much. My ego is so big, overpowering, infantile. I am subject to moods, up and down in terms of energy. I have no more belief in "the ordinary world." I've seen how it operates. Power, sex, money, competition, revenge.

And yet it seems like I'm in a good place. The job is the best I could hope for out here. California itself is still a discovery. But where is all this leading, if anywhere?

10 June 1980

"Sunya" said Keeler, he drops the Bhai, "is now with us again," and he goes into his usual introduction.

Sunya says, "The Viking raid on the gangster city of Chicago where they now call me"—he pointed to a big blue badge on his kurta with the words—"*Mr. Nobody*."

Only a small core of the never-changing houseboat faces laughed.

"It's not words that matter," said Sunya. "It is the Silence

Sunya meets the Alan Watts Society at Crank's Ridge, Almora, India, November 1973

Sunya in his garden, Crank's Ridge

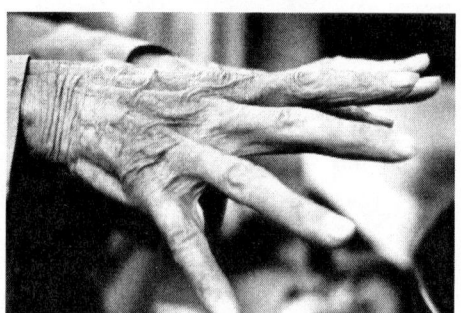
Sunya's hands

Sunya and Sri Wuji

Bill Keeler brings Sunya to America 1978

behind. And that is my specialty."

With that, we all sat with him for a half-hour before he began speaking. When question time came, he so often seemed to repeat himself or talk about nothing. Personal questions he often answered by talking about his own experiences, his large veined hands sometimes flowing in space as he talked.

"He can bore you to death," said one young woman smiling at me.

I agreed and yet it was like nothing I'd ever experienced in the Work or any place else. As I just settled in and stopped expecting and relaxed more, I felt the deep space of the silences.

Afterward, spoke to Bill Keeler and other members of the Alan Watts Society. They were quite open about Sunya and how he had come to California. Alan Watts had told them there were a lot of people who had become spiritually realized but weren't known, so Keeler and some others of the Society had gone to India in 1973 with the intent of finding these unknowns. Lama Govinda was giving a seminar at his home in Kalimat, a high ridge about three miles above Almora, which locals call "Crank's Ridge," so they went there.

In the town they met Professor M. D. Pant, formerly head of the Post Graduate Sanskrit Department in the Government College, and asked him to be their guide. Afterward, Professor Pant, who had known Sunya for more than twenty-five years, asked if they would like to meet "A rare-born mystic, who lives what so many of the Masters talk about." He then led them about a mile away on the hilltop of the ridge to Sunya's stone hut at Kasar Devi. Here they were greeted by a hedge with a sign saying SILENCE and below that SUNYATA. Speaking with Sunya, they were so captivated by his good and simple nature and emptiness, they invited him to visit America, but he told them he had "Nothing to teach, nothing to sell." Bob Shapiro, the group's leader, replied, "That's why we want you!"

When the group returned to America that November, they found that Alan Watts had passed on the very month they met Sunya. After more prompting, Sunya agreed to come and in late

1974 he flew to California for a four-month visit. Not long after he arrived, they booked the then 84-year-old mystic on Berkeley radio station KPFA's show "The Roots of ∂∂." There he sat surrounded by lights and mics along with a 72-year-old lifelong disciple of Rudolph Steiner's Anthroposophy teaching, and a moderator who noticed and commented upon the difference in the quality of vibrations between the two. The vibrations he had felt many times, but Sunya's seemed of an entirely different nature. There was the consciousness inherent in the I Am presence of a developed Individual I, and then there was the I Am of Sunya's unitive awareness, which is beyond the individual I. At one point, Sunya told him, "There's a little ego left but not enough to be any trouble." Later in the radio interview, Sunya spoke of the difference between "Nothingness" that the Steiner disciple spoke of and "No-thingness." This sent the disciple into a coughing fit.

Afterward, the Society had Sunya travel to Esalen, Claremont College, Palm Springs, Chicago, Buffalo and New York giving informal talks and answering questions about his Crank's Ridge life and Himalayan culture. The expectation was that he would take up where Alan Watts left off. But Sunya displayed no stunning intellect, great powers, *Shakti* radiance, or charisma. He did not talk to the ego. Or cultivate it. It was a very dry run. Few recognized Sunya's full, solid emptiness, a silence of desire, willfulness and ego-antics. As perplexed as the Society was, Sunya felt that "California is where a new intuitive, silent race is being born. And Silence is my specialty."

When he returned to Almora and his hilltop hut, Sunya wrote of his experience, but in the third person:

> In the year of Grace, 1974, Sunyaji let Him Self be kidnapped from Himalayan Crank's Ridge life to the terribly externalized Yankeestan realm of technical and scientific perfection and there to hobnob with Bhagavan Sri Dollar and the pleasure and power-oriented rhythm, the affluent food-fuss, body cult, emotional and mental sex-play, the terrible conditioning by the press, radio and

tele-vision. Within a few weeks of arrival, he was pushed up to broadcast his Himalayan consciousness to the world from Berkeley. It was an utterly new experience for him: new surrounds, new personalities and new scientific and mechanical gadgets—and noises around him, but he was not nervous, tense or bewildered by questions from the consciousness, values and views of completely strange fellow way-farers. The silent sadhu had to perform and he did respond and relate spontaneously and simply.

It was a broadcast dealing with consciousness and Enlightenment. One question Sunyaji did not try to elucidate or explain fully was: "Is ego not necessary?" His answer was brief: "Yes, it is necessary." He could have said the illusion is, and is due in *Swa Lila*: "Yes, Sin is behovely"—in the Life play—in our quest for Enlightenment, Salvation, for awakening into—Grace awareness. Elaboration was expected, but was not forthcoming as there was no clarity to comment briefly on radio to strange people. Did they have the same vocabulary, values and meaning of such word symbols—as ego, sin, God, Self, Mind, Reality, goal and Grace?

We are all unaware—unconscious, blinkered in the sin of ego. Ego-oblivion is Self awareness. But the ego-sin is behovely, is necessary, in *Swa Lila*. Without it there would be no awareness of division or of bondage and no urge to regain or re-aware consciousness and from the dream which egojies call life. The "Fall" is due and happens in each individual consciousness—and in maturity, there is transcendence of ego and duality-consciousness. Egoji dis-integrates into the undivided, indivisible—individuum, what some doctors of dis-eased, ailing psyches call individuation. Our Pilgrimage is a Homeward journey, a re-awakening into Self-awareness.

But there had also been many changes building up for years on Crank's Ridge and these were quite different from what he had been accustomed to. At one point, he wrote:

> Here on the silent—Himalayan Ridge-Crest we are completely away from the Hectic—western-conditioned—Shakti-business and no aggressive or lusty human noises but here there has been excessive focusing on the dis-eased hippie-cult and its destructive or negative Shakti-business, power-antics and ego-lust, because it is so near upon us in the former sanctuaries. This hedge-boundary may give a certain privacy, but did not prevent the noises and the stink to penetrate.

The English author of books on Tantra and sexual secrets, Nik Douglas and his companion Penny Slinger, had found the Ridge and in time their cult of followers arrived. Sunya they saw as a weird phony. When Sunya passed by walking down to Almora, Douglas would scowl and once even spat in his face and thought to give Sri Wuji the poisoned meat he died from.

Sunya wrote of this in his *A Wuji Biography*:

> Recently Sri Wuji has been subjected to a kind of asuric attack from a western-conditioned Hippie Head, who is allied with Naga Mahant, tantric tricks and black magic against our Ridge-Harmony, and also allied with the mighty Bhagavan Sri Dollar! Wu! However His Wholeness and Sri Essence seem to be immune to the assaults, so the missiles may 'return to sender,' like a faulty addressed letter. If God did not have the Devil as a play-mate, there would be no play, no *Swa Lila*, says Wuji, and if He did not exist as our play-mate, he would also have to be invented. It is by contrasts and differences that we appreciate God, Grace or Self and Be more consciously aware of Reality. Wu!

With all this going on months and then years passed and Sunya received a number of letters from the Watts Society but no direct invitation. Finally, Sunya wrote to them—"It's now or never." So in late March 1978 the Society had Sunya return to California, settling in Mill Valley in Marin County near Watts' houseboat where he would give weekly darshans.

He had a friend, Dr. Aggarwal, "Bhaiji," he called him, in New Delhi to whom he wrote many letters. Sunya writes:

14 October 1978

We are reading Franklin Merrell-Wolff's *The Philosophy of Consciousness Without an Object*. The first half describing his experience of time and his aphorisms are good. But the intellectual explanation of them in the second half we skipped lightly. Why all these explanations of the ineffable Experiencing, the non-dual flight in inner space or rest in the Plenum Void, the radiance in the full, solid, concrete Emptiness?... John Blofeld has left for Bangkok. He is charmingly English and delightful as is his autobiography, *The Wheel of Life*. But even when he spoke of microcosm and stated that "Everything is within ourselves," he pointed at his head, not his heart and his Wholeness. He had been Headucated. Wu! Perhaps we have told you that the return ticket has expired, given up its valid ghost. So we are here illegally. Money-free. Time-free and Care-free and will be pushed again into Himalayan cave man's life when Shunya Silence and Wu-antics cease to radiate and be sellable. Wu!

28 March 1979

Last Monday evening we went to have a near darshan of His Holiness Bhagavan Muktananda. He has been here for several months in big business. Each evening apparently thousands of Yankee guys and girlies stand in line and file by his lotus feet two abreast, bow low or kneel, offer their gifts and get a bash of peacock feathers. (Perhaps the plunge was beyond thought.) Now it seems that the West eagerly prostrate to the East in the form of Yogis. Gurus and Himalayan Holiness (or rather bow up to them). So Shunyaji also Namaskared the Holiness. (We are equal to the lowest, says Wuji) and lo behold! It remembered the Viking Body from Delhi and said so. Perhaps it was our radiant blue turban! for later on it got us double blessing. We squatted by a gangway and in the darkened hall people were passing and suddenly the head felt a hand pressing upon it! Only afterwards we were told that it was He. The Bhagavan holiness! We felt no electric shock or power-transmission. But we have written Him a nice letter of appreciation. Really we have a much better impression of Muktananda then in Delhi. No radiance. But there he was smiling, lively, joking and quite human.

1 August 1980

Today I finally understood what EEPROM was — *electrically erasable programmable read-only memory*. Good gawd! I'm on my way into this techie world.

13 August 1980

At Sunya's darshan Joseph appeared, white hair, beard, with a long, colorful, striped robe. Did we know what happened in 1967? he asked. That was when he left his body, "my space suit," and went beyond time and space. He was resting on his thighs, licking each of his fingers one after the other, as he told his story. He seemed to have traveled extensively in India, knew all the spiritual gossip. "Who am I?" he asked. "I am Joseph — there's only one Joseph." Then he added, "You know, in history, once you are someone once, that's who you always are." Ahh, yes, Joseph and his brothers. Am I going crazy?

Finally, I asked Keeler if I could see Sunya personally.

30 August 1980

Went to the house at 43 Woodside Lane on a hill above Mill Valley. The Watts Society had rented the upstairs floor for him. Outside his bedroom and bathroom there was an outer back room whose window ran along the whole room giving great views of the valley below and rolling hillsides in the distance. An old wrought iron bird cage, empty, stood in one corner. The window sills were lined with greeting cards, postcards and pictures from Sunya's friends. On one wall there were photos of Ramana Maharshi and Nisargadatta, along with one of himself, and a small crystal that could fit in the palm of a hand. Books, his writings, typed sheets of paper were everywhere. Plants, too, on the floor, in a plant stand.

We talked for a bit, him in a white wicker couch next to the window, me in a white wicker chair opposite him. "Your throne," he told me.

I asked about the crystal.

"It's a symbol of sunyata," he told me, "full, solid, emptiness, the plenum void." [See Appendices, "The Plenum Void."]

I noticed on the floor a tape recorder. He said he would read his favorite poems into it and what "gushed up" in him.

He handed me a poem, *The Man of Tao* by Chung Tzu, which Thomas Merton had translated. It was a long poem which began:

> "The man in whom Tao
> Acts without impediment
> Harms no other being
> By his actions..."

And it ends with...

> "The man of Tao
> Remains unknown.
> Perfect virtue
> Produces nothing.
> 'No-Self'
> is Time-Self
> And the greatest man
> Is Nobody."

Sunya asked if I had ever read Merton's *The Seven Story Mountain*?

I had started, I said, but did not finish it as I had known what he would come to and I was put off by Catholicism.

"What religion are you?"

I told him I supposed I was Presbyterian.

"As a youngster," I said, "my mother made me go to Sunday

School. One Sunday I was given a passage from the Bible to read to the whole Sunday Worship. It made people cry. I felt nothing myself, felt like a hypocrite, and never went back."

"Someone was reading through you," he said with a smile. "Did that ever happen afterward?"

I didn't know, but I told him about everything I felt to be of any worth in my life: the acid trip where I felt I had died, the experience of a rebirth, discovering the Work, Lord Pentland, the inner sound, the heat sometimes in the spine.

He made no response.

So I found myself telling him about how my father had paid little attention to me as a boy and so I saw now I had unconsciously been in search of a father and yet my independence made me something of a father to others.

He said—sort of scoffed—"Why couldn't you let the Void be your father?"

He gave me some of his writings to read. He mentioned the word "Wu" which in Japanese meant both "yes" and "no."

"My inner guru," he told me, "is named 'Wuji—Sri Wuji.'" He had a dog by that name in India but it had died.

I am a reader and so is he obviously, as the place was filled with books. As I looked through them, he told me he had known Sri Krishna Prem.

I found myself asking him to go to lunch and, not knowing where to take him, took him home where Barbara prepared a beautiful meal for him.

When I took him back to Mill Valley he lent me a copy of Prem's *Initiation into Yoga*.

2 September 1980

At the darshan, he talked about the inner guru.

I asked about Satan being the false inner guru and the temptations. It seemed to startle him. He wiped it away saying it was all part of duality. Afterward, it seemed as if he wanted me to come up and talk to him, but I didn't.

Who is he really? Is he what he purports to be—enlightened—or some quiet fanatic who bought into the idea of Oneness? Why does he so often repeat the same things over and over, tell his life story again and again, and why does he exude no great light or power? Is he living on a realm so high that it is beyond all this—or hasn't he reached it?

But soon, every Saturday, I would go to his home and take him to lunch. Once we went to a restaurant in Mill Valley set up against a hillside so when you left you had to turn right, toward the street, otherwise you would walk into the hill. We leave, go outside after lunch and he turns to the left! He says he is always aware but can rarely remember the restaurants we've been to many times. But I really liked being with him and hearing his stories, even if they were the same stories, same words, same tempos. I kept wondering what it was all about, whether I was wasting my time.

My relationship with Sunya was developing. Felt very good when I left him, a real warmth.

11 October 1980

Sunya gave me a letter from Sri Anirvan, the Bengali guru. He had lived for a time at Crank's Ridge and they had become friends.

> My Own Sunyata,
> Why do you address me as Swamiji? Am I a Swami, a grabbing possessor or a tyrannous over-lord—whatever that odious term may mean? For some years I had to bear with it, because I found myself free, I dropped it, as a tadpole drops its tail. Now this is simply Anirvan, the quenchless fire, born of the travail of the Earth and leaping every moment into the sky and losing itself in Sunyata. So it is a Brother calling to a Brother, losing anirvan-fire, losing itself into the Void of Sunyata.
>
> How androcentric or ego-centric our ideas are, instead of being theo-centric or self-centric. We put so much stress upon our doing something—(of some body!), our hurrying to some goal or bustling along like busy-bodies without for a moment awaring, that we are being driven all along

by a secret stream working within and behind all. The only thing that matters is to recognize the drive, the push or pull, and force [here Sunya writes, "free??"] the joyous sweep of the mighty stream. We are being used—led and guided, so surely and need not entertain the blinkered, or blin ding conceit of agency. Neither fear nor choice are real—if we awarely innerstand. Wu!

You remind me of a splendid line of Shankara's describing the free souls as "*Vasantavat Lokhitam Chorante.*" They wander about doing good to the world by being what they are, just like the spring coming after a dreary winter. A fine imagery! The spring in our Being comes not with an éclat, but softly, silently, breathing life into the seeming dead, warmth into the cold, making the seeds sprout. The bare trees put forth leaves and blooms, bringing gladness to the heart of all. It is just like the advent of the Spirit: Somehow the purpose of Creation seems to be silently fulfilled in one, and one becomes the promise of a new dawn without even knowing about it, far less talking or lecturing about it. What happens, happens quite naturally without trying or power-display, and it is the total scheme of things, if you innerstand it—that way. "Ye are the Tao." Wu! or the Tao Is!

[There is no signature.]

Sunya gave me another letter he had just written to Mrs. Boshi Sen in India:

Our Lama has given us the recent news of you. When you gave the name of Crank's Ridge to that holy-crest, some of us naturally took it as a compliment: There are ball-bearing cranks that help the wheels of Life—in the *Swadharmic* play, *Swa Lila*, to move softly and silently; but perhaps that was not your meaning of the epithet?—

We do not know what we do, or are, so we may be forgiven, says Wuji. We awared that you did not favor 'that Sorensen' among the cranks, but we were unaware that you, during these 40 years *and still this year*, felt, said and asserted "This Sorensen is a hypocrite, pretender, parasite — disguised as a woman in fancy dress." We naively felt that your mind had mellowed — to accept our Wuness.

He then invites her to his "Sunya darshan" on the 27th of October 1990, along, he says, with Margrethe, Queen of the Danes, Empress of India, Lila of Greece, Prince Peter and others. [Later he included Lottie Rose and Betty Camhi.] "Yes," he says, "he is very patronizing, elective and selective: He invites You too—. Wu!"

Other letters were from Albert Bouwmeester, a young Belgian who had worked at a leper colony, spent time at Rajneesh's ashram, and lived with Sunya for a year or so. One letter he wrote to a friend about Sunya, which he had copied and sent to Sunya.

Sunya was very much at home everywhere, and it was a delight to observe and share his cavorting skills: the playful, the unexpected, the gratuitous, the unawares awaring, the serene serendipity. Though so much younger than him, I simply could not keep pace with him as he went quantum-jumping as a mountain goat up the Himalayan slopes through the forest to barely discernible footpaths. So much quicksilver-awareness gave him a very nervous nature. He was very much alive, mischievous lights sparkling from his eyes, fussing about, relativating himself, the universe, every mood, every concept. Being alone, he was everywhere as Wuji (Wu meaning beyond 'Yes' and 'No' and ji meaning reverend) and egoji, playfully interacting along the spectrum, splitting, love-playing, always serenely amazed.

It was there in the eyes of his Tibetan mongrel-doggy whom he named Sri Chow Chu Wuji, Sri Wuji for short, as it was looking at Sunya, this incredible depth of space, this silence, this endless falling/sinking into ego-oblivion, "falling in love." Sri Wuji would remind through cascading inner dialogue that "Ego-Oblivion equals Self-awareness."

Let it not be said that Sunya did not love his egoji. He

did. And how many of us can say that? Sri Wuji brought him home, he accepted himself, loved himself, redeemed himself. That is quite a silent explosion; what remained was nothing but play, play, play. Sunya's halo was mostly askew.

12 October 1980

Spoke with my mother today. She is 79 years old. She has been living alone since my father died in 1978. She's amazing. She was a chain smoker but gave it up, knowing it was too dangerous to smoke and live alone. Other than the fellow who delivers the groceries once a week and telephone calls and infrequent visits from my sister, Marjorie, and me, she has no one. She is finally thinking of putting the house up for sale and moving to Pittsburgh to be near my sister.

Last week began a rewrite of the book. *Lord Have Mercy*. I'd finished a first draft last December and when writing the last scene I became aware that the body had tensed and wanted to cry—so I let it cry, all the tears pouring out and all the time just watching. It had felt disloyal in some way, like I was betraying something.

I remembered telling Don Hoyt about this and he told me, "You've reached a milestone in the Work, something that only comes after having made many, many efforts."

I realized that this inner separation between body and mind had also happened with my father's death, which was why I initially wanted to write a book about how my practice of the Work had allowed me to act as I did.

17 October 1980

They're dead at *Industry Week* in Cleveland. I wonder how long I'll be able to hold this job. Ordinary people don't like creative people because they work for their muse, not the money. To be creative is to be a rebel. The rebel is either eaten by the father—the prevailing ideas—or the mother—the caretakers, believers in the ideas. Or he eats *them*.

Colin Wilson speaks about the rebel in his book *The Outsider* who either falls victim to drugs or alcohol, or creates his own world.

"Nothing to teach, nothing to sell." 33

18 October 1980

Finished the nude snake woman painting. She'd come to me in a dream, arms outstretched coming to the sides of her head, a white snake on one arm, a black snake on the other. She was standing on a chess board. In painting it, instead of standing on a chess board, I envisioned her coming out of the crown of my head and standing atop it. A moon was on her left side, Venus on her right. Hovering behind her was a bright red glow of a large red heart. I called it *Glory to God*. It was good, but painting isn't a possibility for earning money.

26 October 1980

At St. Elmo LP had us really come to ourselves in the sitting and then put all our attention on the limbs, one by one, then the centers. Then he had us breathe into the third eye and in exhaling follow the particles of the breath down into the stomach.

Donna called. Lord Pentland had moved to Manhattan to be closer to the Foundation, and Lady Pentland had invited her to come live with her up in Riverdale. So she's really moving in the Work.

27 October 1980

Gave Sunya a rainbow shawl for his birthday. He now wears it over his Mr. Nobody button. Sunya is even more of an enigma to me than Lord Pentland, and being with him so much I came to realize what it was that I had missed: the emptiness. It seemed like he was "dead," emotionless. And he had no light around him. It wasn't a place I wanted to be. I told him about this. He said simply, "Take it as a positive, at least neutral." And later, "It is full, solid, emptiness. Not a vacuity. Not a negativity. I accept everything and everyone as they are. Such beautiful differences." He didn't take any manifestation to be real, "It's mostly shakti-business." Of ordinary life, he would say, "It's more than a dream, but it's not real. Not anything to get upset over."

November 1980

Sunya writes of his birthday:

"Sri Wuji is still a little dazed and distraught after all the dissipation in wordiness. There were no candles on the cake at all, only in large letters: 'Sunyata: Ego-free Understanding.' There were present 90 lovable egojies, all enlightened, though only a few of them aware of being luminous in Self radiant Light. We quoted Ramana Maharshi: 'You who wish to celebrate the birthday, seek first whence was your birth? One's birthday is, when he enters THAT which transcends—birth and death, the Eternal Being. To seek one's Self and merge in the object of the Self, that is wisdom.'"

3 December 1980

Finished a restructuring of the book. I should finish the second rewrite at the end of the month. A violent side is coming out of me. Hadn't seen it before moving out here.

16 December 1980

Sent Mother a cat for her birthday but she wouldn't let the pet shop woman in the house. She's 80 years old today. She's had a tough life. She said to put on her tombstone: "I got a dirty deal."

And she did. A middle sister, both sisters, Marie, the oldest, and Peg, the youngest, jealous of her, as she was quite beautiful and personable. When she married my father she went to live at his parent's home. His sister, Ossie, and her husband, Bill Newbaker, also lived there. Ossie had graduated from Indiana State Teacher's College, rare in those days, but, like my mother's sisters, Ossie was jealous of her. It wasn't long before my mother packed her bags and went back home, but her father told her, "Mabel, you've made your bed, now sleep in it." When Marjorie, my mother's first child, was born, Ossie, who was childless, acted like her mother. Thirteen years later, when she had me, Grandmother Patterson told her, "This one's yours, Mabel."

1981

"We are always aware, Sunyata."

13 January 1981

    At Mr. Gurdjieff's annual celebratory birthday, I was put on the team holding trays to serve everyone Armagnac for the ritual toast. Don Hoyt came up to me, took a glass, smiled and lifted the glass making a gesture of a toast toward me. The glass was empty.

    Oddly, last year I was also a server with the last glass on the tray being for me, but the tray was one glass light and so everyone but me drank a toast. On the wall I noticed a saying of Gurdjieff's, "Don't sit long where you shouldn't sit."

The reading this year was from the *Third Series* where Gurdjieff speaks of God throwing Lucifer out of heaven as a reminding factor so as to continually activate His awareness.

18 January 1981

At lunch I finally said point-blank to Sunya what was bothering me—

"Why do you have no power or radiance?"

He laughed, "What a question to ask me."

He told me that to get the deeper awareness you are not the doer. "We think we push and pull but we are being pushed and pulled all the time."

26 January 1981

Industry Week published my first feature story, a piece on semiconductors. The same week got a scoop with a news piece on "The World's First Listening Chip." That was sheer luck. Just talking to an engineer who let it slip. But it rang bells in Cleveland.

29 January 1981

At St. Elmo the theme of the Work day was "Self-enquiry and the Search for Inner Freedom." It seemed like just so many words. Or is this only a state I am going through?

30 January 1981

Stan Modic sent me my six-month report card. "So far, good," he says. The meaning? I'm still a question mark.

31 January 1981

Forty-four years old today. Waist at 38 inches, hair thinning. "When you're falling, dive," says Jung. So I shaved it all off. Felt good. Barbara could hardly look at me.

Mother sent a birthday card and twenty dollars. Bought two canvases, a brush and a can of turpentine and began to paint again.

Started in '72 but had mostly stopped when I first came out here.

Went to see Sunya. He asked me to tell him about the essence of Gurdjieff's teaching. I didn't want to speak about the exercises, so began speaking about the enneagram, the laws of three and seven, the triads. At one point I heard myself and realized how ridiculous this was to speak to Sunya about it. I stopped abruptly and told him—

"I find it hard to believe you are who you say you are." He readily agreed.

We had a big laugh together and I found myself inviting him to go to lunch with me.

I asked about doing.

"I don't know what I am *doing*," he told me. "And I don't care. I let them kidnap me. I had no wish to go anywhere. It had to happen. It was my karma that had to be fulfilled. We have to accept it. We can only change our attitude toward things, not the things."

2 February 1981

Dreamed that Hoyt told me to inscribe on each step of St. Elmo's one of Gurdjieff's aphorisms. I didn't know whether to do it or not—it meant, of course, becoming involved.

Have been reading my second sci-fi novel, John Brunner's *Players at the Game of People*. It's about being "called." But the "hero" had sold his soul to the Devil.

6 February 1981

Dreamed Hoyt and someone I couldn't see were carrying this enormous snake/dragon in their arms. It was very powerful. Also so very ugly and grey. I cautioned them not to let it get away, because once it was out of their grasp . . . then I realized that the snake was my ego.

7 February 1981

Bought *The Androgyne Journal* by James Broughton, a local poet and artist. Thought I might learn something about Sunya.

14 February 1981

Went to Watts' houseboat to hear Lama Govinda speak about the I Ching. Govinda had made it part of his life's study. He is a small man and had to be helped onto the platform. He has a long Fu Manchu beard, broad forehead and before speaking clutched his cane as if he were a small bird gripping his perch. When he began to speak he changed entirely — he was strong, engaging, in command, and quite knowledgeable. His wife sat to one side, made sounds, and finally reached over and put a watch in his lap to let him know he was speaking too much.

2 March 1981

Feel such a strong creative spirit inside me that I wonder if I would ever subsume it to any system or idea of nothingness; at least until it's played itself out. Or is this merely another form of ego — yes, of course, but should all egos be annihilated in total awareness before they've had their play in the world? Yes, bliss is nice, wonderful, but what is the price? It's not "absolutely free" — it's the most expensive "thing" one can purchase. Can't this happen with me beholden to no system or person but only to the Holy Ghost itself?

4 March 1981

A question: there is Ramana Maharshi with his egoless-bliss at one pole and Gurdjieff and his ego-suffering at the other. Both use self-enquiry and attention-awareness as the basic practice. Why annihilate the ego? Why regard it all as a dream? Why not act in the world for the sake of experience — bought, of course, with the conscious acceptance of all the pain and suffering contingent of life?

18 March 1981

At St. Elmo I told Lord Pentland, "When you came into the movements hall I was asleep. I wasn't trying. I felt like a jerk."

He told me to speak louder. The room was very large.

"I was enraged," I told him.

"What?"

"*Angry*. This isn't an isolated instance. My anger is so quick and big, so mechanical. My wish is too small. I'm still on the level of personality. I'm not mature."

He told me that emotions were caused by tensions in the body. I should try to relax more. Then I would be able to see the emotions—I would suffer with them. My black thoughts would not pollute others then. I would see the jealousy, envy, injustice, justification.

"You've said the right thing," he said. "Spoken from the right place."

19 March 1981

Sunya told me, "You don't know what pure awareness is yet. It's beyond idea or anything you've experienced."

14 April 1981

Gave a small party for Sunya. One crazy, blown-out girl came, said she wanted to go and clean toilets in Reno, talked about the Demon of Death.

A fixated ego—is that a mark of madness? Fixated and unrelated to the environment. But we all exist in varying degrees of that.

He seems to attract such strange people. Am I one of them?

Spoke to Sunya about the two types of spirituality—the Gnostics who believed the world existed in an irredeemable fallen state and those like Aurobindo who believe the Holy Ghost should be brought to Earth—that matter should be spiritualized.

When Maharshi was told of Aurobindo's ideas, he asked, "Will it ever leave Pondicherry?" [This is where Aurobindo lived.]

15 April 1981

Took my first John Lilly float today at the Samadhi Center in San Francisco. Doing a story on it for the magazine. A very *est* atmosphere. Feeling of weightlessness was interesting. Felt tightness in the neck, shoulders, bottom of spine. Could hear my heart beat—that was the only sound. There was a little fear. The ego uses the mind to talk to itself when it feels fear.

17 April 1981

Another float. Did a little of the dolphin breathing John Lilly suggests. Did breathing exercises from the Work, too. Had much more awareness.

25 April 1981

I have received a great deal from the Work and LP, but now my heart is with Sunya and I see that I have been waiting for the right moment to leave. LP once said, "Few people leave the Work in the right way."

28 April 1981

At the St. Elmo meeting I had been asked to help set up the chairs and intentionally gave a neutral "No." The fellow's eyes blinked. He couldn't believe what I said. I felt his energy come into me. So the shocker gets the energy, if the shocked can't keep it for themselves.

Don Hoyt wasn't there. Ann Burns, his assistant, took his place. I asked her, "When a person is shocked and they do not have the presence to assimilate the liberated energy that the shock creates—where does the energy go?"

"I am astounded," she said, "that you could ask such a question. It's so narrow."

So she didn't know the answer. And I received her energy, too.

[Gurdjieff said there were two ends to a stick. He shocked people to awaken them to their sleep. In doing so, he was taking the bad end of the stick consciously. If students identified, rather than awaken, then all of their negative energy was projected on him and he had to process it.]

7 May 1981

When Sunya makes his "Chicago raid" he is hosted by Dr. Arvind Vasavada, a Jungian psychiatrist who had studied in Zurich with Carl Jung. Vasavada said he had met Sunya during his first visit to America at a retreat sponsored by the Human Dimensions Institute near Rochester, New York, at which Sunya was their guest of honor.

When I first saw Sunyata he was walking—I spotted him from the back and I was instantly struck by his speedy "Himalayan Power Gait." When I saw his face I was taken by his eyes—and, like many, thought him to be a woman—and much, much younger than his chronological age. Very quickly my whole inner being started to be absorbed by this strange, wondrous person. This, in itself, is extraordinary, as in those days the intellect was my pride and joy—I showed off the mind like other women show off their designer clothes. I do remember strange tugs in my heart, tears welling up, and finally my urgent and private question to him: ". . . You really think all will be well?" His answer lodged forever in my consciousness—*"All is well. All is always well."*

Vasavada held weekly Friday evening meetings for his students, other therapists and psychologists. When Sunya came, it was a darshan that he had Sunya lead.

8 June 1981
Moved from Corte Madera to 77 Tamalpais, an old, one-story red-framed house in San Anselmo, a long block from the downtown. Looks like a small barn. Located on a corner lot with plenty of trees, rose bushes and out back a large L-shaped deck.

July 1981
Alan Watts' houseboat was sold. Sunya's weekly darshans are moved to the Omphalos, another docked houseboat whose only available night is the same evening as the St. Elmo meeting. Fortunately, the weekly Work meetings ended in the summer and don't start again until September. What to do? I had to make a decision. Did I really want to leave the Work for Sunya?
[In Greek mythology, in Delphi, omphalos is a black ovoid stone set on the spot where two eagles loosed by Zeus crossed paths at the Earth's nexus. It marked Delphi as one of the greatest power centers of the ancient universe.]

18–24 July 1981

Went to the Work week at St. Elmo. Each day Lord Pentland gave a theme: *Saturday*—Being open to the movements of energy and manifesting accordingly. *Sunday*—I wish. But as soon as I face the demands of life I disappear. I am nothing. What is my work? *Monday*—I need more energy for my work. What is the real study of and work on moving-instinctive center? *Tuesday*—I came here voluntarily. Today my wish is confronted with resistance. Am I willing to allow the two parts to approach each other?

Wednesday—Do you find the task useful? *Thursday*—can't remember. *Friday*—Being awake to the signs and symbols.

One day at lunch Lord Pentland said, "The Work promises to show you yourself. Now that the Prince sees he is a frog he wants to become a Prince again."

He then spoke about King Konuzion who explained to fawning courtiers that he could not stop the tide, as his power was not equal to that of God's.

27 July 1981

In the meeting I blew up, telling everyone they were just making book reports. Hoyt agreed with me and mentioned what Gurdjieff said in *Views* about how to know something. I looked it up:

"The secret is small and very easy—we must learn to work like a man. And that is when a man does a thing and at the same time he thinks about what he is doing and studies how the work should be done, and while doing it—forgets his grandmother and grandfather and his dinner."

Reading Nott's book *Teachings of Gurdjieff*, I suddenly read "'great men' are those who in reality are immersed in vanity, self-pride, self-love and egoism to the point of madness." So that's what LP meant about my coming to California! Too subtle for this "great man."

2 September 1981

Dreamed Sunya was very powerful. And there was something

not human, or beyond human, that was normal to him. We were going to sit—and from his mouth came a popping sound and an *Aumm*....

5 September 1981

I was with Sunya from 10 a.m. to 4 p.m. We spoke of Maithuna, of not wasting seed. I saw, felt—understood—that he really was sunyata—full, solid, emptiness.

He is nothing. It is extraordinary.

"Expect nothing, get nothing," he says.

All else, everything else, has some orientation and therefore some limitation—some frozen aggression, assertion.

That Nothing makes its appearance in a "Something" [Sunyata, him, her, itself] is without parallel. A contradiction. A mystery. A rare-born mystery. Sunya is the appearance of nothing.

My thoughts were so heavy I felt like I was being crushed.

We went to the Pelican Inn by Muir Woods for lunch.

He is an Arahant—one who lives the truth without proclaiming it, who accepts all for all is God, all is perfect just as it is. There are not two, so what is there to change?

The mystery is that nothing is something; that what cannot make an appearance—in that it is nothing—has made one. It is sitting there before you, talking, joking, eating, playing. But nobody is there. *Only Mr. Nobody.*

Another paradox—if he is nobody why is he always and exclusively talking about himself, his story in the world? And why is he always repeating the same stories, old stories, as though nothing is happening currently? Are the stories all that remain from a large "salutary death"?

The beauty is that being with his nothingness one sees his somethingness—all thoughts become crushingly clear. Nothing swallows everything.

After lunch we went to see the Rajneesh film. On leaving, I kissed Sunya's hand and he bowed to me. He joked that I should watch that I didn't lose my mind.

6 September 1981

Went with Sunya to see the second Rajneesh film. I gave him an offering—a big tub of popcorn and a coke. When we returned home Sunya read to me a letter he has written to Rajneesh, who is now in Oregon. He wants an invitation.

15 September 1981

I was leaving the meeting when Don Hoyt came up and shook my hand. He is a good man. I trust him. He repeated what he had said at the meeting—that we could ask any question we wanted. I told him every time I asked a question I felt a deep condemnation, so I've shut up. He said he thought he knew what I was referring to. I said I wanted to talk about the inner sound and the energy up the spine. He said he thought the group had come to a place where it was possible for real work to begin, so I could ask about that.

I feel like it is too late. I feel drawn to Sunya.

19 September 1981

Sunya came to our home for lunch. It didn't go badly and I filled in any long spaces. On the way back to his place I told him I was thinking of leaving the Foundation. He said, "If you doubt, don't do it."

I told Barbara about leaving. She said she didn't relate to Sunya and didn't want to leave, but finally said it was up to me.

I thought about it many times. Lord Pentland had a powerful presence and intellect. He was a master teacher and man of real will and knowledge, the consummate spiritual warrior. He was that rare combination of a man of the world and a man of the spirit. Like St. Paul, he had devoted his life to establishing the teaching of The Fourth Way throughout America, as Gurdjieff had asked him to do. In the true sense of the word, he was my spiritual teacher.

Sunya was what? He had been born so, had never had to dominate himself. It was true that he had nothing to teach and nothing to sell. But in the true sense of those words. That's what makes it hard to talk about, because it is beyond language, beyond the subject-objective dualistic life that we all live. Sunya's only admonition was his oft-mentioned, "Be still and know that I am is God." He was neither a man of the world nor of the spirit in that he took his stand on the groundless ground of sunyata, what he called "full, solid emptiness."

The Work, as presented, was an ancient progressive path of self-development with many concentric circles of self-remembering, each leading to deeper and deeper being and self-knowledge, an esoteric teaching that was simple yet rich and elegant in the subtlety and extension of its principles and axioms. As this developed, so did understanding, leading from conscious egotism to the individual I to the soul, which is immortal within the solar system.

Sunya had no teaching. In fact, mention the word and he would laugh. At one of the darshans a fellow who existed by raiding the trash of the wealthy and selling the contents at weekly flea markets gave him a second larger Mr. Nobody button. Sunya loved it and wore it ever after, even signing the many letters he wrote to friends with those words. His interjection of the word *is* in the admonition "Be still and know that I am is God" and not "I am God" is brilliant as it returns the assertion from the personal to the impersonal. That could only be true of a Mr. Nobody.

When I was with him I felt a true emptiness and silent being rarely experienced with such depth. Later, a doubting would come, wondering if I was just being conned. Weird as I felt among some of the stoneheads who attended the darshans with happy smiles and liquid eyes and memories like Swiss cheese and the others who were hurt or confused by life, I had come to feel comfortable among them. I had questioned what the Self was, and while it had not been a burning question, it was a haunting one which I saw now as leading me here to Mr. Nobody. As in the chess game I had once played with Lord Pentland, and seen a forced mate if I left a bishop hanging, I had to trust my intuition.

The dream I had after three years or so in the Work came back to me.

I am in Lord Pentland's apartment. He hands me a large square white envelope made of sturdy, expensive paper.

"It's one of the original invitations," he says.

I open the envelope. There is a white card, inscribed in calligraphy. It has my name on it. It is from someone named "Charles Fort."

"But I don't want to leave!" I cry.

"I'm afraid you have to," says Lord Pentland.

He is sitting next to the window in a large Queen Anne chair. He gestures broadly with his hands.

"You see," he says, "there's nothing to be done."

"But I—."

"I'm afraid it's not a question of what you or I want, if you see what I mean?"

"You mean . . . you mean—it's fate?"

Lord Pentland nods slowly, impassively.

I want to cry. I feel such love for Lord Pentland, for all that he and the Work have done for me. Then a sense of responsibility comes—of my having to go on, and to make the best of it.

It is then I realize I am in a dream, that all this is happening on another plane. I have to remember the man's name who has sent the invitation, so I keep repeating it to myself—"*Charles Fort! Charles Fort!*"

I wake up with the name on my lips. *Who is he?* Thinking he might be a writer I went to a local bookstore. I found his work in the science fiction sector. I hated science fiction. But there it was—*The Book of the Damned.* Good gawd! How did that relate to me? Was I going to be one of the Damned? Fort wrote about all the factual things that happen which science has no explanation for and so are scoffed at. Perhaps, I thought, I was being told that sometime I would be called upon to leave the Work. To become one of the damned.

With that, I recognized that sometime—*I would leave the Organized Work.*

Lord Pentland had always said few people had ever left the Work in the right way. Most simply found some excuse not to continue and simply left or sent a note. It became clear that I had to leave the Foundation, its organization—the inner Work I could never leave. It was me.

11 October 1981

Went to St. Elmo to pick up Movements shoes. Mrs. Titus was there and wondered why I was taking the shoes. Told her I was leaving the Work. She is thoroughly committed to the Work. She got *All & Everything* and had me read The Five Obligolnian Strivings.

13 October 1981

I went to New York and told Lord Pentland I was leaving. [Described in detail in Part I of *Eating The "I."*]

14 October 1981

Bloomingdales has Irish flags flying everywhere. Watched a short film, *Brendan's Voyage*. In the ninth century Brendan makes a journey hoping to find the Isle of the Blessed. Supplies go overboard, so he decides to go off course and hits an underwater iceberg and lands on an island which turns out to be a giant sea monster, but he does manage to eventually get there. Is this what my "voyage" will be like?

I went to see my old painting teacher and friend, Don Stacy, and told him what I had done. "In leaving something," he said, "you can't know if you are right or not—you can only know the risk of giving up what you have, and probably not even that!" When I left, he gave me prints of his drawings Sol and Luna. Sun and Moon together. So that was the aim.

15 October 1981

Went to the Sign of the Dove for dinner. The woman beside me asked the piano player to play "Follow" from the play *The Fantasticks*, the first play I'd seen in New York back in 1960. He played "Try to Remember" instead. She was reading a book, *Initiation*.

19 October 1981

Flew down to Florida to see my mother. Left my Gurdjieff books in the taxi. When I got out of the taxi the song *Moon River* played.

What is going on?

21 October 1981

First night back I dreamed of Lord Pentland. I was driving up 3rd Avenue. I saw Lord Pentland at the corner of 34th. He was waiting for a bus. There was a terrific downpour and he was getting drenched. I didn't see him until I was almost past him. I stopped, backed up the car and he got in. He said nothing. I almost told him I wanted to come back to the Work, but said nothing. I drove into a lot of white fluff or gauze. The car had sunk in up to its wheels. I got out and was so angry I picked the car up and put it back on the road.

22 October 1981

Picked up a book, *Messengers of Deception*. It was about UFOs and mentions Urantia and the Order of Melchizedek. The book said a new myth was being born with UFOs and that the people who reported them were likely hypnotized by aliens.

Donna called, at her meeting Lord Pentland had said there are four reasons why people leave the Work: Grandmother, Digestion, Money, or Sex. Then he added, "The Work works on deep levels and once we've experienced it, we are poisoned forever."

27 October 1981

Took Sunya to lunch. Instead of wearing a kurta or dhoti he wore a robe and said, "I'll be your girlfriend."

I told him what happened with Lord Pentland. "I couldn't have done it without you," I said.

He raised his hands and shook his head in a gesture of "I had nothing to do with it."

I told him, "When I feel good, I really feel good. There is a lot of space. But when the fear comes . . . ."

"Oh yes," he said. "But you'll get used to that."

"Yeah, I know," and repeated one of his favorite sayings—"delightful uncertainly!"

We both laughed.

"You know Sunya, seriously, I couldn't have done it without you."

"I did nothing," Sunya protested, mildly.

"Yeah, and boy was it powerful."

We both laughed again.

When we returned to his home I noticed a small postcard-size picture of James Broughton, the author of that *Androgyne* book.

7 December 1981

"Here, you'll like this," Sunya said to me today. He put a book in my hands, *Neither This Nor That I Am* by Jean Klein. He told me the writer put it as well as Nisargadatta Maharaj.

I read it at one sitting. The thought was so clear, precise, penetrating, without embellishment. He wrote easily about that which cannot be spoken of. I was immediately taken, but then realized this Jean Klein, the author, was in Europe.

"I'd love to meet him," I told Sunya, "but . . ."

"Well, who knows," Sunya said. "People suddenly appear."

I asked about the book that Neil Vanover, Vasavada's student from Chicago, was going to write. He hadn't heard from him.

"Why don't you write the book?" Sunya said.

And so I began asking questions, reading some of his writings, letters, keeping notes about Sunya's life. I've put in narrative order all that I originally learned.

Sunya took "body birth" about five miles from Aarhus, in northern Denmark on October 27, 1890, on a small and rather isolated farm. His father was Soren Sorensen, 60 years of age, and his mother, Maran, about 58. He had two sisters, 12 and 14, Mary and Jeusine. He was named Alfred Julius Emmanuel Sorensen. He writes:

> I was born into Silence and it never left me. There was no reaching out, no ambition, no trying to know or to become or share even. There was a Unity-Awareness, a certain wisdom — not knowledge — that was there from childhood, a

pre-ego consciousness which is completely and harmoniously integral. It is not aware of itself because there are no contrasts. Then at about seven years old ego-consciousness emerged with its sense of separation, multiplicity, subject-object relationship. It usurped and to some extent blurred the inner light. I felt like I had lost something. Still the two modes of values coexisted unclashingly. Egoji was not assertive or bumptious in likes and dislikes—or in craving willfulness—nor in any lusty curiosity to know, to excel or to become this or that. Everyone thought I was a simpleton because I was so unassertive, so uninterested in their ego-antics and shakti-business. In my childhood there was no talk about sex. Some of my women friends had desires, or at least were curious. I had no sex on the mind because I had no mind—at least no mind to trouble me.

The village school was delightfully mediocre and we suffered no exam or intelligence test. No hectoring and brainwashing or mind-shaping and no promotion. I left school early after eighth grade so had no headucation. Neither did Churchianity attract me. Its dogmas and doctrines, rites and rituals, were mere beliefs, concepts, abstractions—divorced from natural life and natural spirituality. God, Christ and the Holy Spirit were nothing outside oneself.

In my fourteenth year the world around and within crashed. The farm, my outside world, was sold to and desecrated by strangers, and from that time I felt uprooted, or perhaps deeper at home within. I discovered my wings and my insertable roots and later on I loved my various homes and was at home everywhere. Ego-consciousness had developed in a kind of self-defense or as a reflection of the mentality and the ego-desires of the humans around me, a contagious disease. Though it had strong and subtle roots within, ego was also provoked, fostered and developed by much tuning in and listening in to the rhythm of fellow-pilgrims when they were in close vibrational nearness. The ego was invoked in imitation, in reflexes and in self-defense, but also, in the same process, it was humbled, crucified and crushed. The intuitive light prevailed and the mental, emotional and physical was no trouble, so *ananda* bubbled up healthily and also in the due ego-deaths, some minor, some crucial and salutary with no outer, dramatic or tragic events. One can learn to die now and then — from time to eternity — and thus experience that there is no real death. No death of the Real that we ever Are, I AM, BEING-AWARENESS, Grace. [See Appendices, "The Awakening."]

When in 1904 his father, Soren, a peasant farmer, sold the farm, young Alfred was uprooted and experienced the "disease of civilization in cities." For five years he served an apprenticeship in horticulture, then worked as a gardener in Denmark, France and Italy. In 1911 he went to England. In 1929 he was working as a gardener at Dartington Hall at Devon, about 200 miles from London, from six in the morning to six in the evening with minimal but sufficient wages, when the Indian poet Rabindranath Tagore came for a rest.

Tagore writes [See Appendices, "*My Reminiscences*"] of having had a transcendental experience in which he suddenly was made aware of the great beauty and joy of the world. He attributes it to his "deliberately suppressing my self (ego) and viewing the world as a mere spectator." On a following morning he had a deeper experience of this radiance and relates, "A thing that happened the next day or the day following seemed especially astonishing." He says that there was "a curious sort of person who came to me now and then, with a habit of asking all manner of silly questions. One day he had asked: 'Have you, sir, seen God with your own eyes?' And on my having to admit that I had not, he averred that he had. 'What was it you saw?' I asked. 'He seethed and throbbed before my eyes!' was the reply."

Tagore says he would "not ordinarily relish being drawn into abstruse discussions with such a person . . . . Nevertheless as he was a harmless sort of fellow I did not like the idea of hurting his susceptibilities and so tolerated him as best I could."

When he came one afternoon, Tagore says, "I actually felt glad to see him, and welcomed him cordially. The mantle of his oddity and foolishness seemed to have slipped off, and the person I so joyfully hailed was the real man whom I felt to be in nowise inferior to myself, and moreover closely related. Find no trace of annoyance within me at sight of him, nor any sense of my time being wasted with him, I was filled with an immense gladness, and felt rid of some enveloping tissue of untruth which had been causing me so much needless and uncalled for discomfort and pain."

From time to time Tagore would call "Emmanuel," as Sunya preferred to be known at the time, to his suite and read him poems. "I recognized in Tagore," Emmanuel says, "an awareness of kindred values, of intuitive insight and of integral experience and I responded with loving gratitude to the simple beauty of language and of feeling tone."

One day the poet beheld him playing Beethoven's last quartets on a gramophone by the River Dart. Tagore listened appreciatively and Emmanuel offered and he accepted the album with the B flat opus 130. In return he offered Emmanuel a casual invitation "to come to India to teach Silence."

Emmanuel had never found "a kindred consciousness" in the West, except in the books of Ibsen, Chekhov, Shakespeare, Keats and the *Oxford Book of English Mystical Verse*, and the biographies of Dostoyevsky, Tolstoy, Lawrence and Huxley. He was a voluminous reader of spiritual texts — he called them "my book friends" — of Meister Eckhart, Jacob Boehme, Angelus Silesius and others of like perspective. Having read the *Light of Asia*, Bhagavad Gita and the Upanishads, he wondered if the consciousness he met in these books could be "a living thing still in India."

Leaving in 1930 for a three-month holiday, Emmanuel said:

"While Shantiniketan was the goal, the chief thing was to sense, intuit and experience the Way, the journey and the various new realms of awareness, of consciousness and of cultures. It was just to move solitary through the various realms and sense one's perceptions and receptions, one's acceptance and reactions in the interplay and interrelationships."

He went to Tagore's home, Shantiniketan, the Abode of Peace. The poet was cordial but not really overly welcoming as he probably did not remember Emmanuel. Undeterred, Emmanuel met and became friends with the Lama Anagarika Govinda [Ernst Hoffman, a German by birth], the author of *Foundations of Tibetan Buddhism* and *The Way of the White Clouds*. Emmanuel found the Indian setting very congenial. "My simplicity was my great asset in India," he said. "I could be at home with anyone. They would sometimes say, 'We don't *feel* you are here.'" In traveling about India, a Quaker couple he met gave him written introductions to their Indian friends in different cities.

In Adyar he donned Indian dress, a style he would continue to wear for the rest of his life. In a Calcutta slum a Bengali youth chopping onions inside a little shop saw him and shouted, "In the whole world, there is nothing but God." He went on to Burma, even journeying to Bamo by the Chinese border on the river Irrawaddy. When Emmanuel returned to Shantiniketan, Tagore now asked him to stay as his personal guest as long as he liked. The three-month holiday had turned into eighteen months before Emmanuel returned to Europe to tie up affairs.

In October 1933 he returned to India, now for good. For a time he lived in a tree on a small island in the Ganges river near Haridwar. He visited and stayed with Bapuji Gandhi at Maghanwadi four times for several weeks. Eventually, his wanderings brought him to Binsar in Uttar Pradesh, a summer retreat of the well-to-do. The Nehru family had an estate there. Tagore had introduced him to Nehru. In Binsar he visited the home of Nehru's sister and brother-in-law where he stayed and did horticultural work in the garden. While staying with the Nehrus, he met one of their friends, the Anglo-Indian philanthropist E. T. Thompson, who owned a large estate at Kalimat Ridge, so named after the goddess Kali, and known to locals as "Crank's Ridge." He was offered a portion of the estate for his life's use. Located some three miles above the hill town of Almora, the ridge with its tall pine trees and chattering monkeys was known as Kasar Devi because it stretched out to the rock of Kasar Devi, a natural hollow where in ancient times human sacrifices were offered. Not far away, on the Nepalese border, Kalimat offered a magnificent twenty-three-mile panoramic vista of the snowy Himalayan mountain ranges one hundred miles north, with deep valleys on all sides some 7,000 feet below the ranges.

Of Almora Emmanuel wrote:

> Below is the Almora town, recently electrified. It is a sea of light in the surrounding dark hills. I rest awhile under the pine trees on the top of the cave. When I awoke, the 'morrow' had come from somewhere and was 'today' and with it came the thought of body needs and daily bread. Take no thought for tomorrow, say the lilies and the birds. But today I have to get water from the well, and flour, dal and vegetables from the village far below my cave.
>
> Natural activities and *dharmic* tasks are part of my constant contemplation, all acceptance and unity awareness. I get good contemplation when I walk in nature and when I write at 3 or 4 a.m. in bed. I also get it when I build and repair 5 or 6 small huts. Yes, food-fuss and cave-cleaning can be a nuisance. I am on good terms with dust! The sun and the pure air disinfect. Emmanuel's body has not seen a doctor here. I enjoy my walks during which I induce good contemplation. Of food, one needs very little when one lives harmoniously. One should eat slowly and masticate well. A day of food fast can make a virtue of necessity when provision is short or when one is traveling. If one takes *satvic* food, one does not expand or waste much. It is good to do deep breathing in pure air. All this is nourishing harmonious growth.
>
> I keep my body fit and flexible in activities such as building huts, caves, cottages and water tanks. This is natural 'yogic skill in action,' without any rigorous tapas [ascetic practices] or special yogic discipline.

In 1935 he built a one-room stone hut, roughly twelve-by-twelve, with two doors, one window, fireplace and chimney on a dirt floor, the stones he carried from a local quarry. The only furniture was a worn-out wooden couch, an old armchair and some upturned wood boxes. There was no electricity or running water. He got water from a well about a half-mile down a mountain trail. He constructed tanks to collect rainwater for washing. These were filled during the monsoon and the water had to last until the following year's monsoon. On his gate he put up a sign, *Silence*, scrawled in large letters. He loved to be naked amid the flowering shrubs, mimosa and blossoming cherry trees, as well as what he said are "the fruitless battles with the monkeys, shadowy footpaths, winding morning glory, stone steps, chirruping cicadas, rustling pine trees, the pine needles everywhere, under the Akasha skies." Twice a week he would make the steep trek down to Almora to buy groceries. Occasionally, he might stop at Dwan Singh's, the Crank's Ridge cookery for tea. Otherwise he rarely left his hilltop hut except during the winter months when he would descend to the plains and visit friends. He says:

> I live on what happens to be available and what comes to me. I feel that I am near heaven. There is vital nourishment in the pure ether and the blue space around. I do not ask anything from anybody but I may accept whatever is offered for my needs in the right spirit. In Himalayan solitude, one does not think or talk about any ailments, dis-eases or ego woes. Within us, there are no sin complexes, frustrations or grievance complexes.

An omnivorous reader of spiritual books, he read Paul Brunton's *A Search in Secret India*, in which Ramana Maharshi is mentioned, and began to correspond with Brunton, who was staying in Ramana Maharshi's ashram at the foot of holy Arunachala, near Tiruvannamalai. He had first heard of Ramana Maharshi from Lama Chow Chuji in Kashmir in 1935 (he apparently named his dog Sri Chow Chu Wuji after the Lama). Brunton invited Emmanuel to come and so in 1936 he arrived there. It was very quiet. There were hardly any buildings other than a Samadhi site Ramana Maharshi had built for his mother after she had passed on. Everyone had their meals together, the meals served near her Samadhi site—there was no dining hall. Ramana Maharshi sat in front of everyone, between the untouchables on one side, the Brahmins on the other. Very few people were there, maybe only eight or nine, and Lakshmi, Ramana Maharshi's cow. At the ashram Paul Brunton noticed Emmanuel dressed in Indian garb squatting by the wall, and motioned him forward to introduce him to Ramana Maharshi. A few words were exchanged, nothing more. Later, Brunton said that the sage told him that Emmanuel was "*jananm siddha*" or "one of the rare born mystics." Of his meeting with Maharshi, Emmanuel wrote,

"He had not before met or re-cognized such ego-free, Self-radiant consciousness in a human body, but was not unfamiliar with it in Himalayan nature—and in the Self."

In 1938 Emmanuel again visited. A dining hall had been built, as well as some small dwellings, and there were many more people, more organization. He was hardly let in.

"I was irritated," said Emmanuel. "In that mood I was ego-bound. Then, his Radiance came upon me, right after I squatted down. He glanced at me—that's what he did with some—and I could not take his Radiance."

On his third visit, in 1940, Ramana Maharshi transmitted to him telepathically—only five words: "We are always aware, Sunyata." They were directly and distinctly heard. It struck him so powerfully, he said, that "I took it as his initiation and from that time I took the name Sunyata."

Later, he said:

> There is only one practice, becoming aware of what you are. So I was struck by the fact that he used the word "aware." But most of all, I was struck by his use of "we." Who is "we"? Is it he and I, or is it everybody? It is both. Sunyata is the void. When in the West we say the void, it sounds like a vacuum, or complete negation. In India,

Sunyata is the full, solid emptiness.

This answered the one question he had had: *are we aware of Sunyata when the body sleeps?* He had had the phrase "Awareness is All" but until that moment he had not realized whether there is consciousness or unconsciousness, there is Awareness, always. The answer of *always* being aware was his completion. And so as he digested all of this, which took many years, "Emmanuel" became "Sunyata."

In 1945 Sunyata began focusing on his childhood. Before, there were not the words to express his experiencing, but now in "the retrospective musings on pre-ego and pre-natal memory words bubbled up," and became his "scribble," later called his "Wu language." Highly idiosyncratic, with playful use of word-symbols, combining English and Sanskrit, obscure literary terms, these joined with his own invented wordage like "joyous ease," "affectionate detachment," "delightful uncertainty," "innerstand," "headucation," "egojies," "ego-fuss," and "Shakti-business," all of which he used in writing *Memory*; his use of Socrates' term "anamnesis," usually translated as "recollection" or "memory," in *Phaedrus* referring to the recollection of a light awareness possessed before birth. He says:

> As a child he vibrated vicariously with the desire-rhythms of talkers .... The ability to listen and respond passively developed a flexibility and an awareness of the beautiful difference among *egojies*. He had his own rhythm and rightness in Silence, and with this as a background, he listened and responded patiently, contentedly, and unassertively .... The child knew—although he couldn't have said it in these words—that the real correspondence is in Silence, beyond and deep within, and the surface flutterings and ego-antics blurred this true language.

For the first seven years, he says, "As I was not very conscious of sexual differences, for me there was no war of the sexes .... It did not then occur to me that there is a feminine truth, complementary, but often contrasting and seemingly at war with the masculine truth....

"Physiologically, we all still have rudiments of the other sex; we have developed from some hermaphroditic organism in the dim past, and it may be that we are being carried along to some hermaphroditic fulfillment in the not too far-off future.... When the male and the female truths function in a complementary harmony within one psyche, the body (as a tool) will remain male or female, but the psyche will aware the harmoniously wholeness of itself, freely functioning in the unitive mode of experiencing."

When he was eight years old, he says, "he gradually succumbed to a sin-complex" and secretly took a large stone by a roadside and stood it "erect like a *lingam*," which became for him a stone of Remembrance. He says, "the Stone did not shout loudly enough. *Memory* became more intermittent in consciousness, and the Viking boy duly fell into the grip of desires." With this there was a descent deeper and deeper into ego-consciousness. When he was eleven or twelve there occurred "an instance of dual consciousness...."

"The mystery of how a unified consciousness can become double is as subtle as the mysteries of creation and growth. In my case, 'the fall' was a gradual affair and ego-consciousness only clipped the wings of *memory* after a prolonged period of time."

He came to recognize that "all thoughts are an extroverted activity of the mind, and the mind is extroverted until it reflects the Self purely. Once you can still your thoughts, they will no longer blur memory. Transcend ego-consciousness and be Self-Aware.... I came to see that the essence of love is not reciprocity, reward, nor requital; not touch, gratification, possessive joys, nor ego-fulfillment, but just this steady seeing and contemplation of the ever-living Beauty that is.... The beauty that we see around us is really only within our own psyche. That which re-cognized its Self is within."

At twelve he had what he called "two fits of prayer" in response to a crisis, the first being with Daisy, the cow, which was dying, and another when a childhood friend was leaving. "The Lord of

Hosts seemed to be a failure. 'He' proved to be sublimely indifferent to the whims and moods and cravings of my ego—and so I gave up my short-lived external image of an exoteric God, and turned instead to Henrik Ibsen who hailed the ego-surrender or ego-transcendence in mystic death as depicted in his dramas *Brand* and *When We Dead Awaken* . . . . Parents and people around me were all anti-Ibsen, so quietly I went to a second-hand shop in the city where I traded my boots and other odd 'essentials' for an unbound *Collected Works of Henrik Ibsen*, a marvelous exchange."

At fourteen, he says he felt no need for ritual, imagery, magic, or even of a language of symbols. "Pastor Gudme tried to 'bully' me into his faith. He demanded that the Viking boy 'explain' what he said which meant he was to repeat them. He thundered hell-fire at me when I quoted, 'Seek ye the Kingdom within.' 'Within what?' he bellowed. Shakeningly but unsubdued, I suggested, 'Within all things.' But he was quite sure the devil was within me prompting me to express such wicked, pantheistic notions."

Near *Memory*'s end he writes:

> Partly due to lingering *memory*, I quietly escaped education, or rather it did not fall upon me, and I did not reach out for it, did not seek it, and felt no urge or desire for its blessings. Likewise, later on I would 'escape' property, marriage, fame, ambition, art, organization, intellect, and—in truth—all ties and attachments. Apparently, in this life, there was no need for the lessons that they have to offer.

[These have been condensations of *Memory*. It should be read in its fullness. See *Sunyata: The Life and Sayings of a Rare-Born Mystic*.]

Throughout all his years in India, he continued to travel regularly all over the country, being befriended not only by the Jawaharlal Nehru family, but spiritual teachers Krishna Prem, Sri Anirvan, and Neem Karoli Baba, the English psychiatrist R. D. Laing, and the Chilean diplomat, mystic and writer Miguel Serrano, all sharing the Silence of "affectionate detachment, joyous ease and delightful uncertainty."

Several times he visited Mahatma Gandhi's ashram in Wardha. He loved best Gandhi's evening walks and the hour or two when Gandhi was at his spinning wheel. "I live in *Silence* once a week," Gandhi told him, "and you live in *Silence* forever." He remembers at Gandhi's suggestion setting off with Olga de Nottbeck, a Dutch lady friend, with brooms and buckets to clean the nearby town, but it was really too dirty for any impression to be made. He didn't accept Gandhi's formal Monday silences, as he believed that the very effort blurs the Silence.

Indira Gandhi had stayed for a year in nearby Binsar convalescing from her early tuberculosis and Sunya and she got to know each other quite well. He had a standing invitation to visit her in Delhi where they shared many teas, breakfasts and lunches. He was also a friend of her father, Jawaharlal Nehru, who once so fascinated Lady Mountbatten with very tall tales about Sunya's "Crank's Ridge life" that she became a friend. In 1953, when Sunya became an Indian subject, Nehru told him, "You have done us the greatest honor by becoming one of us."

His most favored companions were two dogs. The first was Lady Yami and when she died he got a plucky little black and white dog brought from Tibet in a sack with a tiger cub. He named it Sri Chow Chu Wuji. He would go with the Viking, now known as "Brother Alfred" or "*Kuttewala Baba*" (the saint with a dog), when he went down the three-mile walk twice a week to Almora to get groceries and pick up his mail. Sri Wuji quickly learned to sit on his hind legs to give a Namaste blessing to local grocers to procure a morsel of meat. One day Sri Wuji ate some poisoned meat and departed for what Brother Alfred calls "the invisible Real." Now the droll and wu-full observations of Sri Wuji begin to bubble up, Wuji saying "Ramana Maharshi is Himalayan. The others are only mole hills."

Anandamayi, whom he spoke of as the greatest Ma of his life, he visited often in Benares. She called him "*Bhaiji*," which means reverend brother. Once she visited his stone hut and spent the whole day. "There was peace in Heaven that day," says Sunya. At her ashram once, Sunya was invited to sit with her in the "silent room."

Wuji went right along inside as well, which sent Anandamayi's disciples into a rage at its doggish impudence. But she waved them off and gave Sri Wuji careful spiritual scrutiny before finally announcing "Wuji is not a dog."

Sri Yashoda Mai, another great Ma, wanted to initiate Sunya, but he had no interest though he was fond of her. Sunya's mother had died in 1937 and Yashoda Mai felt that he needed a fleshly mother, so Sunya became one of her many children without *diksha*, an initiation by a guru. Said Sunya, "She was one of the only ones who intuitively innerstood and effortlessly re-cognized that a mystic needs no diksha." When she passed on, Krishna Prem, the British-born Ronald Nixon, author of *The Yoga of the Bhagavad Gita*, took over her ashram. Sunya liked him, thought him sincere and earnest but too mental, "still stuck in words."

Over the years, Sunya attended a number of Krishnamurti's talks. He felt Krishnamurti was "very tense on the platform." Sometimes Sunya would break into a parody of him, raising his hands to his chest, scrunching his face and saying loudly—"Ohhh, if you would only listen!"

Having been blessed by Ramana Maharshi, Sunya was concerned with what was happening at his ashram and in 1945 wrote an essay, "Darshan," much abbreviated:

> The aim of the Shakti-cult is knowledge rather than wisdom, power rather than freedom, and some of its tenets are opposite to Advaita. From the very beginning of Ramana Maharshi's appearance in the outer world of worldliness there were two schools of beliefs among the devotees. The adherents of the Shakti-cult were actuated by a firm, powerful resolve to take over full control of the Maharshi's teaching, so that they could interpret it in harmony with their own faith or at least could tone down the Advaita trends of the teaching. Unfortunately for them the Maharshi kept on living in his body, and living the Advaita Experiencing. His Silence radiated out from it, and he spoke out from it rather than about it. He was

It—consciously aware, and death-free in Life.

The chief hindrance to the Darshan in Self-awareness is ego-concepts, ego-consciousness in false identification and the ensuing conceit of agency, the dust of ego-fuss in noisy duality. The sediments which we stir up and the values and gods that we create and worship hinder us in reflecting purely. Thoughts and mind usurp to blur the light of the Eternal, the invisible Real, while awareness in that which ever is evokes the Strength of no desire and the *Karuna* experience that is more than Love, as it cannot be jealous, clinging, possessive or exclusive. Eternity seems to play in time.

As Ramana Maharshi said, "There is no way so sure as Self-inquiry and that of a mature Sadhu's company for this purpose. The simple, natural spirituality of the Sadhu provides the needed Strength unseen by others."

Sunya's Silence was recognized by a wealthy Indian who offered to support him with 20 rupees a month (about $2.50 U.S.), but he would accept only five rupees a month.

Said Sunya: "I do not find it so difficult to live on a precarious income of Rs 5 per month in India (an allowance from a good soul), which is spent somewhat like this: milk (1/2 seer per day) Rs 3; atta and whole wheat, 12 annas; gur (sugar), 4; and the one Rs left goes to vegetables, fruit, oil, stamps and 'pocket money.' In a month it suffices, and many a fellow pilgrim in India has less to manage on."

Later, in 1950, his name was recommended to the Birla Foundation in New Delhi which helps babas. They wanted to give him 100 rupees a month but he would only accept 20. "It was more than I needed," he says, "but I thought prices might rise." The monthly rupees and his garden and the occasional kindness of strangers more than covered his material needs.

In the 1940s Sunya had met Lizelle Reymond, author-to-be of *My Life with a Brahmin Family* and later *To Live Within* and *Shakti*. Sunya introduced her to his good friend Sri Anirvan, the Bengali sage who became her guru. They rented a cottage on Crank's Ridge which they called "*Haimavati*" from the *Kena Upanishad* meaning "immaterial whiteness," which they hoped would serve as an ashram. Enough students failed to come, so, finally, after five years Anirvan closed the ashram and sent Reymond back to Europe. A few days before her departure he handed her a book, telling her it had just been published and he had read it in one sitting.

"Read this carefully," he advised. "It contains ideas that are very dear to us and that have been your food in these past years. Look for the people who are working in this direction; they are living for a conscious reality."

Before Reymond left she went to say goodbye to Sunya. She showed him the book, Uspenskii's *The Psychology of Man's Possible Evolution*. He thumbed through it and nodded and told her to remember the Self in all her self-remembering. Then he closed the gate and went back to his garden. Reymond returned to Switzerland where she met Madame de Salzmann and joined the Work.

Later, in *To Live Within*, she wrote about her time with her guru, Anirvan telling her:

> All life is from the Void which is the matrix of universal energy. One has access to it by four stages. The first stage is to realize the plurality of 'I's; the second stage is the recognition of a single 'I'; the third, is no 'I'; and finally the Void. Uspenskii speaks about the first two stages in *Search of the Miraculous*. He remained silent about the last two because he had left Gurdjieff. The writings of Gurdjieff [*All & Everything*] open for us the frontiers of the two last stages. These are cleverly hidden in his mythical narrations.

Besides Sri Anirvan, Kalimath, or Crank's Ridge, drew many prominent residents. Walter Evans-Wentz, translator of *The Tibetan Book of the Dead*, became a friend and neighbor. Lama Govinda and his wife Li Gotami, a Parsee, rented from Evans-Wentz a house with abundant acreage that lay at the extreme tip of the ridge, about a mile away from Sunya. Others on Crank's Ridge included Taoist John Blofeld, painter Earl Brewster, psychiatrist R. D. Laing (who committed suicide there), Orientalist Alain Daniélou and his married lover Raymond Burnier, New Age visitors Timothy Leary, Alan Ginsberg and Ralph Metzner, and Tantric hippies like Nik Douglas and his sex crew. Most every Sunday Sunya, and a few others, would come to Lama Govinda's for tea. (The Lama's wife was cordial but had little interest in Sunya.)

"The inmates in and around the ridge lead solitary lives," said Sunya. "They are friendly but are inclined to avoid listening to the radio. They study Sanskrit, yoga, abstract painting and indulge in other spiritual pursuits." As guests would come to visit, he eventually made three other stone huts. In the morning, he would get up, make a fire, prepare tea and sit in the sun, letting guests do as they liked—meditating, reading, speaking. Without visitors, the days were mostly full of Akasha blue skies, but the nights he especially liked in Kalimath where, as he said, "the Ghostly Whole" spread itself over everything. He would bring his gramophone with its big horn from the hut then place his creaky records from the 1920s on it, Beethoven's last quartets being a favorite. Of these he wrote:

> When first these heard melodies and unearthly harmonies swam into our conscious ken, it was our habit to let them play themselves, while we were actually writing or doing things. When we are ego-freely alone, there are no clashes in the seeming dual consciousness. The attention to needle and changes is no break. The music goes on and is responded to—aye, merged into—by the deeper Ground of consciousness, while the surface-play—activities and thoughts—go on co-existingly. There is full conscious awareness, and the deeper aware unconsciousness. Wu.
>
> These four or five last quartets of Ludwig von Beethoven reveal his deepest and most real Awareness, there was the grand acceptance, the supreme Affirmation. Simply, stilly and ego-freely "go with" and Be them, and you will be aware. They play you into freedom, into full

acceptance and, so, into the essence and beyondness, immanence and transcendence, that is joyous ease. These four quartets are as if bodied forth to Himself, rather than to public appreciation and sharing, while in his earlier, violently storm-swayed and powerfully discordant compositions, Ludwig is definitely asserting and sharing his subjective truths, agonies and pain-joys. In these quartets the Ananda and the Advaita-mode prevail. The ninth symphony may express the same Victory, but loudly, assertively. How stridently, aggressive even, until it breaks into the human voice in gladness, in *"Freude,"* and in the *"Seid umschlungen, Millionen."* Acceptance. The quartets are pure contemplation.

1982

"You are tired of the phenomenal."

1 January 1982
Sunya wrote:

Mere beliefs are a hindrance. One must have Faith and, more so, experience—until one can awaken into Experiencing. Allah's chief prophet advises: "Die before ye die." When it was suggested to Nisargadatta: "You will die" — the Gnani's reply was: "I am dead already. Physical death will make no difference in my case. I am a timeless or time-free being. I am free of desire and fear, because I do not remember the past or imagine the future. Where there are no names and forms, how can there be desire and fear? With desirelessness comes timelessness and time-freeness. I am safe because what is not cannot touch What Is. *There is only life*: There is nobody who lives life."

Sri Ramana Maharshi's egoji died when his body was sixteen years young. Sri Wuji says, "Sri Nobody was born dead. Wu ha da! A *Maha Rishi* re-cognized a rare, born Mystic and reminded him: 'We are always aware Sunyata.' Egoji is the disease. Wu!"

Sunya quoted Nisargadatta's *Dhyana Yoga*:

> Sit in the open air every day in the morning in a simple asana for a half-hour to one hour. Keep your eyes half-open and see your nose tip. This is only to withdraw the mind's attention from the external sense organs. Then be aware of the Seer, the Self that is sitting. Do not think about the sense organs. Do nothing, have no thought. BE — only aware the One, that which is sitting in Dyana. If the eyes close, let it be.
>
> Experience inner space. True birth is when one enters THAT which transcends birth and death, the Eternal Being.

When pressed still further Sunya would quote Sri Aurobindo intoning like a bell chime:

"In the beginning, ego is the helper, then ego is the bar. Effort is the helper, then effort is the bar."

2 January 1982
Went to see Barbara's parents in L.A. over Christmas. Coming home came down with another asthma attack.

Early 1982

A large, black rabbit with one white paw was sitting by my car. Its coat was rich and luxurious. It had large chestnut eyes and seemed unconcerned that I was watching it. Mentally, I realized that the black rabbit was an omen, but there was no feeling of the mythological.

13 January 1982

Gurdjieff's birthday—the first time I had missed since I joined the Work. I felt funny all day. Dozing off that night I dreamed I called my answering service (which we don't have) to see if I had received any calls. A distinct female voice said: "Mr. Gurdjieff called for you."

Later dreamed Gurdjieff had come to town and was staying with us in an attic, living behind a set of screens. That night there was to be a dinner for him. All the Work people were there and every table was taken. I noticed a waiter setting up a new table down by the stage and so gave the waiter a five-dollar bill to set up a table for Barbara and me, but he made a big face handed the bill back to me. It was only a one-dollar bill and so apologizing I gave him a five.

Gurdjieff was dressed as a sort of medieval peasant or craftsman in knickers, shirt and vest, all very colorless. He seemed oblivious to all the people there and acted as if he were totally alone, taking no heed or notice of anyone. He seemed, perhaps, as if he had lost something, for he walked up and down and even scratched his head at one point.

I made a judgment of him as being an old fool and just then he looked up at Barbara and me, first looking straight at her and giving the two-fingered cuckold sign behind his head and then giving me a cutesy-nice face. With that I woke up.

That day Barbara was reading D. H. Lawrence's *The Plumed Serpent*. She said Lawrence mentions "the black hare of witchcraft."

16 January 1982

I wore my St. Paddy's day hat and navy blue pants and jacket in contrast to Sunya's Hindi attire. He said I looked like a black magician.

I told him about the rabbit. "Black," he said, "is a mystic color."

19 January 1982

Still think of returning to New York. In some ways I feel the experiment out here is over—in others that it is just beginning. Certainly from almost every angle San Francisco is better for everyone, that is, except for my reentry into "the arena." I feel the need to give and take, the intellectuality, the power of self-expression. Here, in terms of my job, I can do little. I've learned as much as I can about the various industries—it seems time to move on: but, the old questions, where?

I may have been wrong about the Work; at least I haven't found anything as strong or serious. But it seems like there is no returning. The guard is changing and I could never accept or be a part of the new guard.

I feel as though I have to find my own way now, and feel not up to the task—yet I have no choice but to go on.

25 January 1982

The black rabbit was in our garden. I threw it a carrot.

31 January 1982

Finished another rewriting of the book.

Remembered when I had finished the first writing and as I was writing the last scene I became aware that my body had tensed and wanted to cry, so I had let it and watched. So there I was with tears coming out of the eyes, and all the time watching. It felt disloyal in some way, like I was betraying something. But what?

When I had told Hoyt about this before, he said, "You've reached a milestone in the Work, something that only comes after having made many, many efforts." This time I didn't cry.

3 February 1982

Dreamed I was at our house in Ossining. Four women came to the house. They acted as if they were ordinary women but it was obvious they weren't. "Who are you?" I asked.

"The Void Sisters," was the reply.

Next I was out in space and in front of this gigantic figure seated in a chair with all sorts of colored lights going off behind him. He, or it, looked like Anubis—very impersonal. A judging figure.

10 February 1982

Learned that Bill Keeler was a Mill Valley lawyer and was absent on business, so Betty Camhi asked me to introduce Sunya at the darshan. I did so, but a bit nervously.

"This is Sunya," I said. "That means full solid emptiness."

"Nothingness," Sunya exclaimed.

"Nothingness," I agreed. "He comes to us from Denmark, England and India."

Earlier I had given Sunya a copy of *Emergence*, a newsletter written by Benjamin Creme announcing the coming of the Maitreya. In Buddhist tradition, the Maitreya is a bodhisattva who will appear on the Earth and achieve complete enlightenment and teach the pure dharma. According to Creme, that the Maitreya stopped the impending California earthquake was "tangible evidence" he had arrived.

Now Sunya began talking about Maitreya like he was already here. Afterward, I asked how could people who are asleep know whether the Maitreya was authentic.

"We couldn't," he said.

"Well, how do you know then?"

Sunya continued to speak positively about the Maitreya.

I wondered what I had gotten myself into. On certain levels he seems like a con artist. Had I made a huge mistake?

My feeling is that the latter half of my life will be nothing like the first.

14 February 1982

Sunya told me that he will have to move. He didn't say why. Spontaneously, without thinking about it, I told him he could come and live with us. I'm feeling he will.

15 February 1982

The black rabbit returned again.

19 February 1982

Introduced Sunya again. The half-hour sitting before the question period was powerful. Body couldn't relax, yet I went deep.

Sunya backed off the full endorsement of Maitreya just a little. The people he attracts are so weak-willed, weak-minded. It seems incredible that I could have made the right choice to choose Sunya; the ego is weakening. But this kind of thing makes me wonder what I have signed on to. More and more I am feeling I am in his hands.

28 February 1982

Wrote a news piece for *Industry Week*, "The Return of the Maitreya." (Yes, Patterson announces the return of Christ in a business magazine.) Gave it to the secretary for typing and said, "Gee, I hope I'm not cursed." Immediately felt as though I had been hit in the stomach.

This Maitreya business seems like a hoax. His messages show no new consciousness, no new phrasing or use of language. In a word—it's dull.

Spoke to Mother. It sounds as if she is thinking of coming to California.

7 March 1982

Woke up to a small explosion at the base of the spine that traveled to my head. I felt like a hurricane had entered the room and I was holding on for dear life.

8 March 1982

Woke up to a pulsating light inside my forehead.

14 March 1982

I hit Sunya with some tough questions.

He says he isn't mental, but he reads a lot — is his reading mental?

He says he is always aware, but can rarely remember the restaurant we have gone to for lunch hundreds of times now.

He says he is spontaneous, but usually tells the same stories over and over again.

His answers weren't all that good, but he wasn't flappable.

2 April 1982

Asked Barbara to read the UFO book *Messengers of Deception.*
"Why do you read books like this?" she huffed.
"I usually don't. What book have I read like this?"
"That Charles Fort book," she said.
This was long ago, *The Book of the Damned.*

4 April 1982

Flew down to see my mother. Over dinner I asked what she had learned, having lived all alone for six years.

"I have come to God," she said in a quiet voice. "There was no one I could turn to, no one that would understand or could understand. I was all alone.

"I thought of committing suicide — only for John and Matthew I would have. It got so bad I thought I would lose my mind. I prayed and prayed. And when I hit bottom He came to me. He walked with me and He talked with me and He told me He was my friend."

She put her hand to her heart. "He's inside me now and I feel so good inside. I know nothing can harm me or take Him from me."

I had the sense we should drive to Key West. It was good to get her out of the house. On Sunday we went to St. Paul's church. I took communion for the first time in years. The Epistle was from Hebrews 5:1–10. The Gospel lesson was John 12:20–23.

"You are tired of the phenomenal."

15 April 1982

Sunya is leaving today for his six-week "Viking raid on the gangster city of Chicago." Before he left he invited me down to the cellar for lunch. The house, set on a hillside, has a kitchen in the cellar. It was a very hot day outside, but the kitchen was so cold I was freezing. The hair on my forearms was standing up, my knees were knocking.

A rickety old table had been set up with two chairs. He motioned to one and said, "Your throne. You ask intelligent questions."

He plays about over the stove. It was rather dark in the cellar. I am seeing these two different realities, or interpretations of it, at the same time. I get the feeling I am in a cave with King Yama, the Lord of the Dead, and am near blue with cold. He brings me some bread that looked like it had been sitting out since the week before, some horrible looking prunes. Then King Yama pours the soup into a crusted old bowl that looks like it hasn't been washed for weeks, with a spoon that's seldom seen any water. He follows this up with a plate of stale crackers, moldy cheese and a half-eaten banana whose skin shows just a little yellow between great splotches of black spoilage.

He sits down and eats heartily, as if it is a sumptuous feast. It's the same food as mine. I've never seen him eat with such real gusto. At one point, he looks up and asks if I'd like some more.

"Sunya, you really eat this stuff? It's all decaying."

He smiles and serves me a plate of noodles, carrots and peas.

He doesn't say anything, so I sighed and gave it a go. But finally I put down my spoon.

"I can't eat this stuff, sorry," I tell him.

"What's wrong with it?" he asks, as if it were perfectly delicious.

He didn't seem to care. In fact, he reached across and ate my blackened banana.

"The death of a caterpillar—what's that to a butterfly," he says.

I took a few courageous nibbles, but by that time he had finished. His bowl and plate were wiped clean.

He smiles, "A little dirt won't hurt you . . ."

When he brought out the dessert I blanched. On the plate were pieces of brown bread with a piece of an old egg (he admitted it had been there since the morning), jelly and slices of dark bananas again.

Sunya's face was very light looking but the hand he served the plate with had a purplish cast. The purple coloring, the veins, the old wrinkled skin — it seemed like I really was dining with Yama, the king of death. I remembered that he had called his first dog "Lady Yama."

"Sunya, how come you're so into death?"

"But it's not the death you're talking of."

"Do you want more dessert?" I shook my head. I hadn't eaten any.

"Okay," Sunya chortled, "I'll risk it." He began to reach across the table.

I waved him away. I didn't want to insult him, so I made myself do otherwise and ate it.

Sometimes I think he is a lovely old man, sometimes King Yama and sometimes that he is who he says he is, Sunyata. At other times I think I am being conned — this is my greatest fear.

I told Sunya before he left that "I doubt a lot."

"It's good you see that," he said.

He handed me a paper when I was leaving, saying "This was written long ago but this might help an Innerstanding."

> I find that by shifting my attention the focus of attention, I become the very thing I look at, and experience the kind of consciousness it has. I become the inner witness of a thing. I call this capacity of entering other focal points of consciousness Love, you may give it any name you like. Love says I am everything. Wisdom says I am nothing.
>
> Since at any point of time and space I can be both the object and the subject of experience, I express it by saying: "I am both and neither — and beyond." Also I have found that some thoughts become self-fulfilling. Things would fall in place smoothly and rightly. The main change was the mind,

it becomes motionless and silent, responding quickly, spontaneously, but not perpetuating the response. Spontaneity becomes a way of Life. The real becomes natural and the natural—real, and above all; infinite affection, love dark and quiet—radiating in all directions, embracing all, making all interesting and beautiful, significant and auspicious.

18 April 1982

Jean Klein, author of *Neither This Nor That I Am*, was giving a dialogue in Berkeley. Barbara and I went. He was slender and bald but with long white hair on the sides covering both his ears. He reminded me very much of Lord Pentland—erect carriage, spoke in a precise, intellectual manner.

Afterward, spoke to Emma Edwards, one of Klein's English students who travels with him. She told me she'd taught philosophy at Manchester University. He had first seen her when she passed outside the window of a restaurant in which he was eating. He immediately came out and introduced himself, his eyes flashing light.

"He turned his 'high beams' on," she said.

She's been with him ever since. Jean was an educated man, she said, spoke four languages, Czech, German, French and English, played a Stradivarius violin, had served in the French Foreign Legion. He had gone to India after the war, met his teacher who initiated him into the Tradition, and when he returned to Europe in the 1950s he had begun teaching.

20 April 1982

Klein was giving interviews so I went to the Marietta Inn down by the Bay. It was a warm sunny day. He had rented a room for interviews and we sat outside on the porch. He spoke about having been in Santa Fe but has come to prefer the California shoreline. He said he would spend five to six months a year here.

I told him about coming from New York, how I had trusted something, but now felt like I was in space. The insecurity was tremendous.

"You are tired of the phenomenal," he said.

Phenomenal. I would have never thought to use that word. But he was right.

"See the fear, let it develop as it would," he added.

I sensed he moved from his intuition. He kept feeling the moment and acting from that. He seemed so natural, open, spontaneous. The image of his face was dynamic, not static.

I spoke of the Work.

"It develops attention with tension," he said. He paused, "It conditions the mind in a certain way."

I didn't want to argue, but it has a different aim, to develop servants of God, so I said nothing.

I talked about painting and through my painting teacher Don Stacy I had learned to paint not from the head but intuition. He told me, "Live your life like you paint."

We talked about morality—"There is no good and bad," he said.

We spoke about perception.

He told me: "You take me in with the five senses—what I look like, my dress, the sound of my voice. But then you think about what I have said... Now you conceptualize. You can't do both at the same time."

I spoke about the inner sound. He seemed to say it was the sensation of the body.

About kundalini, he said it happens when you are ripe.

I spoke about Rajneesh equating Christ with Hitler. "Rajneesh is stupid," he said. He repeated this a few times.

He spoke about putting people in mental frames and agreed with Sunya that there was no witness.

He got up quickly and we shook hands twice. He patted me on the back and said he'd be back in California in December and would like to see me then.

It was a wonderful, very full conversation that lasted an hour and a half.

Constantine Dies, 1/1980

Capturing the Moon

Man and Lion

Glory to God, 11/1980

Only the Shadow... #1, 4/1982

Only the Shadow... #2, 4/1982

25 April 1982

In Chicago, Vasavada was having Sunya lead the Friday evening meetings at his home, but realized:

> To most of their questions, I embarrassingly found that Shunyabhai was not replying to them directly. As the evening continued, my embarrassment increased. But in the course of time I began to feel that, even though there was no answer to the question asked, whatever was coming from him was authentic and, at least for me, penetrating my whole being. He was talking, not talking to us, but talking to the Self in us all. He was speaking the language of Silence. Silence was speaking to the Silence.
>
> The bond that I felt with him was very different from what I felt towards my first two Gurus. Shunyabhai was a friend; there was no awe, distance, no putting him on a pedestal. Yet all along I always felt, and still feel, that he was a very different kind of holy man than I have ever met. He was really a born mystic, he was so childlike, innocent and never felt embarrassed when he had no answer to a question asked by an enquirer. He would plainly say, "I did not experience this. I do not know. I am not mental, I do not have language to answer."

Late April 1982

I felt I had died. Nothing there. [I did not write down what happened and have no memory of it.] Finished two paintings entitled *Only the Shadow . . . #1* and *#2*. Both very dark, almost completely black, hard to see. The first one had a series of mountains in different colors, their tops formed into gullies like they were once volcanic. The second had a ring of parrots overlooking a dam with two figures fighting far away. Behind them stood a single larger parrot with his head cocked to the heavens, as though waiting to hear something.

I painted *Constantine Dies* in January 1980. And then came *Capturing the Moon*, *Man and Lion*, and *Glory to God*. With *Only the Shadow* . . . , I have no idea of what happened, why I "died."

[The last painting before I left for California shows a woman with a man behind her riding a horse. He is frightened, she is not. *Taken Into The Unknown,* I called it. Stacy said it was my best painting in that all the images were locked together.]

15 May 1982

The young woman from whom the Alan Watts Society had rented rooms for Sunya had become more agitated with his "nothingness" and wanted Sunya to leave, but she had signed a rental agreement. For him to break it, she began prancing around the house naked. When that was fine with Sunya, she then began to have sex with boyfriends on the couch in front of him. That, too, was okay, but he realized his acceptance was driving her up the walls. So, when I again invited him to move in with us, he first said to ask my wife if she agreed.

Barbara, a private person, didn't want him. I was adamant, but that night in bed my hand touched her abdomen and it was in knots. I realized if I persisted, she would get sick. So in the morning I told her it was okay if he didn't come. My releasing allowed her to release, so she said it was okay.

18 May 1982

Sunya is to move in tomorrow. After much discussion, we decided to give him our large bedroom, which is at the end of the corridor and out of the way. We could put in a few chairs and he can receive people there. We would move to the den, which is much smaller, and the kids would be up in the loft area.

19 May 1982

Bill Keeler moved Sunya in. His whole worldly belongings consisted of several cardboard boxes tied together with string and some bags of clothes, many threadbare and in need of stitching, which Barbara quickly took care of.

31 May 1982

I was waking up in the middle of the night. I felt oppressed. I told him he would have to find a new place to live.

1 June 1982

We had a sitting in his room. Afterward, I saw Sunya as I had before. We joked and laughed and I told him he could stay.

Most nights after dinner we would sit on the couch together in the living room. He would read me the letters he received from people around the world. Sometimes I would help edit some of his writings. Often they seemed like poems to me so I began putting some into poetic form and gave him a booklet of these entitled *Sri Honesse*. One poem was *Samata* which means sameness in its best sense. [See Appendices, "Samata."]

Sometimes I would point out how a word he used had more than one meaning and the meaning he meant wasn't exactly clear. "The words just bubbled up," he said, and he wasn't for changing them. Then the game would begin. I'd insist. He'd give ground but not to the point where he changed anything. Logically, I'd back him into a corner. Conceptually, he was between two walls. Whatever he said would be wrong. But then he would just jump into an opposite corner, like everything he had agreed to up to that point didn't matter.

"Sunya," I'd say, "you can't do that!"

"Yes, I can," he'd retort with Danish impishness. "In fact, I just did."

"But it makes no sense. It's not logical."

"Mere logic," the Great Nobody would mutter.

"Sunya!"

"So I contradict myself," he would intone, drawing on the words of Walt Whitman, "I am vast . . . ."

Then he'd say, as if looking into the inside of my brain, "Anything else?" Then he would pick up the stack of letters and toddle off down the long corridor to bed.

He did have a sweet tooth. I would say, "We're having dessert tonight. Do you want some?"

"Wu," he would answer, meaning beyond 'yes' and 'no.'

"Sounds like 'no' to me, huh?" I would tease. His knee would give a little knock against mine so I'd relent and he'd get dessert.

One evening I came home from work at *Industry Week* and was exhausted, angry at the day's events. It is one thing to see your teacher at a group meeting or Work day or having made an appointment, and quite another when exhausted and angry from the day's events and there is Mr. Nobody in all his "full, solid emptiness." You are completely full of the day, he is just the same as when you left him in the morning, having brought his tea and toast to his bedroom, in a word—empty. The moment is searing. You are totally identified with your story. He has no story. So, you begin telling him of your day. He listens. He apparently is interested in a way that might be called an empathetic disinterest. You try to make him understand what happened, pull him into your pain, justify your state. He smiles and nods, even laughs a little, but he remains unaffected.

One day after months of the same, you finally get it—your suffering is yours alone and you can either go on suffering, or you can drop it. It's all the same to Mr. Nobody. A simple quiet clarity strikes through all your centers—*suffering is a choice*. You don't have to suffer psychologically. As Gurdjieff said—"The last thing a man will give up is his suffering." And so I just dropped it and realized I could.

I asked if I could meditate with him, supposing that he meditated every morning as I did. He seemed surprised but agreed. The next morning I went to his room. He was lying in bed and made no motion to get up but instead motioned that I sit down. At his age he was incontinent and the urine smell from the rug and bed was overpowering. I was deep in meditation when the image of three cobras appeared, their tongues flicking out at my face. There was a simple watching, no reaction. Not fed, they disappeared. It was then that a space, a deep silence, was awared and I found myself beyond the body.

Afterward, I related this to Sunya. He seemed no more interested or disinterested in this than he was in my person's story.

"You are tired of the phenomenal." 83

When I mentioned the urine smell and also how messy his room was, he told me good-naturedly that I had "a sin-complex."

People always wanted to know what Sunya recommended as the way to come to Real Being. His answer, "The method is to be still," didn't satisfy them. He was asked about meditation. I don't recall what he said, but this is what he once wrote:

> To Wuji meditation seems to be negative in as much as thoughts are kept away—concentration on one thought. His sadhana has been contemplation not meditation, concentration or *neti neti*, not shutting out, but rather an all-acceptance, a passive positivity, negative capability; and receptive sensibility, specially when he is ego-freely alone in nature and in the Self. In such a mode of contemplation there is no concentration, no effortful elimination or holding onto one mantra. Thoughts may come and go: he is thought-free, not caught up in thoughts, concepts or abstractions, but free in those and in the graceful Self-interplay and mutual interpretation.
>
> Meditation on forms—or on concrete or abstract objects, concepts and ideals, is said to be *dhyana* meditation, while Self is *vichara* or *nididhyasana*. Wuji's natural mode of *Sadhana* seems to have been contemplation, rather than meditation or *vichara* inquiry.

People would come to see Sunya at all hours of the day or evening. One early morning a young fellow turned up looking distraught. He'd given a fierce knock and had blazing eyes. I was going to tell him to come back later, but Sunya called out from his bedroom to let him in. Concerned, I trailed after him and with Sunya's nod, sat down and listened. At first he was okay, but then it seemed when he felt no rejection, no criticism, no judgment he did as many people did in experiencing Sunya—he just unloaded everything he was carrying. It got so wild and weird, so heavily charged with energy, that I thought of saying something. I looked over at Sunya, but a quick glance of his blue eyes told me to accept it all. So I just sat and watched as the fellow really went into a psychic whirlwind, the long suppressed pent-up energy flaring. Metaphorically, it was like this acceptance was sending him to the edge of the cliff. Was it going to make him jump?

This is where everyone steps in, but Sunya said nothing, made no gesture. The fellow hesitated, looked at Sunya. There was no judgment, only space, conscious space. He became bewildered. If he was going to go crazy, it was all right. That was his choice. He stopped talking, moving erratically, his face became still, and he sat down. It was probably the first taste of sanity he had felt in a long time. He sat back, then another person, another "I"-of the-moment, began talking calmly. Then he thanked Sunya, as if nothing had happened (and it hadn't) and left. We never saw him again, but he had the blessing of No-thingness and Sunya's Wu!

I told Sunya sometimes life is like a minefield and you don't know what your next step will bring. "Step by step as thou goest, the way will be shown to thee," he would intone.

"But Sunya sometimes you take a wrong step . . . ."

"A little death now and then is salutary."

6 June 1982

Besides the Maitreya, Sunya now talks about a book someone sent him, Swami Omananda's *The Brother: Teachings of the Holy Hierarchy Given Through 'The Boy.'* How weird is this going to get?

8 June 1982

A beautiful dancer at the meeting said she had a dream of her being Eve and that she would meet the new Adam and they would produce a new race of more conscious people.

Her boyfriend, in cowboy boots, said he had taken her up the mountain and made the sun come out and the clouds part. He said he was Christ Consciousness and working on Buddha Consciousness. I asked if he had heard of Maitreya but he couldn't pronounce the name. But he did have plenty of energy and obviously something had happened to him. Probably acid.

12 June 1982

Some five years of Sunya's darshans had been taped by the Alan Watts Society. Though I've edited it, here is one that gives a real taste.

> *Do you conduct meditation?*
>
> I never conduct anything. (Laughter) I let it be. We have one hour of silence before these meetings. I'm not aware of the silence. *I am* that Silence. Anyhow, you make me talk, talk, talk. So ask some questions.
>
> *What about the mind?*
>
> I was never mental. The mind did not develop. I never had to study. It's so troublesome here. You're so mental here. In India there is an intuitive awareness. They are not 'mental' in your sense of the word. The mind-ridden ego. The ego-ridden mind. They are very much the same.
>
> I've been in good health all the time. Never needed a doctor. And not a psychotherapist either. (Laughter) That is your guru now. This is all a body-cult and a ego-cult here. Power-power.
>
> *What about your childhood?*
>
> I was not aware of consciousness, though there was consciousness. There was no contrast. So why is all this? It is what is called "*Lila — Swa Lila.*" Self-play. God that plays in all this. There is nothing but God. The first time I came to India I passed by a slum of Calcutta and in this little shop was a boy chopping up onions inside and he shouted, "In the whole world there is nothing but God!" That's India. The intuitive light reveals reality. Not intellect and not trying...
>
> T. S. Eliot has the phrase: "Where is the wisdom we have lost in knowledge?"
>
> *What about Emmanuel?*
>
> My peasant mother gave me that name. It was my secret name. I did not know because I do not use the mind, but I was aware that it was the in-dwelling Christ.

How do you mean that?

I mean it is the sense of the beginning of St. John's Gospel: "In the beginning was the Word! The Word was with God and was God." That Word was Emmanuel. That's the Logos, the Sophia. E-mman-u-el! All the prophets and all the archangels had the name ending in *e-el*. Something to do with the God within.

"Ilya, Ilya, how thou has glorified me!" Not: "My God, my God, why hast thou forsaken me?"

And then just later *Consumatum est*: "Joyful!" Not: "It is finished." Very tame.

How do you see people in our mental culture?

Wuji feels that the deep psychic dis-ease in modern man and woman is the diseased, atrophied condition of the intuitive faculty. There is a whole world of life and beauty that we might enjoy by intuition and by intuition alone. We ignore the source of intuition, the light of our intuitive, central "Shiva-eye," the source of the intuitive life and the insouciance which is so lovely in free animals, in plants and tree-friends—and in ego-free, age-free Being.

What do you experience?

I find that by shifting the focus of attention, I become the very thing I look at, and experiencing the kind of consciousness it has. I become the inner witness. I call this capacity of entering other focal points of consciousness Love, but you may give it any name you like. Love says: I am everything. Wisdom says I am nothing.

11 July 1982

Betty Camhi drove Sunya and me to see his old friend Lama Govinda and his wife, Li Gotami. We stayed about two and a half hours. Having suffered several strokes, the Lama was now sitting in a wheelchair. He seemed smaller than before. But the head was still large, balding, long white hair, glasses, a small tuft of beard.

He is painting, using watercolor and charcoal, scenes from the Tibet he saw fifty years ago. "Once I concentrate on an image, give

"You are tired of the phenomenal."

myself completely to it, I can always call it back," he says.

I could feel the power of his mind—he would be carried away by it when he was speaking. He had just finished *The Inner Structure of the I Ching*, which he considered his most important book, and didn't know what to do next.

Sunya, who had said nothing all this time, spoke—"Just be, Lama, just *be*."

His voice was deep and ageless.

The Lama moved a little back and forth in his wheelchair. It was as if he were digesting what he had just heard. Then when he began to speak again, Sunya said quite definitely, "Just be, Lama, just be."

And the Lama visibly relaxed in his wheelchair, slumped a little.

Li Gotami served tea and cookies. Some old times in Almora were recalled and then the Lama and I got into a discussion about language. It was interesting to witness the transformation from the child of before to the intellectual powerhouse. He spoke directly and uncompromisingly. There was no "space" in his argument. In other words: he knew.

I had always thought Lama Govinda to be enlightened. It was obvious that evening who was liberated and who was not. Certainly the Lama was a great soul but not fully released and realized.

2 August 1982

Went with Sunya to *Midsummer Night's Dream*. Shakespeare was conscious—the whole play is about sleeping, waking up, being what you are and knowing that you are nothing.

20–26 August 1982

Betty had interested the *Pacific Sun* in writing a story about Sunya. Now its cover featured a large photo of Sunya with the story line:

"At Age 91, Mystic Sunyata Has Followers and a Wealth of Knowledge, But He Remains a Humble and Reluctant Guru."

It was excellent, considering the writer knew nothing about him or what he is.

25 August 1982

At the darshan, having seen the *Pacific Sun* story about Sunya, another beautiful young woman shows up. She informs everyone she is "Alexandra, Queen of the Nile, Empress of Egypt" and her boyfriend "Jesus Christ Incarnate." Later, she accused Sunya of being phony, a representative of the Beast because he had not appropriately recognized her.

Sunya gave her a wonderful smile and apologized. Then he added, "There was a Sufi who ran around saying, "I am God, I am reality, I am Truth—and got his godly head chopped off. He was not mature enough to be quiet."

With puzzled looks on their faces the Queen and Jesus Incarnate left.

The Queen is not much different from all of us really. She believes herself to be some ancient personage while we believe ourselves to be some currently named incarnation—Patrick Patterson is much more acceptable than the Queen of the Nile, but, in reality, what is the difference? Both are illusions. She got caught inside a Halloween mask and never came out and we are inside some manufactured personality.

1 September 1982

Queen Alexandra and Jesus Incarnate showed up again and caused such an incessant uproar that I had to call the police. When they arrived and the two were asked to leave, Jesus said to Alexandra—"Who are you?"

"The Queen of the Nile."

"Then why are they doing this to you?"

That stopped her for a moment, then—"Schmucks!... they're Nazis!"

5 September 1982

Went to New York. It is such an ego town, everyone intently into their own story. Saw the play *Faust* and the film *Mephisto*.

"Come, let us plunge into Time's rushing dance,

"Into the roll of Circumstance!" *Faust*

"*You are tired of the phenomenal.*" 89

"*Blood is a quite peculiar juice.*" *Mephistopheles*

13 September 1982

Sunya said that you became more than human by stepping through the person.

"But it could be said, too, that one becomes less than human," I said. "From the egoji's point of view he doesn't know."

Sunya agreed.

"So, in a sense, there is no difference in giving your life to God and selling your soul to the Devil?"

Sunya agreed.

It followed logically then — though I didn't say it — that one passed beyond good and evil; these terms only apply to ordinary life, the lives of souls, the *jiva*.

18 September 1982

As usual in the morning, I went to Sunya's room and gave him his tea. His gown was open to the waist. The next day I went and it was open to his knees. He is hung like a bull. I turned quickly away, my face full of pain; it was something I didn't want to see, a way I didn't want to know him. I went to work and my eye developed a sty. The next day he was fully dressed and yesterday inside the morning paper he buys and then puts out for us to read is a book on neo-tantra by a disciple of Rajneesh.

Sunya had said at some point that he had had sex only twice, once with a woman, once with a man. "That was enough," he said.

I wondered if that was true.

21 September 1982

Sunya wrote something about it not mattering if one light bulb burns out in the city of light. I told him Wuji was a plagiarizer. He at first said — or pretended — not to know what this meant.

I told him that Nisargadatta had written this in *Seeds*. "Well," he answered, "Wuji says that same thing."

Why does Sunya have no light around him. He said once it was because he never had to dominate himself. What in me is questioning, doubting? Only the mind? Or something more?

22 September 1982

Betty and some of the people who came to his weekly darshans had gone up to Oregon for the weekend to be with Bhagwan Rajneesh. She was given the name "Layena."

The *Pacific Sun* reported, and she and the people confirmed, that instead of collecting expensive watches as he had in India, Rajneesh was now collecting Rolls Royces. Up to twenty-one at the moment.

Afterward, Sunya told me he wanted one, too. I couldn't believe it—all this talk about materialism and now he wants a Rolls! I thought he must be joking but he kept mentioning it.

He wrote about the Rolls, ". . . all standing in a disciplined row—and a thought occurred that one of the Rollers might be given to Sri Wuji, but Sri Himself rebuked our levity, saying 'Do not want, do not anticipate or expect: The new Beatitude is: 'Blessed are they who expecteth—nothing.'"

28 September 1982

Woke up with the experience of the perfection of imperfection; that imperfection is a necessary part of perfection. We are all perfectly-imperfect.

Spoke to Sunya about it. He says an old fairy tale says you must accept three times, on three different levels, body, mind and spirit.

"I'm not used to being a speaker at all. I've always been a listener, a spectator in the background. Until I was 'kidnapped' here, I didn't know I had a language or anything that could interest people. I never learned any of the Hindi languages. I didn't need it. There in India there is an intuitive language. The language of Silence, the language of Being, not of doing. Here you are doing-doing-doing . . . ."

We spoke about the stages of consciousness.

"*Turiya*," he said, "is not the fourth stage; it is what underlies the three stages, but people do not readily comprehend it, therefore it is said that it is the fourth stage and the only Reality. In fact, it is not apart from anything, for it forms the substratum of all happenings and it is the only truth. It is your Being, the three states appear as fleeting phenomena on it and then sink into It alone, therefore they are unreal. 'We are such stuff as dreams are made on.' Wu!"

30 September 1982

Dreamed I was in a long line in a cellar. Something to do with the Work. A young fellow stepped out of line and began to do intense mudras. Finally, he projected an astral hand and arm from his physical parts. I was intrigued. He asked if I wanted it sent to me. I agreed. I watched it leave him and come toward me, but when it got near it scratched me. He said it was because of the difference in our vibrations, that if I closed my eyes that wouldn't happen. I did and the hand came and touched mine, grasped it. It was like an animal's hand, an ape's hand.

7 October 1982

Rowena Pattee, a visionary painter and writer, came to a darshan. She had given Sunya her book *Song to Thee: Divine Androgyne* and he had "responded most enthusiastically," she told me, and asked to buy more copies. She came to see him many times afterwards and he would always call, "Pat! Rowena's here!" and we would sit on the floor and tell stories and laugh together.

5 November 1982

Went with Sunya to hear Benjamin Creme in Berkeley. Small with thick white hair, he had power, a lot of light around him, pulled down a lot of energy, had everyone holding hands. But I don't trust the whole thing.

He said that the Maitreya calls on mankind to accept the principle of sharing, that there can be no true peace as long as hunger exists anywhere, that the products of the Earth belong to all people everywhere and so the food, energy and raw materials are to be redistributed, and this will mean no third world war once the media makes this known.

During the question session, I told him, "You and the Maitreya must be hopelessly naïve if you think the media bigwigs would allow the use of their airwaves."

Creme said, "The media was created for just such a thing."

He seems sincere, but he is hypnotized and doesn't know it.

16 November 1982

Sunya said he had written to the Buddhist author Christmas Humphries from Almora and they had exchanged correspondence, and when he was going back to Denmark for some family matter they had met in London for lunch. Nothing came of it. He had expected that. The same happened with Gerald Heard, the poet. Few see him. Westerners expect spirituality to have a certain power, a presence, to have a "weight."

Sunya is air. He is like a picture frame with no picture. You can look right through him. He says it doesn't bother him, although he is too quick to give his credentials, to tell his story—there must be some pain there. To have people think one thing and then completely discount you upon meeting would seemingly hurt. How odd to be put here enlightened but with no mind, no strength of conceptuality or memory. Why does he repeat himself so often and use the very same words, gestures in telling the same story?

6 December 1982

Sunya and I went to Lama Govinda's home in Mill Valley. The Lama and his wife, Li Gotami—Sunya always calls her "Darling," but privately refers to her as the "Dragon Lady"—were interested in Rajneesh. The Lama was still in a wheelchair and Li was suffering from Parkinson's disease but said it was getting better. She said her left side was bad and the Lama's right side was bad.

"We make one whole," the Lama quipped.

They both were dressed in dark red robes. They reminded me of two birds—he a parrot and she a raven or blackbird. They seemed very vulnerable but alive. Sunya seemed so young beside them and yet he is ten years older.

The subject of karma came up and how with calendars and the I Ching when a 'bad' day or 'bad' throw came it wouldn't be accepted. Karma makes the circumstance compelling, but we didn't have to accept the compulsion. We have a choice, especially in our attitude toward what happens. By raising ourselves above the compulsion, we can either not manifest it or mitigate it. Also, in making new karma we have to give our will, our intention, to the act, otherwise it is not karmic. "We kill ants when we walk," said the Lama, "but we do not make any karma."

In a poke perhaps at Sunya, the Lama spoke about those who do not care for anyone else. "They are egotists," he said. "Conscious but icicles." He wanted to feel for others. Otherwise life was not worth living. Yet it wasn't dualistic. There was only one consciousness. I didn't feel Sunya completely agreed with him, but nothing was said.

Someone had given them a framed print of a Gauguin painting. Odd to give as a gift. Li, a painter and writer, asked me what I thought of it — two women, one a redhead, plus a devil-like character behind them. Very black magic looking. I told a story about Gauguin finding a key in a fish's mouth. His native friends laughed because it meant his woman there was sleeping with someone else. Also, I said, he was into black magic and had venereal disease.

The Lama spoke, too, of water finding the lowest level and passing on, not being stopped by obstacles but going around them. I feel he is more Taoist than Buddhist.

I felt today that I had a choice as to whether to be conscious — aware of the moment — or to go with my thoughts. I've never had that strong a feeling about it.

I asked the Lama why if I can will a bad thing — why can't I will a good thing? Why can't I will myself to be conscious. He said it was a matter of maturity.

15 December 1982

Jean Klein returned as he said he would and was giving a dialogue in Berkeley. Sunya went with me. While I parked the car, he went ahead of me. Hurrying to the building I suddenly stopped as I saw both him and Jean Klein approaching one another but from different directions. I emptied out. When they were about to meet all I saw was a white blur. Their images disappeared. Just this emptiness. Then they reappeared. I don't remember what happened thereafter.

Jean Klein spoke about the witness. "Memory is only a way of thinking," he said. When the dialogue was over he left the main room. Sunya and I also left but rather than go to the car he took me to a small adjacent room, and went in to speak with Jean. When he came out he shoved me through the doorway with such force that I half ran in and fell to my knees before Jean Klein, who was sitting in a chair. He told me, "Don't go out to things but wait for them to come to you." Then he invited me to a weekend seminar he was having at a retreat center in Santa Barbara.

On the way back from Berkeley we passed a billboard that had been whited-out in preparation for another ad. I'd kept the thought of Sunya wanting a Rolls Royce, but hadn't seen how it could ever be fulfilled. Now the thought suddenly struck—*rent a Rolls Royce for Christmas!*

17–20 December 1982

Barbara and I went to Jean Klein's weekend seminar at Casa de Maria, a lovely retreat in the Montecito hills above Santa Barbara. I hadn't expected a lot. Not because of Jean Klein, but because I had already been touched by Sunya. He was my teacher of nothing. I had come because Sunya seemed to favor my going and I was attracted by Jean Klein's gift for speaking so clearly about that which cannot be spoken of.

For the early morning meditation, I went into the chapel and sat down directly in front of him. The marble floor was cold and before closing my eyes I took in the morning light streaming softly through the stained-glass windows, lighting the large carving of Christ on the cross. Beyond the windows was a graceful tree, its trunk so thick it gave the impression that it had always been there.

It was quiet in the chapel and there before me sat a slender figure dressed in white yoga pants and white sweater with a white or cream-colored scarf turned once around his neck. His face was strong, the chin, the nose. The forehead large. The figure was very light, relaxed. I had the feeling that in some way he wasn't there. I felt like I had never seen him before.

Then I closed my eyes. The moment was so fully, palpably alive. Very soon this great tide of energy streamed into me. My first impulse was to fight, to hold on, as I felt it would sweep "me" away. But I trusted, relaxed, accepted and opened to the energy. Soon, there was this tremendous sense of well-being, of wholeness and harmony.

"Jesus Christ," a voice inside me roared. "This is for *real!*"

Yoga was another surprise. Jean Klein teaches yoga in the Kashmir tradition that forgoes the gymnastic approach and works directly on the energy body. It is a yoga which moves the body-mind through space very slowly, all one's attention devoted to the movement. The postures are taken in silence, eyes closed, the attention on sensation-feeling-breath-movement. There is to be no effort, no struggle, no end-gaining. It was unlike any and all I had done before.

At the dialogue on the last day someone asked a question about the point of doing all this yoga — after all, wasn't it another "thing," and therefore transient and unreal?

The question took everybody's attention.

Jean Klein just sits there, gazing into the marble floor of the chapel. In the shadows of the evening sun, his face takes on a different form. I wonder: *Who is he?*

Finally, he begins to speak: "It's a pretext," he says simply.

A pretext!?

"... a pretext to share the Silence."

And with that everything fell away: and we are all just sitting there: empty-minded on a marble floor in the hills above Santa Barbara.

When we left Casa de Maria and got on the highway heading north I was almost immediately pulled over. The cop came to the window and asked — "You on drugs?"

I told him I wasn't.

"Well, you're only going twenty-five miles per hour on 101. It's a highway!"

I told him we'd been meditating for the weekend.

"Now that's one I've never heard before." He laughed and wrote out a warning.

When we came home I told Sunya about the seminar. He nodded as if it was nothing to get excited about. "Expect nothing and get nothing," he murmured and the rare born mystic went off to bed.

25 December 1982

After Sunya celebrated Christmas with the kids, Barbara and myself, I told Sunya his real gift was outside. He was truly perplexed — a wonderful sight, for once. I opened the door and gestured toward the white Rolls Royce, complete with chauffeur standing by the open rear door of the car. He giggled —

"Oh my, my carriage," he said.

Sunya was wearing his rainbow-colored shawl along with a new turquoise-colored kurta he had received as a gift from Chicago. It all worked perfectly with the turquoise leather seats, walnut paneling, push button windows.

As we drove off, I gave Sunya a large model Rolls Royce and ten small Rolls, each gift wrapped in Christmas paper for his friends. First, the chauffeur took us to Lama Govinda's house in Mill Valley. Sunya told me to go in and give him the gift.

"Oh, no!" I laughed, knowing that behind that door was the infamous "Dragon Lady." No one simply visited the Lama. You had to ask her for an invitation.

Sunya implored. I resisted. "Perhaps we should send the chauffeur?" I said.

"We'll both go," said Sunya finally.

It was a brisk but clear, sunny Christmas morning. I knocked. The sounds of the Lama's wheelchair creaking across the floor were heard. The door opened and the Lama beamed with delight at seeing his old friend. He began weeping with joy.

From a downstairs room his wife shouted, asking who it was. She began to come out and was fully dressed in an Indian sari.

"But I'm not dressed!" she thundered.

"It doesn't matter," Sunya told her.

She told him that unless he apologized, he would no longer be welcome.

He maintained that he could not apologize for he had done nothing wrong.

He handed the gift to the Lama and we left, with him in his wheelchair shocked and in tears, and her steaming.

The chauffeur then drove us to other devotees' homes. We had the chauffeur honk until they came to the car window. Then Sunya handed them their little packages, saying—"I've got a Rolls, you should have one, too."

Some students believed that Sunya had actually received a Rolls, so I made out a Wuji Chauffeur Application:

> If you are interested in taking manifestation as a chauffeur upon arrival of Mr. Nobody's Rolls Royce, which will be used for Sri Nothingness' rolling contemplation, please fill out this questionnaire. As to compensation, should that question arise, remember the Wuji maxim: "Expect nothing and get nothing." Seen from the vantage point of Advaita Vedanta the gift of nothing, or no-thing, as the individual case may be, is of course the consummate gift surpassing all else in the purity of its emptiness. Should you expect some type of "something" that, of course, immediately disallows your incarnation this supreme satisfaction or *anand*. Better grace next time. And remember, says Sunya, "All is well."

Later, Sunya wrote a short note to Lama Govinda, who replied that they both should now abide in what was eternally real, Silence.

They never saw one another again.

Sunya

Sunya meets the Queen and King of Denmark

Sunya and Pat at lunch

Sunya with his Rolls Royce

Pat and Sunya at Mount Vision

1983
"My God. This is for *real*."

1 January 1983
Sunya had never been to Pt. Reyes and so Rowena Pattee invited us to come. We arrived after noon and Sunya told stories of how he had been giving away Rolls Royces for Christmas to Lama Govinda and "the regulars." Rowena said a great white heron had landed in her front yard and stayed all morning. She said she had seen that the Earth would go through a time of travail

and then children would be born who would be more spiritual. She served us a hearty soup and then took us over to Olema and up to Mount Vision for a walk. She was surprised at how Sunya walked with such "gracious ease." There was the most wonderful golden light at sunset.

[See Rowena's documentaries on the internet *Soul Fire* and *Vision for 21st Century*.]

10 January 1983

Jean Klein gave a dialogue again tonight.

"The question is never answered on its own level. The question is dissolved in living being. So it is not to put emphasis on the words."

His way, he said, is listening.

I asked about direct perception—"If what arises in consciousness is one's self, what of suffering that is outside one's body?"

"That is you—the perceiver's—as well," he said. "All points to the Ultimate Subject—consciousness as well as ignorance, joy as well as suffering. When you see pattern without images you give the other person the opportunity to be free.

"One has to see what they feed the body—both in terms of food and impressions.

"Fear—you localize the fear in the body. You see where it is located, how it is affecting your joints. Do not escape from it. Face it directly. Go into it. Give it freedom to express itself, to tell you about itself.

"Tradition—what is transmitted is tradition. It is not in words."

I asked about how not to identify with another's disharmonious energy. He spoke about eating the right kinds of food. In other words, not eating that energy.

There are two types of memory—psychological and functional. Each of us should read 'our book.'

Sunya and I went in to see him afterward. I could not speak. Klein touched my elbow.

31 January 1983

Jean Klein was staying at the Durant Hotel in Berkeley, a few blocks above Telegraph. He was on the sixth floor. He mentioned the weather. I gave him the Peanuts cartoon showing Snoopy singing to himself with the music bars but no notes. "I see in this some of what you've been saying," I told him. He smiled and nodded.

A small number of Klein people had formed a group and met on Sunday. He asked if the group had entered the silence or made an object of it. I laughed and said it felt more like an object, at least for myself. He said I should not come to conclusions so fast. Conclusions will come but I should not make them.

His noting that I came to conclusions was so accurate that it broke open the conversation. I told him about hearing the sound, "Nada," and sitting and coming to the blankness. I said I needed a direction, that I wasn't coming to anything, although, of course, there was nothing to come to. Still, I felt I needed something.

He said not to listen to the sound, to let it go. That it was a result of my desire, stay with the body's wholeness or well-being. He said I should make no efforts. "Stop making an effort, focusing yourself. Let go, relax. Make no effort to become the Silence. Do not come in from the periphery so you have this idea of there being an inside and an outside. Allow things to happen. Human beings are quite mysterious, if we don't come to conclusions but allow the moment to unfold, then perhaps we will come *to the moment that is not a moment at all—it is out of time.* We have no boundaries then." He said I should just allow this moment to happen to me during the day. He said it would happen.

There will be no inside or outside or separateness, but it will all be of the same ground or background. Things will appear in this ground, or consciousness.

At night before going to sleep he told me I should lie down flat on the bed and notice the points of contact between my body and the bed. Then I should see the points as one point, or feel them altogether; the heels, calves, behind, back, head, etc. Then I should experience the temperature of the body. That experience will be there waiting when I wake up—I will wake into the same fullness.

I told him of my experiencing as a child with being called or taken away by some force so that I would go up into the woods and run around nude with an erection. Then I would be released and return to my playmates. I spoke of waking up at night and told to go places, etc. I said I didn't trust the Universe. That though evil was ignorance there was a conscious evil, perhaps people with power who had strayed off the path. I felt I needed some kind of confirmation.

"Anything given intellectually," he said, "could be countered. The experience would have to come of what I have said, 'All questions will be resolved in this.' Watch for the gaps between thoughts. They are not nothing."

I told him about my asthma. It's psychosomatic, he said. Comes from having an overbearing parent. He said I should eat no cooked fats. Put the oil on the food afterward. Also, very little sugar and especially the fats. No acids either. Cook the vegetables in water for two minutes and then cook them in new water.

Yoga—breathe consciously. Relax into the position. The *Kumbhaka* at the end of the exhalation and the end of the inhalation. Watch these two points. He again repeated to watch for the gaps between thoughts.

2 February 1983

At the darshan with Sunya I was quite cruel—hurling one question after another. "Stop," I said at one point when he was looking for a word. "Are you aware now? You look like you're unconscious to me, like you're searching for a word."

Outside, I asked if he still wanted me to go on asking questions.

"If you like," he said, "why not?"

"Well, I've been throwing them past you, Wuji. You haven't hit one yet. Struck out every time."

"So," he says with a wry smile, "what's wrong with that."

At which, of course, I died again.

13 February 1983

At the Klein dialogue a Da Free John devotee went on and on

with an intellectual blueprint, ending by asking if the heart was on the right side as Ramana Maharshi had said.

Jean dodged and weaved around the question. He did say that one took energy in through the eyes and focused it at the back of the head in the old brain.

I spoke up talking about the materialism of spiritual experience, the formulations, blueprints.

"Stay out of the psychic realm," he said.

16 February 1983

At Sunya's darshan a woman asked about the Anandamayi story he often tells. After he spoke about it, she then read the same story in Paramahansa Yogananda's *Autobiography of a Yogi*. Sunya had said that he had never read the book, but here it was. He just nodded.

Why does Sunya lie? This is not the first time. He uses what Nisargadatta has said, too, as his own. I am very tied to Sunya, but I might have made a big mistake. I wonder if he is just simple minded—he wants to be there and isn't. When he went to India his simplicity—simpleness—was taken as spiritual and so, as he says, "I fit in." But then I talk to him—he is so gentle. Maybe he doesn't recognize any real separation. To him we are all one and the same really. So maybe whatever he relates to that someone has said or written is really him as well. There is no difference.

6 March 1983

I am seeing more and more of this dark side of myself. It is becoming so transparent. I have really hurt people with things I have said to them. I am becoming embittered.

At work I am running into the "old scene"—I'm doing such a good job, independent of any direction, that it is frightening those above me. "Tough to manage," says Stan Modic. That translates as I question orders, follow my own direction. The same thing happened at *Food Management*. All around it is the same—everyone is afraid of giving me power. Or, rather, acknowledging that I have it.

2 April 1983
   Received a letter from Don Stacy:
   Keep your eyes open and you will surely meet yourself! Whatever touches you—is you—outside of general things that touch, or would touch, everyone.
   All those special, unique reactions are exposures of the self.
   And fate is said to be made of that which is unknown.
   This is the "hidden gold." The self to be revealed!

3 April 1983
   Fischer, a Jewish psychologist from Boston, had appeared at darshans. Asked Sunya to give him a spiritual name. Sunya asked what his middle name was. "Isaac," he said. Now Isaac takes Sunya to Easter services.
   Lottie Rose, a new person, greeted Sunya saying she had first met him in 1975 in Buffalo when she was "in pain and utter despair about life." She said he had told her "All is well. All is right that seems most wrong" and "His answer lodged in my consciousness."
   She had just moved to Berkeley and by chance she heard of the darshan he was giving. Seeing him again now made her realize "In a split second that my own essential nature had its center in restless, tireless doing—whilst Sunya Bhai was totally, peacefully, perfecting, centered in Being."

7 April 1983
   At the darshan I noticed Isaac did not look at me as he usually did when I came into the room, always sizing me up. A few nights before I had told Sunya I was repulsed by Isaac—by his arrogance, pushiness, the gamesmanship. After the darshan Sunya gave Isaac some xeroxed material. Isaac told him in a voice loud enough for everyone to hear—
   "I'm glad, for otherwise others would be jealous."
   I knew then that Sunya had told him what I had said. I felt naked and betrayed and blew up inside but said nothing. All throughout the meditation I continued to explode and erupt like a volcano. I was going to speak to Sunya about it, but it would lead

to nothing but ugliness. We drove home together in silence. Yes, silence is best but something is broken. It was good to say nothing, to contain it all. It gave me great energy.

Lottie Rose came again and brought a car full of gifts—cookies, jams and jellies, candles, flowers, clothes. He called her "Abundance."

14 April 1983

At the darshan Isaac answered questions for Sunya. As Sunya said nothing, even seemed somewhat interested, people began to think Isaac was enlightened.

17 April 1983

Reflecting on his time in America, Sunya wrote:

> Sri Wuji and Co. are as well as ever and ready to go home, be it to the Real Home—or to the *Turiya Nivas* in Himalaya, and there BE at joyous ease. In this wee Viking-body we have now been in this predominating extravert, mental and Power-pleasure oriented Yankeestan five years. After the sessions and satsangs aware Yankee guys and girlies do seem to try to squeeze the life out of the wee Viking-body. They kiss its face and say that they love it. Yet no harm is done and no insult. At first the Himalayan Wuji was surprised and somewhat "shocked" at our seeming sex-appeal at 90, but he awared that in Yankeestan you can *make* love and fall into it and often make a sorry mess, and that it always implies sex. Sri Wuji is the Divine Androgyne and thus Wu! The Real Marriage is always within the individual-wholly-fixed in the Individuum. All is right that seems most wrong to clever-egojies. All that happens in *Swa Lila* happens providentially—by its Self. It is *Swa Dharma* and *Swa Darshan*. Compassion can be condescending. Co-passion cannot. It is Empathy Experiencing and profound Gratitude in the divine, mystic and Ghostly Whole.

P.S. Do keep joyously well for the Alan Watts celebration in November. Now, coming to mid-April, we are due to sally forth in annual Viking-raid on the gangster-city—Chicago. Neilji is projecting a "Dance with the Void"—with two periods of Shunya Silence. At present we are reading Connor Barrett's auto-biography in the form of poetry and graphic wood-sculptures—after 50 years of rich Silence.

30 April 1983

Sunya left for Chicago's gangster city. He'll be back in six weeks.

2 May 1983

No matter how we dress up our anger and no matter how much we believe we understand what we are saying or doing—the fact is that we are calling that up in ourselves with all the residual reactions. Even if we dress our devil—the ego—in charming clothes and benign appearance he is still what he is. We have given him the floor and he will take our time and energy in any fashion he can, drenched in duality, fears, angers, etc.

The Queen of the Nile and her boyfriend again turned up in Mill Valley and fortunately Sunya was in Chicago. She made the *Mill Valley Record* this time, descending on the Mill Valley City Council declaring her sovereignty over the town, and saying, "All of you have been taken over by the headquarters of the Fuhrer of est. From now on there will be no psychiatrists, psychoanalysts or psychiatry in this town. Mill Valley is for the chosen, holy people. There will be no more poverty throughout the land. I have cursed you. I have blessed you and now I love you all. We have abolished poverty on Uranus, you know." She was then led away by four uniformed policemen, who she called "Nazis!"

3 May 1983

Patterson is all this horseshit of thoughts, etc. But then the board is swept clean of all that—and there is only awareness of being. I tack onto it either an I-thought or a witness-thought. That way I am still in the ballgame. But if Patterson only exists in ego, then Patterson is not the witness. Who or what is the witness?

This kind of question has the ego as its refinement. It is not a question of the witness except perhaps when the I-thought remaining in the witness postulates and asks: "Am I the witness?" Or, more sharply, "Is Patterson the witness." No. But that "no" is an intellectual "no"—it is not an experienced "no." The mind is still playing tennis with itself.

When ignorance asks about itself—no matter the question or the answer—it "wins" because it is taken to exist, to be real. Patterson can keep on being ignorant all his life and that is stupid. He keeps "winning" and all the time "losing."

There is no witness because "I" takes itself to be the witness. "I" shuts the witness making more ego. The ego's identification with the witness heightens the intensity of duality, heightens the suffering.

Is the way of Gurdjieff to suffer the "I" out of the witness into the individual I and then to the Self?

18 May 1983

I dreamed of Lord Pentland—the first time he had appeared in my dreams since October 1982. No, there was one before I left the Foundation and he was going to give a lecture and I recoiled inside at the thought of hearing him. (I realized how much pain I still carried in leaving.) Now, he and I were walking up some steps. He asked me what I had told people about my leaving the Work. I avoided a direct answer and said I'd been very careful to not speak to many people. We embraced and I nuzzled his face and I realized how much I cared for him. Next I was walking and carrying him on my shoulders.

21 May 1983

At Vasavada's in Chicago, the questions now centered on Sunya. Neil Vanover, a student of Vasavada's, taped one of the darshans with Sunya that centered on Wuti-Wuji.

"My God. This is for *real*."

Sunya, tell us about the dog.

During my 40 years in India I usually had a small dog, four of them in all. The first was eaten by a leopard. The second was famous. I named him, or he named himself, Wuti, which was the sound he made when he barked. I got him, or he got me, in 1950. He had come over the mountains from Tibet in a sack with a lion cub.

Well, Wuti lived for nine years. The cleverest dog you ever saw. Without being taught, he could Namaste. He went to the butcher shops in Almora and sat outside with his paws pressed together. An Indian finds it hard to refuse that gesture. And they had never seen a dog make it.

When Anandamayi, the Holy Mother, was visiting her ashram in Almora, Wuti and I would walk down the mountain a few miles to her ashram. We would sit in silence there for hours, both of us, and the dog, too. One day after Anandamayi had sat with us for a half an hour. She then repeated it: "That. Is. Not. A. Dog."

But she did not say what it *was*.

Wuti became famous in Almora. I was a Nobody. In fact, people started calling me "The Dog Sadhu." Indians had seen Holy Men and Holy Women but never a Holy Dog!

Wu! He had been a man also, but he told me he much preferred being a dog.

You could speak to him?

Intuitively, yes.

In words?

No, not words. But meaning was there in innerstanding. Not mental at all. Intuitive awareness. After almost ten years he was poisoned. It was one of those drug pushers who lived on the Ridge and put some poisoned meat outside his door. It was time to go, and so Wuti went. (Sunya chuckles.) But after that he's still here.

(Sunya pats an empty chair. Laughter)

He's my invisible friend, my spirited friend, my

inspiration. He's my alter ego. And yours. Everybody has a Wuji, which changes from time to time. For me, a dog star, for you, a sentient typewriter, talking mirror, wee small voice, your secret playmate from the beyond the beyond.

Is Wuji here tonight?

Certainly. But you are not aware of it unless you become spiritually Aware, see him clairvoyantly, with the Intuitive Eye.

He is here.

Is Wuji a consciousness?

Yes — a playful, impish, sex-free and god-free consciousness. Or conscious awareness.

Is Wuji an Angel or God?

Yes. Both. And neither. Wu!

What is Wuji really like?

Wuji is like no thing on earth or heaven. One of his name tags is Sri No-thing-ness.

Does everybody have a Wuji?

Sri Wuji, Sri-No-thing-ness is not possessive, nor a possession; neither a have nor have not. He innerstands at joyous ease and awarely. He intuits and appreciates, apperceives and is Real-ly sex-free, body-free, birth-free, and death-free. Wuji is ego-free in non-dual One-ness. Or wu-ness. Wu!

Why did you change his name from Wuti to Wuji?

He needed less bark and more bite! Adding *Ji* to a name is what is done in India to show respect.

(Later, he told people if they would like to see how animals communicate with each other and people who understand them to read James Allen Boone's *Kinship with All Life*.)

13 June 1983

Drove up to Rajneesh's community near Antelope, Oregon, with a letter from Sunya asking to be invited up. Had to leave the letter with the chain-of-command, but I was told I could see

Bhagwan Rajneesh, for every day he drives one of his Rolls Royces down a long road and all his disciples line the road. I stood waiting for him. When the Rolls was about six feet away I self-sensed, breathed, emptied, divided the attention. The next thing I saw was the rear end of the Rolls. The same "disappearance" as when Sunya and Jean had met.

23 June 1983
   Sunya spoke often about spiritual death, liking to quote Ibsen's "The victory of victories is to lose everything."
   I often wondered how Sunya actually saw life. Intellectually, I thought I understood, but what was the experience like, what was it really?
   He said there were two consciousnesses, the cosmic and the ego and they can exist together unclashingly.
   I intuited that his identification was with the cosmic, not the ego. He always saw things as 1) being unreal, that is, temporary; and 2) occurring within the Ur ground, the Self.
   Of things happening and not happening, he would say that on one level the happening reigns supreme; and on another level it doesn't matter; and on a third level it never happened.
   I asked him what he took himself to be.
   "Dead," he said, with a glint in his eye, meaning from the ego point of view.
   "Then you're not human?"
   "Supra human," he answered.
   "But that's only from your point of view," I said kiddingly.
   "What other is there?"
   "Huh?"
   "There's only the Self," he softly declared, as if it were as obvious as the fire that crackled in the fireplace.
   "But what about me? I'm real, aren't I?"
   "Of course," he said, paused, gave a smile—"so it seems."
   "You mean to someone locked into duality?"
   He nodded as if it were a horrible condition but an amusing one nonetheless.

"I dunno," I feigned a sigh. "I'm not sure if I want to be in the place you're in. It seems a little remote, if you know what I mean?"

"I know nothing," he quickly answered.

"Yeah, yeah, but still you know what I mean."

"I suppose so. But it's not mental, this knowing. Here in the West you are so mental. Dr. Jung talked about 'psychology-mentology.'"

Sometime afterward we went to see Ibsen's *Hedda Gabler*. The characters and actors fit their parts perfectly. All at once I found myself "inside" the play. That is, there was a suspension of disbelief. And with that the play came up in my consciousness—the play was living me. The characters could be nothing different from what they were. Each was true to him- or herself. There was no urge to change their lines, be critical, somehow intrude my own small ego into the play. No, I was just pleased to be effortlessly watching, taking in, what was happening. It wasn't a momentary experience. It lasted throughout the whole play. It wasn't that 'Patterson' was missing. It was more that he was passive and the witness, the choiceless awareness was active. Or as said in the Work 2-3-1 or 3-2-1.

At the end of the last act I said to Sunya—I could sense that he could feel, innerstand, where I was—"So this is how you see 'life'?"

He smiled and nodded.

"Wow!" I exclaimed.

"It's more than a dream. But it's not exactly real either," whispered the rare-born mystic, taking my arm as we descended the steps leading outside.

Once there I said—"So what's real?"

"Why nothing, of course."

"Nothing is real?"

"Take it in a positive form. Void doesn't mean vacuity. It means full, solid, emptiness. Not blandness."

"It's the plenum (full) void?"

"There's no understanding. Only *innerstanding*."

At his darshan Sunya would often open by saying, "I have Nothing to teach, Nothing to sell. Just be still and know that I Am is." Often he repeated the same answers, even down to the gestures.

The mind fought it, but once it stilled one took in what was behind, as Sunya said, "the play of words." People asked all sorts of questions, mostly about their lives. Some asked about "enlightenment." Sunya held that everyone was so, they just didn't know it. He would repeat Shankara's statements—

> I am That,
> You are That,
> All this is That,
> That Alone Is.

Some people began to believe they were That and acted so. Now Isaac, the New Age psychologist from Boston, not only answered questions but began interpreting. Sunya didn't mind.

"But they came to hear you, not him," I told him.

"What's the difference, really? Besides, I like to hear the answers."

An intrinsic problem with Advaita—or, rather, with people attracted to it—was that it held that everyone was the Self, realize it or not. It takes a great deal of spiritual training and maturity to come to the necessary self-sincerity to observe and admit to oneself just how far from that one actually is. As Gurdjieff said, "Sincerity has to be learned." Not grounded in that, Advaita became a conceptual drug in which the egotism deftly defended itself by adopting the stance of the Self coated with spiritual imagination.

7 July 1983

Isaac has left. A wealthy woman asked him to give darshans in Temple Terrace, Florida. I almost miss him.

14 July 1983

Bill Keeler was sick so I introduced Sunya. A young guy, a friend of Isaac's, came to the darshan. He accused me of being an "Orchestrator." My stomach burned in flames, but I didn't identify with it, kept it below the neck—my consciousness never became fire. Afterward, I invited him to come again. Said his name was Justin.

16 July 1983

Justin comes to see Sunya. He says he is an actor, his mother is the Devil, his sister, an angel. He talked with Sunya for two hours.

24 July 1983

At the seminar at Casa de Maria in Santa Barbara I asked Jean in the dialogue about that point where the body relaxes yet the very relaxing tends to make one more sleepy.

"Take note," he said, "that you do not experience the whole body. There are zones that open up and the relaxing of these zones creates thought. As one relaxes deeply an alertness appears and an inner structure."

25 July 1983

This morning at the 6:30 a.m. meditation I sat down before him. Suddenly, I was engulfed in a flow of subtle energy. I had to swallow. It was enormous like a wave. A voice again said, "My God, this is for *real!*" And then quickly, the voice, "What have I done?" The wave kept flowing the whole time.

Then he had us sense our limbs—"Don't produce the feeling," he said, "allow it to come up into the listening."

We started with the hands, then the face, feet, legs, shoulders, abdomen, lumbar region, shoulders again and feeling the body's weight on the floor. Then we "felt" the ears and went in through the channel. Next the eyes and inside from the left eye to right hemisphere and vice versa. Then we felt that point in the lower brain where the eyes meet. Afterward we expanded the back of our head. We were instructed to keep the shoulders low.

This was followed by breathing exercises, left nostril, in and out; right nostril, in and out. Then an exchange of nostrils and finally a very quick breathing in and out with the stomach held pressed against the back.

He had us close our eyes and go into the yoga movements. But instead of taking them, we first visualized our subtle body taking them. Then we would slowly listen, feel the whole body, and slowly move ourselves into the position. And hold it. "Explore it," he said. "Pretend you are in a dark cave and you have only your senses. Don't force or use the will, if so the muscles in the subtle body contract." We then "felt" the space to the front of us; to the back; left and right sides.

26 July 1983
   Asked a dumb question about our bodies being our karma and how hopeless it seemed. "Don't make a tragedy," Jean Klein said. "And in twenty years who knows? You might have a new body."

27 July 1983
   The artist is the channel, not the Doer. He is the witness. It is all right to be the witness, as long as he does not say, "I am the witness." There is still a separation with the artist, he is not completely out of time. And so there is a residue — something that remains. And it is this which can be expressed, that forms the basis for expression.
   "I have answered your question somewhat from behind," Jean said.
   "From behind?"
   "Yes, behind."
   "But, good!" I said.
   I had asked Jean what was missing in artists like Van Gogh, Pollock, Rothko that they had committed suicide, stood before the Unknown but were eventually done in by it.
   Earlier he had said the difference between the scientist, artist and truth seeker was that with the scientist and the artist the witness remained. In the case of the scientist to express the laws of material objects, with the artist to express, celebrate, joy and peace. But with the truth seeker there was no reflex. He was consumed.
   "In pure action there is no residue, no time."
   With Mozart, for example, his music came out of Silence and was returned to Silence.

28 July 1983
   I asked a question saying, "Jean . . . Jean . . ." each time louder.

It was so hard to call him by his first name. It was so intimate.

"I read your book *Neither This Nor That I Am*. I was surprised and elated to find in the first paragraph you mentioned René Guénon and said you went to India to find a living Tradition. What does tradition mean in reference to your having said just now that 'Yoga was a pretext'?"

His answer was something like this: Tradition means the living transmission of Reality. There is the positive way that was taught by Krishna Menon where the transmission comes from the lips of the guru. This is the negative way showing you what you are not. *Neti, neti.* I would say to you that you should observe the objects that enter consciousness but come back to the subject and from there the Ultimate Subject. Do not react . . . .

His face changed throughout. There was such a seriousness and directness to what he said, I felt it was coming straight from the Source.

"Yoga," he reminded me, "is a pretext for sharing the Silence."

"What about ideas?" I ask."

"Ideas are nothing," Jean answers.

Nothing. I am shocked still.

Finally, I tell him—"But what about principles?"

He tells me the same—"They're nothing in terms of consciousness."

A deep anger flares up in me.

I want to leave. But I am sitting directly in front of him and there are a lot of people between me and the door . . . .

Now, there is only space between us, silence. Suddenly, I see he is right.

Yes, *there is only Consciousness.*

29 July 1983

Jean ended the meeting by saying that "Whatever we see we should touch—you look at the sky, touch the sky—you look at the sea, touch the sea."

11 August 1983

The word must have gone out, for now with Isaac out of the picture here is Justin, a curly-tousled young punk rocker with a cherubic face, quite articulate, and he, too, fully convinced he is the Self. Sunya did not dissuade him. Like Isaac, he soon took to answering questions for Sunya.

He would come to see Sunya during the week, tape recorder in hand, and spend hours telling Sunya his life story.

6 September 1983

Like Isaac, people began to believe Justin was enlightened. I was among the few hold-outs. Before the darshan started, he ran up to me and, pounding on my chest, cried out—

"Why do you resist Me?! Why can't you see Me?!"

"If you are really the Self," I told him, "what does it matter?"

That evening when we returned home I told Sunya what happened. He smiled but made no comment.

"Sunya," I said, "people are beginning to think he is enlightened. He's started answering all the questions for you like Isaac did. He's leading people astray."

"So, what is enlightenment?" the impish aspect of Mr. Nobody asked.

I could say nonduality, oneness, consciousness. But all these were just words, attributes, not what it was. I hesitated a moment then blurted out—

"What it is, I don't know, but I sure as hell know what it isn't!"

"But, of course he is. And isn't," Sunya observed.

"Yes, of course, the 'person' can never be enlightened. But what isn't the 'person' is."

"Who's to say who is enlightened?"

"But why agree with him then?"

"Why disagree?"

"Because he's crazy and you're making him more crazy."

Sunya adjusted his turban. "I'm not doing anything. I don't know what I do."

"Well, if you don't know, then you do now because I'm telling you."

"I don't know what I do and I don't care either."

Sunya sat up straight and clasped his hands together and pursed his mouth like a little boy who refuses to believe he has been bad.

"What's enlightenment?" he asked. "Are you enlightened?"

"No."

"Then how do you know whether he is or not?"

"Got me!" I answered.

"If you know what it isn't, then you must know what it is. Not 'know' but *innerstand* what it is."

"Yes, I agree."

"So be your innerstanding and all will be well."

Sunya had often said "All is right that seems most wrong," and I had added the clarification "*to egojies.*" He liked that and so now I repeated it.

Sunya nodded, gave me a little twinkle and toddled off as usual to bed.

On another night I brought up Justin again and 'enlightenment.' The conversation, if that's what it was, was the same but this time Sunya got up, his face red, and went off to bed, only this time he shut the door with a little jerk that made a gigantic sound. I never persisted again. There was such awesome strength in that little shutting of the door. I realized I had no idea of who or what I was playing with.

4 October 1983

Sunya and I were invited to see a Yogi Mahajan from India privately who was staying in San Rafael. Yogi Mahajan had known Sunya in India and they spoke about friends they had in common. Then the conversation came in my direction. There was something about the Yogi I hadn't liked. Perhaps it was the certainty with which he talked, giving ideas that were rather shallow or obvious in a tone of "truth." As he kept coming at me, I finally began to ask some questions — how could consciousness have a desire?

Wasn't opening up the chakras of immature seekers dangerous? And didn't Ramana Maharshi say that awakening the kundalini was "preliminary to self-realization"? His answers were not impressive and I was glad when it came time to say goodbye.

I thought I was done with it, but that night I suddenly woke up to find my spine ablaze. There was an energy pulsating that I had never before felt. I was perturbed that such a thing could happen with someone I didn't trust or feel any affinity with. I had to see what this was about.

5 October 1983

The next day Sunya and I went to see him at the seminar he was giving. Five hours later—five hours of feeling the fingertips, twirling the hands and tying astral head knots—we left and once again I thought that was that.

Yet that night the spine was again all fireworks.

13 October 1983

The Yogi's guru, Shri 5 Nirmala Devi Srivastava, a sixty-year-old Indian woman, was speaking at the Sausalito Presbyterian Church. She looked like a beautiful young girl, but when she sat down in the front pew she looked quite different. When she spoke I felt her incredible primal energy. It was as if I was a young child in front of my own mother. She was a great Earth mother in energy. Her face was massive, very strong, high cheekbones, very thick, a long nose and dark eyes, very bright, and a big smile. She talked of going shopping but keeping the attention inside. Then she denigrated Rajneesh and Kirpal Singh as false gurus. Kirpal's people, she said, had too many heart attacks.

Again, I was unimpressed—someone had told me, "She's not the latest in intellect"—and it was true. But once more I was awake in the spine, all aflame. Mataji was giving a weekend seminar in the Santa Cruz mountains. On impulse I called and made a reservation and again the spine started up.

14 October 1983

That night Mataji led a meditation. I went to bed feeling very aware. I hardly slept but my body was filled with light and light streamed out of the top of my head. I wondered if I would ever sleep again. I began questioning whether I should let the crown chakra be opened, as I had read somewhere that it was very dangerous.

15 October 1983

Mataji talked the next day. Again, it was a tirade against Rajneesh. When time for questions came I asked, "Mataji, in your last incarnation, who was your guru, and when did the kundalini awaken, or was it always awake, and when did you know you were the 'Mother'?"

That was exactly how the question came out and without aggression. She said she did many times have gurus and went on to list them. Her father had said when she was born that a goddess had been born into the family and he was her guru and that the kundalini had always been awake, but the last chakra, the crown, had only opened on May 5, 1970. She then ended by saying, "You could be my guru."

It was a long but not very impressive answer, but I still couldn't explain what was happening to my spine.

That evening Mataji was a completely different person. Looked different. Spoke differently. Was very gracious, humble, charming. She answered my question but in much more detail and much more convincingly. I felt a great affection for her.

16 October 1983

The next day was a *puja*. Mataji entered the room without looking at the audience. She had obviously prepared herself, or so it looked. She wore a fine sari, lush crimson red with a blue border with gold trim. Her feet were washed first in a large gold bowl. A little boy went up to her. Her eyes and facial features were so loving and her innocence matched the boy's. A tide of emotion came to me. I looked away for a moment and the Yogi caught my eye—did I want to wash her feet? I choked for a moment and nodded. I got up and waited my turn in the line of people that had formed. Muscles in my stomach danced up and down and I had to breathe quickly and continuously to keep from crying. I bent down to wash her feet. The water was all red. Her feet were young and strong. I washed one foot and then the other. Then she put a red *bindi* on my forehead. Her index finger really pushed. She withdrew her hand and I looked into her eyes. She was smiling and her eyes gleamed.

"You'll get it later," she said.

The day ended with a fire ceremony in which we threw our remaining negative energy into the fire. It began at 2:30 p.m. and was still going at 4 p.m. when I left.

Before I left, a woman told me that I looked as though I had been converted. I said the ceremony was very beautiful but that I had felt nothing. She said she expected me to be made head of the center they were starting in San Rafael. I told her, "Please don't wish that on me." She said the Yogi had told her that I needed to love.

When I returned home I told Sunya what had happened. "You weren't ready," he said.

1 November 1983

Told my mother about Sunya and mentioned that he had spent forty-five years in India. "I know about Indians," she said, "They worship *cows!*"

I awoke to a rotary motion in the *Anahata* chakra. Became frightened and turned it off. Stupid.

26 November 1983

A Watts Happening at the Palace of Fine Arts in San Francisco to celebrate Alan Watts. Went with Sunya. Among the known names attending are George Leonard, Fritjof Capra, Toni Lilly, John Lilly, James Broughton, John Blofeld, June Singer, Virginia Satir, Al Chung, Claudio Naranjo and Sunya. Gary Snyder and Ram Dass sending letters of regret, nothing from Timothy Leary.

Of all the speakers, the most interesting was John Lilly and his

Toni. She was in a red dress, he in a black jumpsuit with a silver zipper running from his hips to his neck. They were sitting in the row in front of us. She is to speak first and before she does, she tells him what to say and he tells her to "Fuck off."

She speaks slowly, beautifully, of Alan, her ex-boyfriend. Lilly comes up on the stage, hatchet-faced, large forehead, sunken cheeks. Something unhealthy about him. Trapped in his head, in the wages of good and evil.

He comes across the stage toward Toni with his hands raised in a gesture of embrace, as though he has not seen her before. She doesn't respond and his hands momentarily drop and then rise again and he turns to the audience and begins speaking. He talks about meeting Alan on his houseboat and being given a mind puzzle—or did he give it to Alan.

(What I remembered from his book was that he gave it to Alan and it took Alan all day to solve it. With Alan caught in his mind, Lilly puts the make on Toni.)

Afterward, Alan told him, "Next to me you are the most ruthlessly intellectual bastard in the universe!"

Lilly said that Alan and Toni and he had first met in the hot tub at Esalen. But Alan had said nothing. Toni told him this was strange because, "Alan always had something to say."

A year later Lilly goes to a party to see Alan, but he isn't there. Toni is. She is sitting on the floor; he doesn't remember her but is attracted so he sits down in front of her—Lilly stops a moment, says he has never told this to anyone—he is stoned on acid. It turns out she is as well. He asks her—

"Where have you been for the last five hundred years?"

She tells him, "In training."

"Love steers people," Lilly says. "Here we are so many years and acid trips, isolation tank trips, solid state aliens, extraterrestrial intelligences . . . later."

The next day it's raining hard, very foggy. Can hardly see out of the windshield. But Sunya is slated to speak so we go. June Singer begins the morning followed by the sensory awakening couple, Charlotte Selver and her husband. A Zen priest follows. Big belly

"My God. This is for *real*."

and matching ego. Goes on and on. A tape of Alan Watts' voice telling a joke comes over the loud speaker signaling it is time to stop, but the Zen priest goes on. Again, Alan's voice. The priest won't stop, so finally Bob Shapiro, the head of the Watts Society, comes out and leads him off stage by the arm.

James Broughton shows his film, *The Bed*. A lot of flesh. Broughton nude on the bed playing a saxophone. Great tits on the girl beside him. An odd film.

Now Sunya, dressed all in turquoise, goes up on the stage with Claudio Naranjo who reads a passage Watts has written. He asks Sunya its meaning. "It is true what he says," Sunya replies, and says no more. Claudio, nonplussed, gives his own interpretation. A question comes from the audience, "Sri Wuji, your spiritual friend, says we are only a mini-planet but we must think of ourselves as a globe." Sunya agrees and that is it.

Afterward, a parade of speakers all talking about Alan the great intellect, Alan, the great storyteller, the wit, the man who introduced the East to the West. Of them all, Al Hung, who finished Watts' last book, *Tao: The Watercourse Way*, speaks the most heartfelt words, saying at the end he could feel Alan smiling now and asking moments of silence.

Afterward, everyone goes to Greens restaurant for dinner. Broughton and his partner, Joel, sit at our table. Broughton gets a yen for me and begins to fondle my bicep and pushes his leg against mine. I guess he's still in his film.

"James," I tell him, "you are married and so am I. Get involved with me and I'm going to be your Angel of Death. I'm going to demand of you a spiritual relationship. No heavy physical numbers."

He turns white and leaves the table, Joel scampering after him.

Betty Friedan sits alone at a corner table. I walked in the first women's lib parade in New York years ago. In leaving, tell her that, and say, "It's said once you get on a tiger you never know where it will take you."

She heartily agrees.

A few nights later Sunya wanted to see Robin Wordsworth

Carlsen, "the World Teacher," who was speaking in the San Miguel room at the Hyatt hotel in San Francisco. I didn't want to go, but he said he would pay my way and did. With tape recorders and cameras all over the room, Carlsen appeared in a tux with white gloves and a Sherlock Holmes coat-cape. "This," he says, "is my performance." He walks the floor, the words spin out ceaselessly, alternating his voice, shouting, clapping his hands, telling the audience that he knows us, feels like he has known many of us before. He talks about no-thing, the manifest and the un-manifest, he berates the audience, teases, talks about splitting our ego like an atom. His World Teacher Seminar may not last long, he says. The two-day seminar costs $350. My impression of him is that he is crazy. There is something almost sinister about him, something violent.

The next day Michael, Carlsen's disciple, comes to see Sunya, who agrees to go with him to the seminar.

I never ask Sunya what happened.

7 December 1983

Our landlord decided she wanted to sell the house. I spoke to Sunya about moving. He said to call Lottie Rose, "Abundance," and tell her we needed a house.

"But, Sunya," I said, "you don't just call someone up and . . ."

He waved me away assuring me it would be all right.

And so I called and Lottie instantly agreed and told me to find a suitable house and she'd buy it.

10 December 1983

Sunya received a letter from Albert Bouwmeester which he gave to me to read. Albert had gone to the hospital for an operation on his stomach. He caught a fever from a rare, very vicious bacillus. The fever grew so high that his lungs collapsed and stopped functioning for two and a half weeks and he went into a coma and was given an artificial lung. The first week he was hardly ever conscious and relatives discussed arrangements for his burial around his 'death bed.'

We lived completely in a psychic visionary world, the journey into the Bardo, the under-world, the realm of the dead, the other side of life.

Archaic, archetypal visions, Biblical worlds, middle ages, worlds, primordial nature, we plodded though monstrous mountain-landscapes, suffered immense colds, crossing seas (the Styx, under-world river) which one has to cross in a small, wooden fishing-boat during tremendous gales. Everything of cosmic dimensions; shattering, terrifying was the way our person was disintegrated. All visions were in black and white suitable to the world of Hades.

The beautiful thing was that we were never one moment afraid (of death or whatever happened) but full of trust and surrender, in the fishing vessel in a gale on the ocean we went trustfully to sleep with a heap of rope as a pillow on the floor, this was because we were not identified with our person, but with the Self. (How poor are words here.) Neither life nor death could touch us and we faced the cosmic calamities going with inner love through the journey into death as on the journey through life. What is the difference?

After three days of traveling in the Bardo on the fourth day there appeared huge chunks of matter racing through the cosmos and we intuitively grasped that these chunks were parts of us, reintegrated, made whole again. More and more of these 'parts' of us appeared (we knew that the critical moment had passed and that we were on our way back again, the journey back from Hades), until after another three days, suddenly we were completely whole, re-integrated again, born a second time, as a baby, but with an adult consciousness—this time.

Once during this week the Self took on the symbolic images of Christ. God became Man and Man became God. It was immensely comforting. A bridge was erected between the Self and our ego-personality. All was well. There was no difference between integration and disintegration. There never was one moment of fear.

1984

"Take me with you."

8 January 1984

Emma Edwards asked me to bring a tape recorder and mic to Jean Klein's talks and seminars. Instead of sitting in front of him I was to sit off to the side. I didn't like that but I did so. As soon as he entered the room, I felt his vibration—right up the spine and darting into the head.

He had spoken about tension that results from energy that is trapped. Attention to this trapped energy, acceptance of its existence in consciousness, dissolves it. An experience of well-being results. But thereafter one feels a certain slackness; they waver between being awake and going to sleep.

Near the end of the dialogue I asked about the attention having "gone down to the bottom of the sea," so to speak, and finding oneself between being awake and falling asleep, if an effort is made that comes from will.

"The reaction," he said, "comes from the ego, now more subtle but still there."

"But if I don't make an effort, I fall asleep, so what is needed at this point?"

He began talking about seeing a tree but not to look at it but the space around the tree. To incorporate the tree with the space, make it one. "And it isn't the space one sees, it is the light," he said.

Then he waved his hand—a motion of an arc from the left shoulder over the top of the head to the right—"But let us not be poetic." He then went into a direct answer which I don't recall. But he ended saying it was like a promise that I would not be falling asleep so much, that I would remain awake, and that there was so much to see.

As I continued to tape dialogues, I would differentiate them by dates and what I thought was the theme. Emma said he was always interested in the theme I wrote.

9 January 1984

As soon as I began sitting, there was a wholeness of energy. I was focused in my forehead, but below there was no tangible separation between my body and its surroundings.

10 January 1984

Sitting the same but not so intense.

11 January 1984

The sitting was even less so, but now there is the memory and certainty that to sit is to move into the space.

16 January 1984

Dreamed Lord Pentland and I were walking down the street in San Anselmo. Not talking but not unfriendly, just being. I pulled out a long fat cigar. Started smoking. So did he. It was like we were together celebrating something. I think it has to do with the rewrite of *Lord Have Mercy* I am doing.

19 January 1984

Had an argument with Sunya over Justin. He said he was willing to leave before and would leave now. Truly angry. "I could knock both your heads together!" he said, making a quick motion with his hands, knocking his knuckles together. I felt there was no understanding of what Justin puts everyone through. "He doesn't affect me," Sunya said. I likened the situation with what happened with Isaac. Sunya tended to blame me for both situations. I wasn't having it. By not telling Justin his questions are really assertions of his 'enlightenment' asking for affirmation he is driving him further into megalomania. Sunya said, "Tell him not to come to meetings." But no one wants that.

15 February 1984

Lord Pentland died of a heart attack yesterday, Valentine's Day. The funeral is on Thursday. I called all the major airlines for flights to New York but all were booked. The only possibility was to go by red-eye, but I couldn't book a seat over the phone so I would have to go to the airport.

As it happened, Betty Deran, who was in my original groups and had been quite close to Lord Pentland, was coming for dinner. I remembered that at a meeting at our apartment she had given him a candied apple. The way she handed him the apple was so beautiful, full of caring and respect. But something had happened between her and Lord Pentland. She'd gotten angry and joined Mrs. Stavely's Oregon group. Now just the opposite had happened and Mrs. Stavely asked her to leave and so she went to Rajneesh in India.

As it was an early invitation, Barbara and I decided to go ahead with the dinner. Betty had not heard of Lord Pentland's death and when told it was as if I had said the mailman had forgotten to deliver the mail. At dinner she told one story after another about him, all negative. At one point I reminded her that he had just died. Betty acknowledged that and quickly launched into another story.

Barbara and I were in a mild state of shock. It all seemed surreal. Then I remembered that this is exactly what Gurdjieff had said in *Life Is Real Only Then, When 'I Am,'* that when someone dies all their friends meet and share their negative memories. So, even if it was in total reaction, this was just right. At one point I even tried to tell a story myself but went completely blank.

When I arrived at the airport I found a long line in front of the ticket counter. The wait seemed interminable. Finally, there was only one woman between me and a man at the ticket counter. When he stepped away, she suddenly passed out and fell to the floor. Without the least consideration, I stepped over her as the people behind me rushed to the woman's aid. I leaned in to the counter, saying — "I've got to get to New York. It's an emergency."

The agent checked her computer screen. There were no flights to New York.

"I've got to get there," I told her.

She checked and rechecked connecting flights but kept shaking her head.

"There isn't anything," she said.

"I've got to get there," I repeated. It was a voice I'd never heard before.

Her fingers tapped more keys, checking schedule after schedule. Then suddenly her eyes widened and she exclaimed — "I've never seen anything like this!"

All the flights I needed to get from San Francisco to New York — Los Angeles, Houston, Atlanta — all lined up with the right boarding times.

16 February 1984

When I arrived in New York I went straight to St. Vincent Ferrer Church at 66th and Lexington where the funeral was to be held. So many of the old faces were there.

Lord Pentland's daughter, Mary Sinclair Rothenberg, tall, slender and erect like him, read from the Bible and then from *Sword of the North*, a novel about Prince Henry Sinclair, their remarkable ancestor of the thirteenth century. The passage she read was of the Prince's death. Her voice was strong and clear and carried throughout the cavernous neo-Gothic church. But when she came to the last line—"And another Sinclair chieftain is dead"—her voice escaped her and the word *dead* shot like a fountain into the high vaulting of the church, echoing down on those of us in the pews.

Afterward, I went to the Kensico Cemetery at Valhalla where Lord Pentland was to be buried. His gravesite was by a tree on a small hill, just above a pond, and looked out upon the Hudson River and the high sheer cliffs of the Palisades. The coffin was lowered into the open grave. A line formed and one by one people walked to the grave and took a handful of soil, said a silent goodbye and threw the soil atop the casket.

I took up a pile of soil in both hands and peered into the grave and gave a last goodbye and prayer to my teacher, my great warrior chieftain, and tossed the soil on his coffin.

Later, I was told he had grown a beard and that he had spoken on Sunday at Sparkhill and told those assembled that they had to work with more precision and to know the time to work, and "If sensation does not become feeling, it becomes power."

19 February 1984

Rowena was with Sunya when I got home. Told them both about what had transpired. She had me pick a Tarot card. It was the Hierophant. I felt it was Lord Pentland's final message to me. I felt inside: "Goodbye, dear Teacher. What a fine warrior, impeccable warrior, you were. Hail! You were the most honest man I have ever known. A man without quotation marks enters the void."

Sunya picked a card. He got Death and Transformation.

February 1984

Our lease will be up in May. I've looked and looked for a house but found nothing. So Sunya tells me, "A Yankee-girlie, Dollar Princess, Lottie Rose, has fallen fatally in knee-deep Love with Sri Wuji and has bought a dwelling to humor his frolicsome antics and 'light' play in Being-awareness — and its Silence." It is only one story in nearby Fairfax but has a large cellar so she is having the house lifted 12 feet to make it into a duplex. There will be two bedrooms and two bathrooms upstairs, plus a living room and kitchen. Sunya would have the bedroom with a bath and a small parlor. The other bedroom would be for Barbara and me and the boys would sleep in a downstairs bedroom. There will be a large room downstairs that will be used for his weekly darshans.

Sunya calls it "Sri Wuji's Palace."

4 April 1984

Sunya leaves for his annual Viking visit to the gangster city of Chicago.

10 April 1984

Mother broke her hip today. She spoke about her brothers Humphrey and Bill who she said she loved dearly. And asked if I remembered them. I told her that Humphrey had always given me comic books, brought Batman into my life. My mother thought I was a dreamy kid and had Bill show me how to fight. He was middleweight who looked to have a great career — "He was known as 'Battlin Bill Scott,'" my mother told me triumphantly. He took me into the cellar and showed me how to make fists, put up my dukes, duck and throw punches, twisting the fist at the end so it would cut the other guy, him moving around me like we were in the ring, throwing some soft jabs and him snorting all the time from the poison gas during the war that had ended his career. At end of his life he had told me, "Fightin' don't get you anywhere, Billy."

14 April 1984

Letter from Sunya in Chicago.

Your Himalayan Viking bhai — in the Wei Wu Wei

mode — is in the annual raid on the swell gangster city. Here Dr. Vasavada is no longer skyscraping. He is grounded in a new lowly abode and celebrates Satsang every Friday. We meet his clients and small groups of lovable-alive egojies. The new intuitive and carefree race is here and some individuals apperceive the Individuum, the Ghostly Whole.

Says Wuji: In intuitive apperception the Shadow of egohood vanishes in the Self-radiant Sun-y-att, in aware innerstanding, divine Wuness or Ghostly Whole.

The wee Viking body's body-mind and ego-soul seem to keep harmoniously whole and pliable at 94. (We are getting near the first century, says Wuji): Age-free, mind-free, thought-free, time-free, lust-free, desire-free and death-free. Wu! So, in Graceful Self-awareness, one can be at joyous ease and in delightful uncertainty also in Yankeestan-cult of externalities and noisy trivialities, as in the Pleasure and Power-oriented rhythm of egojies and their blatant worth-ship of the mighty, but not All-Mighty, Bhagwan Sri Dollar. Wu ha da: Sri Hönisse.

Im-man-u-El innerstands at joyous ease. No un-ease, and no dis-ease — but affectionate detachment, regarding things, events and egojies. "Only because of the Atman — the beloved form is dear." All is Right that seems most wrong to egojies — to busy-bodies, split minds and dark nights of ego-souls. We are more than human, mortal personal-masks says Wuji. We can re-awaken from images. Ideals-concepts and day-dreams into intuitive apperception of Divine All-Rightness in the Ghostly Whole. The Source and I are O-ne, a non-dual ego-free — says Wuji: re-awaken honey egojies, apperceive that I AM (Being) is always with us. Be of good cheer. Stilly, maturely re-awaken into serene Grace-Awareness and profound Gratitude in what IS and what we are for ever and ever in Divine Wuness.

So all is accepted in affectionate awareness and serene contentment. There is no regret, no pity and no fear. All is

"Take me with you."

forgiven, all is comprehended. There is nothing to forgive and no one, no entity, to give or to forgive in Anandaful Grace-Awareness. Death is the secret of life, not its opposite. Our Pilgrimage is a Homeward journey. "We" merge in the Ghostly Whole.

In the "*Gospel of Thomas*," Jesus said: "If ye knew how to suffer ye would not have to suffer." Suffering is not spirit—wu says Wuji. God does not suffer. Deep is woe—but Ananda Grace is deeper still than woe can be, says Wuji.

Karuna, Agape, Grace and Gratitude from Viking-bhai Emmanu-el and Hönisse Wuji.

17 April 1984

Won the Publisher's Award. Flew to Cleveland and was given a 9.3% raise. Stan tells me it is "big for them." Five years now and am now making the same salary as I made at *Food Management*.

Work going slow on Sri Wuji's Palace. Raised up to create a second floor.

20 April 1984

New foundation was poured at the Palace. I put a Law of Three symbol into the still soft cement in three places.

21 April 1984

Chuck Turner, the contractor, a squat powerful looking guy, was furious at me. Nothing said. It was all in the looks. I had ruined his foundation with the Law of Three.

30 April 1984

Had talked to Chuck about the job being late and his drinking on the job. He continued, beer bottles all around, so today I told him, I don't know anyone who could drink on the job and still do a good job. He ran out, filled with anger, and zoomed away in his truck.

Then he came back and called me an "Asshole!"

I absorbed his energy, didn't react, but just asked calmly, "Why do you say that?"

Shocked, confused, he shout-gurgled something, and ran off.

1 June 1984

Sri Wuji's Palace was supposed to be ready for us to occupy but still needs work. So we vacated our San Anselmo house, put our things in storage and put up a large tent in the backyard of the Fairfax house to sleep in. The kids loved it.

6 June 1984

Sunya returned from Chicago. I went to the airport to pick him up. He was all dressed in purple and looked radiant. He didn't see me and so I said mockingly—"Sunya, remember me?"

"Faintly," he replied, not missing a beat.

The house was still not ready, so he would stay at a devotee's house.

27 June 1984

The silence in Sunya's darshan was strong and Sunya spoke with an added verve, and when he came to words that were special for him, even bouncing in his seat as if riding a hobby horse. There was something about what he said that seemed different. He seemed to be manifesting a new strength.

In a letter he wrote, he says:

> There are dreams within dreams and all are contained within the cosmic dream. As Alfred Tennyson asks: "Dreams are true while they last and do we not live in dreams?" Yes, we are being dreamt, agrees Wuji. Life dreams its Self.
>
> Egoji does not awaken. How can a shadow awaken into the reality of the Ghostly Whole? Egojies vanish in the Self-radiant sunlight, the translucent darkness, the trinity beyond being and non-being. It is the Self, not the 'me,' not the egoji that awakens into aware Selfhood, the inherent

understanding Christ Emmanuel, the Noumenon in phenomenon, The Whole in the part play, the sea in the dew drop. It is ego consciousness that vanishes with Grace Awareness. It is the non-dual experiencing. Ego oblivion is Self-Awareness.

When Ramana Maharshi reminded us, "We are always aware, Sunyata," Sri Wuji nodded approval with the curl on his wagtail. Yes we are always aware in Sunyata — the calm, unjudging witness — until "we" merge in the Beyond — the name-free, time-free and space-free Sunyata. Being, Awareness, Grace. *Sat Chit Ananda. Tat Twam Asi.* Grace awareness has no opposite nor has Life, the Ghostly Whole, have any opposite. One could not be conceived of without the other. Like all the other pairs of opposites they are not opposed to each other but constitute a Whole. The one could not be without the other. They can harmonize and blend in balanced polarity in unicity, integral health, harmony and Wholeness in the Ghostly Whole. Wu!

1 July 1984
We moved out of the tent in the backyard and into the Palace, though there was still work to be done shingling the outer walls.

11 July 1984
Sunya was moved into the Palace while I was at work. Seeing him, it was like he had never left.

Everything was complete with the Palace except for the shingling. The bang-bang-bang of that throughout the day together with a two-week heat wave Sunya calls a "heatmare" were difficult for him. All those years in the Silence of his stone hut and the twenty-three-mile vista of the Himalayas, Sunya could take the cold, flu and other contagions without a ripple but heat was an opponent. Fans and air conditioning were offered and rejected. He scoffed at them as "artificialities" but finally relented.

With all the heat and noise Sunya said he had almost died. I asked what that was like. Sunya looked at me a long time and then spread his large farmer hands out about two or three inches from his body, as if this was his ordinary experience . . . and then slowly the hands moved further and further out into space as far as they could extend . . . as though he was going to leave the body. He didn't live contracted in the body, as most everyone does. There was "body nearness" but he lived outside it.

"Consciousness is not in the body," he said. "The body appears in Consciousness."

Wow!

19 July 1984

After dinner we were sitting on the couch together, leg-to-leg, shoulder-to-shoulder, his hand holding mine. It was so assertive on his part, the first time he had ever been so, total body nearness. I remembered him saying, "Beware when the Prince of Denmark is acting strangely."

I had always abhorred homosexuality to the point where I saw it was a hang-up. Wuji was frightening on that account and also because I felt so often he was someone else, someone we couldn't see or know.

20 July 1984

Barbara left to visit her parents in Los Angeles. I took everyone to dinner. The kids went to bed. I found myself afraid of being alone with the "Prince of Denmark." He had gone to his room but I could feel his vibrations as I had the night before. I thought of going to his room, not out of lust but curiosity, to finally find out, to end the game, if there was one. But I didn't.

The next morning when I took him his tea he did not look at me as he usually did. I sensed that he felt guilty, but was I projecting?

Later that day I said something about being "queer."

"Oh, we're all a little queer," he said.

"But some of us are *a lot* queer," I laughed.

He laughed, too.

And there it ended.

25 July 1984
Silence was strong during the forty-five-minute sitting. No one moved for a long time. Then Tom Fox, who had attended darshans with Sunya since 1979, speaks to Sunya about his Swiss girlfriend.

"Oh," Sunya says, "what you mean is she's not your friend anymore."

Tom, disturbed, later says he takes it as, "Sunya was on me about my impure heart."

Two new people attended. Shakti, a huge 300 lb. rhino-looking woman with flaming red hair, and her thin husband, a former Trappist monk, who she tells me she "enticed from the robes." Now he has had a stroke and lives in silence.

29 July 1984
I have a vivid dream of a young, sensuous woman, my soul mate. Then a pot-bellied man in a red t-shirt appears "You know that old fellow that lives with you," he says, "Well, he has gone his way."

I tell Sunya about it and he laughs—"Where would I go to? I Am is always with you."

1 August 1984
At the darshan someone had tipped over a lit candle and previously the one-eyed fantail gold fish someone had given Sunya died. Sunya seemed quite concerned. Very unlike him. He has always promised to celebrate his 100th birthday with everyone. Now he says that attendance may be only for those able to leave their body.

Tom Fox talks about the story he heard in India that Sri Yukteswar, having died, then rematerialized as his disciple, Yogananda, who helped a great many people from getting stuck on one level go on to the next. He finishes by asking Sunya—

"Are you working on the next level, having mastered this one?"

"No," Sunya answered and asked, "What people call their love—What is their love? Do they own it?"

"Your love is purest," Tom says and jumps up and runs out of Sri Wuji's Palace as if he was set on fire.

I heard later that he went back home, found a bug in the kitchen, told his girlfriend, "You could help it evolve, if you killed it." Instead, she throws it out the window.

3 August 1984

Barbara and I and the kids were all about to leave for Jean's five-day seminar at Mt. Madonna Center when I remembered I had left something and I went back into the house. I heard Sunya upstairs and went to the landing between the two floors. I looked up. There was Sunya in a light blue turban and orange kurta, all shimmering light as I had never seen him before, his blue eyes soft and alive.

"Take me with you," he murmured.

I smiled and nodded and went down the steps.

"See you in a week. Now don't get lonely," I called back with a laugh.

But his words stayed in my ears . . . *Take me with you*. He had never said that. It gave me a funny feeling. I brushed it off, and left.

I asked to take photos of Jean during the start of yoga and he agreed. There was a wonderful experience of space and Jean saying to experience the sensation of the body and then radiate it out into space. Know the body as light and air. Keep the mouth empty, having tactile sensation of it. Assist the energy to move up the spine.

Justin arrived late Friday evening and got into an argument with someone and demanded a "sincere apology." It was never *sincere* enough for him. Saturday morning he refused to pay for the seminar. "I'm enlightened, too," he declared. Jean had him come to his room. I stood outside just in case. Jean told him to pay or leave. Finally, he returned his check and told him to leave. Justin refused to go. Jean said he would have to call the police. It was quite a dust-up. Only with that threat did he finally leave. Jean said, "He's crazy."

Jean said to me later, "My nature is not violent. You may think I am a weak man . . ." I touched his elbow and assured him that I knew differently.

5 August 1984
   We returned home from the Mt. Madonna retreat. It was too late to see Sunya.

6 August 1984
   Monday morning I went up to his room with his tea, as I usually did, knocking on his door, expecting another Sunya-style meditation, me in a half-lotus on the floor, and him in bed asleep and sometimes snoring. But there was no response. Opening the door, I saw the room was empty, the bed still made. My first thought was that Justin had "kidnapped Sunya." But where was he?
   On Sunday morning, I later learned, Jean Klein had had a dream of "a terrible car crash." He had Emma call all the local hospitals, which is how it was learned that Sunya had been admitted the previous morning to the Ross Valley Hospital in Kentfield, about ten miles east of Fairfax.
   I went straight to the hospital. Jean and Emma were already there sitting in the waiting room outside the Intensive Care Unit. I sobbed. Sobbed uncontrollably. Then I heard this low steady hum. It was Jean Klein talking. It seemed like small talk. All this emotion was roaring inside me, but now there was this hum, too. It was drawing a line through my consciousness. Suddenly, I found myself watching myself cry.
   A doctor appeared. Said Sunya had given his full name when admitted—*Alfred Julius Emmanuel Sorensen*—and seemed quite lucid, made jokes, and had the skin of a young boy.
   Betty Camhi arrived just as the nurse admitted all of us into the Intensive Care Unit where Sunya lay in his bed.
   "Sunya, "I said softly, "it's Pat and Betty."
   His blue eyes were open but stayed on the ceiling.
   "Sunya!" I said more loudly, bending over his body and placing my hand in his. His eyes came to mine. There was only the merest dot of self-consciousness. A small tear came up in the corners of his eyes.
   "Sweet Sunyata," Betty said. "Sweet Sunyata."
   A male nurse came and asked how much effort should be made

to keep Alfred alive. He said the left femur was badly broken, and fat tissue from the bone marrow had leaked into Sunya's bloodstream, causing strokes. The way his left hand and arm were turned in signified brain damage. He asked if we wanted "active measures" taken to keep Sunya alive.

Betty and I told him to let Nature take its course.

"He never wanted anything to be done to his body," Betty explained. "He's a holy man. Nothing should be done to damage the body."

Jean agreed, telling him, "Do not manipulate his body. Let Nature take its course."

Jean and Emma left then and Betty went along with the nurse to tell the doctor.

I stood holding Sunya's hand. He always had such big hands. The hand was warm and spongy. There was no self-consciousness, no resistance, in the hand. Still, I could feel Sunya was present.

I took a deep breath and the words bubbled up — "Sunya..." the voice was low. "Sunya, I'm sorry. I was afraid to love you. There was so much fear. I was a coward."

I remembered once when I spoke about death to Sunya he had said, "Where could I go to? I am *IS* always here."

I called people who were close to Sunya. Should I call Justin, crazy Justin? I do so but with concern.

When I leave for a while, Justin appears. He bursts into the ICU and threatens the doctors with a lawsuit if they do not immediately hook Sunya up to a respirator, pump out his lungs, and do everything they can to keep him alive.

Put on life support, Sunya survives. A doctor says some color has returned to Sunya's cheeks and lips, his condition seems to have steadied.

I am allowed back into the ICU to see Sunya. Now plastic tubing is running out of his nose; sensors are taped to his body; behind his bed, a row of machines monitor vital signs. I go to his bedside and sit and meditate, as I had in the mornings. I lean over and speak directly to him, asking if he wanted to come back. I tell him that if he does I would connect with him and act as a guideline and help him come back, if that is what he wants. Telepathically, he tells me, "No, had enough, want to go home."

7 August 1984

I heard that Justin, after being kicked out of the Mount Madonna seminar had gone straight back to see Sunya and railed at him for hours about the injustice he had suffered. Had this unhinged or disoriented Sunya in some way?

I got hold of the Fairfax police report. It says on Sunday, August 5th, at 9:14 a.m., Sunya was at the corner of Sir Francis Drake Boulevard and Azalea Avenue and began to cross when a tan 1972 Toyota approached from the west. Seeing him, the car swerves into the oncoming lane to avoid hitting him, but Sunya, instead of staying put or returning to the corner to avoid the car, ran into the oncoming lane. The car skids to a stop but hits Sunya. There are nasty scrapes and bruises but nothing serious looking. At the hospital it is seen that the femur is broken. Later he has strokes. At midnight he goes into a coma. There are repeated strokes and now visible signs of brain damage.

Later, Officer Baker, Marin CHP Accident Investigator, reports, "The car's skid marks show it was driven at a speed greater than 30 mph and that the driver should have been able to stop for pedestrian Sorensen."

The driver's statement says: "I saw him standing still on the edge of the crosswalk. I was about fifty feet away when I saw him. Suddenly, he darted across the road. I don't know if he looked or not. When he darted across, I hit my brakes and swerved to the left. I hit him with my right front."

The driver turns out to be Tom's Swiss girlfriend, Sharon Burch. She was not prosecuted.

8 August 1984

Sunya's condition continued to stabilize, it looks as though he will live, though brain damage is a possibility. His blood pressure rises when they move him.

"This is a good sign," says the head nurse, a big blonde-haired woman, "because it means he is feeling pain."

She stroked the bottom of his right foot several times with the same quick deliberate gesture used to strike a match, and each time she got a "light." That is, the leg moved involuntarily.

"There's no movement in his hands or arms though," she noted. She ran a finger down his arm, lifted up his hand, moved it from side to side. "Nothing. But the breathing has stabilized. All his organs are in good shape. The doctor says he expects him to recover."

"What about brain damage?"

"Oh that, well, there may be some, but people have recovered from that." She brought up the blood pressure again. "He's in pain and that's positive."

Noting the concern this caused, she explained, "But we give him morphine so the pain doesn't last long."

"Morphine! Isn't that addicting?"

"We give him very small amounts. Nothing to be alarmed about."

She went to Sunya's bed. This is the first time I'd seen him without a turban. He was mostly bald as expected. She methodically checked that everything was in place: the tube coming from his nose, the large plastic aqua-blue tubing and mask that gave oxygen, the various intravenous feeding devices, sensors attached to his heart, stainless steel traction that kept his left leg from moving, a steel rod through the leg a few inches below the knee. She swabbed that area with a sickly yellow solution the way you might take some bird droppings off a car windshield.

This is becoming a technological crucifixion.

10 August 1984

Sunya is taken off the respirator. Lottie Rose, his "Dollar Princess," brought him a tape player and tapes of the Gregorian chant and Tibetan bells he favored. I brought him his recordings of tapes he had made of Albert Bouwmeester's letters to him.

The events of the week have finally hit. Feeling very tired, emotionally blown out. Drained. Empty.

12 August 1984

An oxygen mask is on Sunya's face. I put a hand on his rib cage, hold his hand, his fingers very Buddha-like. Face changes. The mask makes him look strange, inhuman.

I whisper to him, "I was afraid to love you, *really love.*"

The nurse, devout in her technologic beliefs, says his blood pressure had fallen a bit, the breathing had become agitated. "He's got to want to come back," she says quietly. "It's up to him now."

I recall Sunya telling me we never had to worry about him leaving the body "unless I go to a hospital."

A sheet had been pulled over Sunya's body up to his neck. It covered him like a great white sail. The ward was bathed in a soft shadow. His eyes were still closed. The breathing was now full out, his lungs pumped with every breath to the maximum. "The Yankee Guy" or the "Body Guard," what Sunya called me, put a hand out and placed it lightly on Sunya's rib cage. He held Sunya's hand with the other. He breathed in unison with the lungs in the prone body. It was full-out with every breath, the body doing all it could to remain alive. "Now is the time. You either come back now or not at all."

The realization came that to really speak to him one had to go to where he was—out of the body, out in space. All the attention focused on his body, the feeling of its outline, the fringe of the skin, the eyes softening and not focusing. Mr. Nobody's face blended with shadows of the room. The face was not human, the features strange yet very still. The face was ancient. Had nothing to do with the body, lungs, fighting for survival. The message was repeated but silently.

The Yankee Guy heard himself admit that he had been a coward, that he hadn't loved him enough, that he had been afraid, doubted and escaped.

His two hands lightly massaged the left hand of Mr. Nobody. "Come back, Sunya. Come back. I love you. I really love you."

All his being and vitality completely focused on the inert figure beneath the great white sheet. "This is the ladder down into the body. Take it."

The strange face looked out at him. This was all quite silly. He realized that only a miracle could bring Mr. Nobody back—a tremendous, one-pointed act of will. He had to give everything. *Everything.*

But the Wu communication came: *It is not to be.*

In the great Silence, Sunya's voice came up from the tape player. He was reading Albert's letter where the Ego has at last come face to face with the Unconscious and is voicing its fear and concern at the "birth" of the Unconscious within its midst.

The nurse seemed surprised that Sunya wasn't going to continue the desire to live physically, but there was nothing, quite literally, for which to remain.

13 August 1984

Monday morning on my way to work the Yankee Guy stopped at the hospital. Sunyabhai's head was cocked back on the pillow, his mouth a hole now. The breathing was even more grasping for air. The body was a marvel of strength.

Twelve minutes after leaving, I learned Sunyabhai had taken his last breath. "There was a funny sound, like choking," the nurse said, "and then a last gasp."

The time was 9:27 a.m.

In the midst of my grief: there was no grief. Another Great Master of The Void had passed into, as Sunya called it, the "Invisible Real—beyond the power play, ego-antics and shakti-business."

Yes, Sunya the extraordinary being who innerstood in joyous ease and affectionate detachment the mystic wholeness of life has returned "Home."

"*Prarabdha* karma," he once explained, "is the karma that cannot be changed in one's lifetime."

So now in the Silence there is ever still the wondrous Sri Wuji intoning—

> Never the spirit was born; the spirit shall cease
> to be never.
> Never was time it was not; Ends and Beginnings
> are dreams.
> Birthless and deathless and changeless
> remaineth the Spirit forever.
> Death hath not touched it at all,
> dead though the house of it seems!

14 August 1984

One funeral home wanted $558 to cremate the body. The Neptune Society would charge $495. Daphne's Mortuary in Mill Valley was $385. A white marble Buddha seated on a lotus atop a square urn was chosen to hold his ashes.

But the coroner, Dr. Hendricks, insisted upon an autopsy. The full treatment. California law demands it when death is by vehicular accident. Not only had the body been drugged and manipulated in all manner of ways but now its cranium, lungs and abdomen would be opened for inspection. Hendricks said he had 60% brain damage but is amazed at Sunya's condition, says he had the organs of a 45-year-old man and could have easily lived to 115 or 120 years.

Sunya's body is cremated and his ashes are sent to friends around the world. A small portion of his ashes is put beneath the statue of the guru in the garden at Sri Wuji's Palace.

Jean Klein is telephoned. He was in Santa Fe on his way back to Paris. He said for a long time he felt Sunya was going to leave his body, given Sunya's continual mention of his 100th birthday celebration, for example. Jean gave instructions on how we were to give an Advaita Vedanta funeral. First, a reading from the *Spanda Karikas*, a giving up of the five bodies, or sheaths, and then a walk or dance around the ashes, followed by a scattering of the ashes.

15 August 1984

A memorial service for devotees was held at Sri Wuji's Palace. On the door to the downstairs room where he gave his darshans a small sign read, "*Silence is the ceremony.*"

Everyone sits together in a long circle on either side of his empty chair, his rainbow shawl draped across its back, and on its seat his urn with the white stone Buddha.

We all sat together in silence.

And then did as Jean had directed except for the scattering of all the ashes, as his body had yet to be cremated.

Get a "message" to go and lie down in Sunya's bed. Take my clothes off and do the androgyny dance. Powerful. Can feel his emanations.

Another message: go to the urn of the white Buddha and do the androgyny dance as he wanted. Then, upstairs sit in his parlor. He is there, too.

It is raining and a cat keeps bouncing again and again against our upstairs door making a big noise. Not cat-like at all. I think of letting it in, but I have now become allergic to cats.

19 August 1984

Only on awakening the next morning does the realization come that Sunya must have taken that cat's body. I go looking for it, but it is nowhere to be found.

20 August 1984

I told my mother of Sunya's death. She said, "What's he ever done for mankind?" and a little later, "Well, how's the Prince of Peace?"

Justin called. Says he has a video tape of Sunya. Has taped all his conversations with Sunya. Tells me I'll be enlightened when I recognize him as being enlightened.

Wants to know why he was not invited to the memorial service. He was the closest of anyone to Sunya. He says he came straight back from Mt. Madonna that Saturday and told all that had happened there. They had talked for hours on end. Then he said he asked Sunya, "What's happening tomorrow?" Sunya said, "I'm open for a disturbance between 10 o'clock and noon." Justin ends the conversation with "I love you."

2 September 1984

Sometime before I last saw him, Sunya told me, "You'll write a book about me in ten to twelve years."

After this, I was going through Sunya's books and I opened Miguel Serrano's *The Serpent of Paradise* and there was Sunya's signature and below it the words "The Brother of Silence." Checking the contents I found that this was the title of one of the chapters.

Serrano, who had a close friendship with C. G. Jung and Hermann Hesse, is best known for his book *A Record of Two Friendships*. Serrano, like Jung, had an abiding interest in the idea of Self, which took him on a pilgrimage to India. There he met Ramana Maharshi, Krishna Menon and Krishnamurti. Then he had this incredible encounter with the Brother of Silence:

> It was during the night when the door of my room slowly opened. A shaft of moonlight played on the floor, and outside I could see the treetops moving in the breeze. Then a shadowy figure entered silently and sat down in a corner. He was a strange monk, accompanied by a small dog, and he was wearing a Tibetan silk tunic and an enormous turban. A rucksack hung from one of his shoulders, and he held a pilgrim's staff in his hand.
>
> He sat down quietly, according to the custom of the country, and for a long time we looked at each other in silence. I noticed that he had blue eyes, and that his pale face seemed untouched by age. Then I began to sense what he was saying.
>
> "My name is Sunya Bhai, the Brother of Emptiness or the Brother of Silence. I live in the high country, in Almora, which is the gateway between Himavat and Mount Kailash. I have lived there for many years, and my friends are the Abominable Snowman and, above all, silence. There is nothing like the silence of the Himalayan mountains, nothing like it in all the world. Men talk and speak, but the truth is found only in silence. Recently you have talked a great deal, and you have been wrong in doing so. That is why I

have come to teach you the language of silence, and to listen to your silence. I am not interested only in what men can say with words. I am interested only in what they can say with their silence. You must realize that men who talk well, and who utter beautiful speeches, usually have a very bad silence. What is really important is silence, for it is a preparation for the Great Silence."

"Yes," I replied, "I have talked a great deal lately, and have spoken haphazardly and pointlessly. Therefore I promise that I will keep silent until I come to see you in Almora. But do you think the Abominable Snowman will let me through, so that I can visit you?"

"That depends on whether you learn the lesson of silence and the language of silence. You are nearing fulfillment. I can assure you of that, for suffering is the best teacher, and you have suffered. Do you know how to get to my place? It is there, up here..."

And Sunya Bhai, instead of pointing outside, towards the Himalayas, directed his pilgrim's staff towards my own head.

We had talked a long time, but only in silence, in the language of silence.

[See Appendices for a more extensive account given in Serrano's *"The Visits of the Queen of Sheba"*.]

12 November 1984

Wrote a quarter page ad for the *Pacific Sun* this week—"Teachers of Nothing" linking Sunya and his death and Jean Klein, both being teachers of Nothing. Mention Jean's seminar December 3–7.

17 November 1984

Ran into a Gurdjieffian. He said to me after a short conversation—"My gawd! You've got a new language!"

Sunya's passing, "Silence is the Ceremony."

Sunya, June 1984

Celebrating Sunya's passing at Kesar Devi, Almora, India

December 1984
Jean Klein gave a dialogue at Sri Wuji's Palace.
There was no essential difference between Jean and Sunya and so while we were heartbroken at Sunya's passing, Barbara and I hosted Jean Klein's meetings at the Palace and helped Emma organize his seminars in California.

14 December 1984
Isaac Fisher shows up at our door. He wants to know about Sunya's passing. After we talk, he tells me his name is now "Isaac Satori."

He was expensively dressed with Italian shoes, well-cut brown slacks, dark brown pullover with large black stripes on the upper arms and around the neck. He had a beard now and an expensive gold watch. He had gone to Tampa and a millionairess had bought it all for him. "She wanted to own me," he said.

He showed me a typeset of a book he planned to publish, "The 46 Commandments of Isaac Satori," a compendium of booklets he had written. He said a stranger in a deli had told him his last name wasn't right and said it should end in "ori." And so, he said, "Satori was born."

It was two years since he had left and he was still in the same place, only deeper. I felt a sadness, a compassion, for him.

Later, under his real name, Isaac Fischer, he sent a beautiful poem, "Sunya's Gift."

18 December 1984
Shakti, the rhino woman, called to say she had made a cardboard dummy of Sunya and dressed it with his clothes, had a life mask done of Sunya and stuck that on his shoulders, and behind him put a light box that when switched on gives him a blue aura. She'd like me to see it. I respectfully begged off. What a way to end the year!

1985

"Absence is the greatest presence."

18 January 1985

Drove to Berkeley to see Jean Klein. Had nothing to say, just wanted to see him. He answered the door, empty as usual, and we sat down in two white director's chairs. He turned to the large windows behind him and motioned outside to the huge grove of redwoods bathed in the soft morning fog, shafts of light piercing the general haze and highlighting the ground, and mused, "Nature

"Absence is the greatest presence."   153

is mysterious, isn't it."

"I love Nature," I told him. "But I don't entirely trust it. I feel a certain ambiguity toward it."

Then something in me just let go and I talked about what had happened to me as a child—how when I was five or six years old it was raining hard and so as not to get wet a friend of mine and I got into the back of an open trailer in his father's garage to stay dry. Lying next to each other, we waited for the rain to end. Suddenly there arose this strange, pungent, sexual atmosphere I'd never experienced before, but then I didn't know what that was.

When the rain ended, instead of going home by the road which was shorter and drier, I took a trail up through the woods. On the way I met a kid from my class coming down from the other direction and he led us to sodomize each other. I didn't know what that was and just did as he did. [Many years later at our 50th high school reunion, I saw he was a homosexual.]

"I feel like I've lived my whole life with this guilt, compensating for something I had no real part in. I am angry at the stupidity of the situation. I've looked at it all I can. Nothing works. This is nothing in comparison to what others go through, yet it doesn't matter."

I felt like a fish with a hook in its mouth. This was a last giant attempt to get the hook out. I gave the problem to him. He didn't take it. Or not take it. But I am stuck with having tried to give the hook away.

22 January 1985

Jean Klein gave a weekend seminar at Westerbeke Ranch in Sonoma, California. I was still undergoing a psychological reaction to all that I had told him. Still, it didn't affect the sittings, which were quite deep. But the words and phrases I had said would suddenly come back up in me. At the last day's sitting a voice came up saying, "Fuck you, Jean Klein."

5 March 1985

Dreamed Jean asked me to carry his violin. He later stopped to inspect it, opening up the old case. I didn't know whether or not it had been carried safely or not. It had been. He had one of those high beam smiles in his eyes.

Have been doing the yoga asanas and breathing exercises and enlarging the sensation. At night I wake to find the energy running in the spine, a strong pulsation in the throat chakra, a gale of wind blowing through my body with me hanging onto the pillow for dear life. The thought is always the same: what the fuck am I doing. I like my life. I love my wife and children. I don't want to lose them. Then in the morning I realize I've blown it again. No courage.

11 March 1985

There was a biotechnology conference in London, the first of its kind, so I convinced Stan that I should attend and write a piece on it. Had no interest in it, but it was a way to visit Jean Klein in Paris. As long as I was in England, I went up to Colchester to see Connor Barrett, a sculptor and hypnotherapist Sunya had told me about. They had met in 1924 when Connor was sixteen and Sunya, known then as "Alfred" to many, was thirty-eight. I arrived at his house about one o'clock.

Connor was seventy-seven now but still looked spry. His face is unique in character, at times having an ancient look. He is balding but wears his white hair long with long sideburns and a white mustache and goatee. The eyes are blue but not clear. He speaks well, mostly just above a whisper. "Alfred," he said, "had called him 'the angel that troubles the waters.'" Alfred had given him many books, "He had a greed of giving," said Connor. He said he was introduced to Alfred in 1924 by Alice Cope, a friend who was a musician and teacher. They all shared a deep interest in Beethoven's Four Quartets.

Alfred suggested to Alice that they should marry. Alice gently rejected the idea, knowing it was only an idea, for Alfred had no sexual urge at all. She was engaged to a young man who was killed in an accident before their marriage. "She wanted to have sex," Alfred said. "More than anything she was curious. I gave her the

"Absence is the greatest presence."

experience. But it wasn't my need. It was hers."

Connor and he kept up a correspondence, but Alfred's were largely abstract—always the same ideas couched in the same terms. Says Connor:

> His career in California emphasized his blatant inconsistencies. The protests about being *no thing*, and the obvious gratification about being hailed as a guru in newspaper articles—what reveals itself is a deal of egotism, which would be fine if it were recognized as such. He was an unloved child and that feeling dominated his life. He took refuge in his head, in ideas, and in endless protestations of self-containment.

His words were sincere and I saw no point in arguing with him, other than to say that a great many others had a different viewpoint, I among them. He took me down to the basement and showed me his wood sculptures. All very strong and sexual, quite compelling. He was a genuine artist.

Michi appeared, Connor's wife, and he introduced me, saying she lived with him downstairs, while upstairs lived his ex-wife, an alcoholic. There was also their Siamese cat, Me-Too, wheat colored with red eyes, not very pretty.

"Michi is a medium," he said. "It's in the family. She is a channel for 'Jacob' and 'The Doctor' and sometimes 'The Stone Man,' a very powerful but no-nonsense entity."

Michi had met Connor in London in a therapy group. She said, "I was distraught from being under psychic attack from my husband. He was a taciturn tyrant who had bought a house for the family in the red-light district." She left him for Connor who neglected to tell her that his ex-wife lived upstairs.

Michi, simple and earthy, but sly, is a very good storyteller. She told how when a small girl there were a few goody-goodies in the school that stuck up their noses at her. They always crossed the street when they saw her coming. One day she'd had enough and called out a big "Hello!" before they could cross the street. She asked one of them if she would "like a sweetie?" The girl agreed and Michi told her to close her eyes and stick out her hand, which she did only to open her eyes and see in the palm of her hand a dead mouse.

Connor and Michi make their living doing therapy and healing work. He wanted very much for Michi to channel Jacob for me. She did, as well. I was noncommittal. I wouldn't resist Jacob's coming but wouldn't request it. There was a strong power in the room, quite sexual, producing many sexual images in the mind's eye.

Several days before, the kundalini in the *Muladhara* chakra had opened and I had breathed it up. A very sexual experience although there was no object. Now here I was with two powerful people who I felt inhabited the lower centers. Was this a test? I was curious about Jacob and a part of me wanted the experience, but I would say nothing to suggest it. It would unnecessarily complicate my life.

And I am skeptical, too, of the spirits. Are they not just parts of our own psyche that can't admit to consciousness in any other way? My guess is that it stops one's development as it divides the consciousness at the subtle level. So that was the cat-and-mouse game that we played until after ten o'clock, with them talking about spirits and me listening.

My train back to London was at 10:34. Michi drove me to the station. On the way she told me she lifts her chin up and goes out through the top of her head. Then Jacob inhabits her. I liked her but she is elemental in many ways. She reminds me of my mother.

The next day I called Barbara to tell her about it. I asked her to check the five boxes of letters, diaries, photos Sunya had left to see if there was any correspondence between them. The next day we talked and she said she had found two letters that Connor had sent Sunya. When I returned I read them. The first was in February and the second in September, both 1983. In the February letter he seems to think now that Sunya has come to America he has money or more access to it through "Sri Rajneesh or any other millionaire friends of yours who would like to divert a little money in this direction and help us found our healing center." He is planning on having a country house costing about 160,000 pounds and "we

"Absence is the greatest presence." 157

need another 100,000 pounds to see us through the first two years."

Sunya either wrote to him in the negative about it or, more likely, never replied. In the September letter Connor writes, "What I hear is the cry of a totally unloved child who had to say 'I need nothing and no one' because no real recognition of his existence was forthcoming. And when he says—with all possible means of publicity—'I am nothing—I am no body' what I am hearing is 'Notice me! I do exist after all.'"

12 March 1985

Went to Zurich. Visited Küsnacht, Jung's home. Could only see the Institute, closed for the semester. Not much energy there. Telling a woman assistant over the phone I was leaving for the day, she said, "Ohh, too bad."

"You have a nice voice," I said. "I would like to have met you."

"Oh, and yes, I have a bad side, too."

That night had a dream. I had been on a small wooded hill and left my wallet that held a lot of money. I was scrambling around trying to find my wallet and all these birds were flying around as someone had forgotten to lock their cages.

Rather than go the long way around the hill, I got a ladder and when I reached the top a small boy took out his penis and pissed on me.

For me the dream was about Connor and Michi. I had talked too much and too freely—had left all my thoughts out (birds) and so had left my identity (wallet, money).

15 March 1985

In Paris I stayed at the St. Louis II hotel. In a light rain found Jean's place, 7 Rue de Tournon, next to a clothing shop, Images. We walked at a quick speed around Luxembourg Gardens. He doesn't walk as much as glide, his feet just touching the pavement. Though I am in good physical condition and nearly half his age, these "glides" through Parisian space-time were at first tiring. Body armor was second nature, quite unconscious. In traffic, I felt like a tank. With his hand he led me across streets, horns honking, people staring at us like we were crazy, I felt like I was a little boy. We stopped and sat on a bench and talked of the magazine he proposed creating, . He said he would come by on Friday at 10:30 to take me to lunch.

16 March 1985

We took a taxi to a pre-Impressionist exhibit. A long line so we walked to the Arc de Triomphe. He walks like he drives a car — fast and rather dangerously but in control. He told me he had spent a year in the French Foreign Legion in Algeria and then four more with the underground in France in the mountains. He'd become interested in oriental philosophy through Gandhi, Lao Tzu, Chuang Tzu and Tagore. He tried the Theosophical Society but found it too sentimental. "Then," he said, "a copy of René Guénon's *The Symbolism of the Cross* fell into my hands. It was a turning point for me." He spoke about Tradition as the principle that passed from master to disciple through initiation. He went to India after the war and after some years met his teacher in Bangalore, Pandiji. Sometime later, looking at some flying birds in the sky, he found himself in permanent awareness in the openness which before had only been a transient state.

We got up and walked again, more or less glided, back to the pre-Impressionist exhibit. He liked one particular Cézanne painting. It was a village scene. I asked why. "The distribution of the rooftop and color. It explodes beyond the frame." Gauguin — he said in Paris he was already preparing for Tahiti in his paintings, "Just look at the colors and forms."

He bought a postcard for Barbara — *In the Garden of the Poets* by Van Gogh.

We took a cab to Indira, an Indian restaurant. "You must learn to eat Indian food," he said.

Conversation was fits and starts. I was feeling the yokel and experiencing the great distance between us.

I told him of the egoji's reaction to our last meeting — "Fuck you, Jean Klein" — that was truthful and the conversation began.

"There is no moment; no beginning and end. There is only a succession of images and not even that."

The object always points to the Ultimate Subject. He did not care for Impressionism as it was "Decorative—too much of the senses."

Mentioned Patañjali—fifth chapter, third verse.

[See Jean Klein's *Transmission of the Flame*, Prologue, i-xxii, for an elucidation of his spiritual experiences, time in India, and teaching in the West.]

Note: There is no 5th chapter, so perhaps I misheard him. The first chapter of Patañjali's sutra, third verse: "Then the seer [i.e. the Self] abides in [its] essence." Second chapter, third verse: "Nescience, I-am-ness, attachment, aversion and the will-to-live are the five causes–of-affliction." Third Chapter, third verse: "That [consciousness], [when] shining forth as the object only as if empty of [its] essence, is ecstasy." Chapter 4, third verse: "The incidental-cause does not initiate the processes-of-evolution, but [merely is responsible for] the singling-out of possibilities—like a farmer who irrigates a field by selecting appropriate pathways for the water." Source: *The Yoga-Sutras of Patañjali*, Georg Feuerstein, Inner Traditions, 1979.]

17 March 1985

Jean Klein called. "It is my Self calling," he said, laughing.

"And it is Himself here . . . as they say in Ireland," I joked.

He insisted on coming to pick me up at my hotel. We walked again. He put his hands on my shoulders and guided me in and out between passing cars and people. I felt how tight the body was, but I relaxed and gave my body to his direction. Not a word was said as we flitted up the Rue de Tournon to the Luxembourg Gardens, honking cars, people staring. Embarrassment came but passed. Gliding through the garden, all the tensions somehow dissolved, the two of us silently breezing along in the cool and bracing Spring air.

We sat on a bench and he told me I should experience the body as much as possible. That was best for now. I should see my functioning—for when something is fully seen it is completely burned up.

I spoke about having had asthma and he said it was a fear disease—that I wasn't fearful now but the reflex was still there. He gave me a remedy to rub on myself in the morning and before going to bed.

He spoke about *Être*, the magazine he would like to do. It was unclear what he wanted—did he want me to do it? I think so, and yet he did not say anything directly.

18 April 1985

We again walked and sat on a bench in the Luxembourg Gardens. He said I was more open now and many new truths would be coming to me. He took me to the Café de la Paix and pointed out where Gurdjieff sat. Then he invited me to his apartment. It is on the ground floor, quite large, and it was elegant and spare. A foyer, study, dining room, kitchen, at least two bedrooms. Done in greys. Several Indian wool canvases of the old tantric period. A vase of red tulips. A music stand. Violin case. Statues of Shiva. He said he had lived here for six years.

We went to his study and sat on the floor. I gave him the silvery-grey cashmere scarf I had bought for him.

"Oh," he said, "such a beautiful color."

He looked at me out of the side of his eye and rolled his head. It was like he was a little boy.

He made me a special tea of five various flower petals and herbs. It was delicious. Every cell in my body drank it. "You'll like it," he told me. I did. Very much so, and drank two cups.

He spoke now about fears and the "listening" needed to pass through them.

A question about time came up. He smiled and spoke rapidly in French, gesturing and nodding to me as if I would certainly understand, though I knew only English. After days of dodging traffic with this 'madman,' I smiled and simply relaxed more deeply and listened to the music of his voice.

He then spoke now in English (he speaks four languages) at a slower tempo of "being in the moment." "In reality there is no moment, no time. When one lives in being there is only... Being."

We sat in that moment together. There, again, was the emptiness I had felt so often with Sunya. *Samata.* There was no difference.

"Absence is the greatest presence," he murmured and we got up. At the doorway he put his hand like a bird lightly on my shoulder and guided me through, softly saying, "Goodbye, Pat."

I could not speak.

19 April 1985

Flew to Wales to cover a business conference. When I arrived, a large group was having dinner at the Celtic Manor with the usual business-boring discussion. At dessert I mentioned to Matthew, the balding engineer beside me, how we could change our view of things by simply seeing and sensing what was before us not as people having a conversation but as an energy exchange, energy rising and falling octaves, needing mechanical and conscious shocks. He was blown away. Anne, the blonde, was immediately drawn in. The sudden establishing of a mental connection quickly brought the physical in its wake. A massive, though invisible, transfusion of energy occurred. Later that night in my room I suddenly felt her in her room. I knew I only had to knock on her door. I was blazing with *Shakti* and could sense a glorious time awaited me. But it would be taking advantage of her, as I knew what had happened while she was simply taken. The next day when we were alone I asked her if she slept in the nude. She did. Said she couldn't sleep all night. I nodded. "You entered me somehow," she said. She avoided me thereafter.

End of April 1985

Jean has been coming to the states since 1976 and still has few students. No seminar has paid for itself and $500 is still owed to Mt. Madonna for last year's seminar. Some people have yet to pay for Westerbeke Ranch. Spiritual wimpism—that's how it seems to me.

Had dinner with some of Jean's students. I brought up the situation and asked people to agree to 1) go to all the seminars;

2) we would all make up the difference, if there were any monetary losses; 3) we would do our best to get new people involved.

"Today Fairfax, tomorrow the world," was one reply. Another, "Just let it happen. If it is meant to happen, it will. You don't have to worry about it." And "Doing anything is having an aim, a goal, and this is to be avoided." And similar responses....

It was so passive, so mental-bound. I saw why nothing had come of JK's coming here all these years. And everyone was quite ready to have me do it all for them—at the same time kidding about Jean "the dictator" in France. The worst of this attitude was that the teaching was used to defend their inertia, lack of responsibility.

Advaita is a high teaching, the highest; it's so insubstantial, gives nothing to hold onto, it can easily be used by the ego to justify with unimpeachable intellectual logic the whims of the egoji. People don't want to see themselves and use the teaching to defend their negativity, lack of courage, toward life. There is this superiority of "knowing the truth" and playing the sweet and light game.

It was all there at the dinner table. This is what I had seen in 3-D with Sunya's people once he had died—and here it was again, brought to the surface not by death but a simple request for group responsibility.

For myself, I don't have the tolerance and patience to lead any group. I'm not a "people person." They secretly think I want control and power and so are wary of whatever I say. They want power themselves but are afraid to reach for it—but don't want anyone else reaching. I see a power drive within me, but it's one that doesn't want people hanging on—I'm an artist, a writer. Certainly there is ego in it. It is not "pure." One day I will act without any thought of the fruits of action, but it's hard to act when there is no support and, worse, everyone is in silent resistance and doesn't see how their fear and resistance and envy drains the life out of the moment.

Yes, there is only Consciousness. I feel so close and so far away.

31 October 1985

Sunya and I often talked about enlightenment—he always pushed me to explain what I meant by that term. None of my answers were satisfactory. Even if I got the words right—not two, non-duality, no separation, etc.—it all sounded hollow. "How can you say someone is enlightened or not, if you don't know what you mean by that word symbol?" he would delight in asking.

Sunya had read Bucke's *Cosmic Consciousness* many times and the margins showed his tiny bullet dots marking expressions. But it was the life of Jesus that seemed to interest him most—Joshua ben Joseph, as he called him. He spoke of him as a "third degree initiate."

He asked me what would have happened had Jesus been able to leave behind tape recordings of his talks. At times it came to me that Sunya, this bizarre Dane in an Indian turban who delighted in boasting of his lack of "headucation," might be the reincarnated Jesus just seemed too preposterous for my logical mind.

Sometimes, though, I would say that perhaps Sunya was Christ returned to see the results of his work.

He would look at me seriously and seem to agree but then ask, "But who would believe such a thing? Better watch who you tell that too."

He would then give a big grin.

9 November 1985

Mother says she feels "like I don't have long to live." She's still on a cane and can see only out of one eye. "Age catches up with you," she says. "If the soul isn't world-weary, the body becomes so."

A friend lent me a copy of one of U. G. Krishnamurti's books. U. G. is a debunker of enlightenment. Thoroughly negative. Believes we always remain what we are—attitudes, beliefs, ways of thinking and perceiving.

My guess is he got there on acid—was "washed" all at once instead of gradually and so had no time to evolve spiritually. He's a dud, a blank shot.

13 November 1985

Went to see Thich Nhat Hanh. His is an "engaged" Buddhism, not the withdrawal from life that Gurdjieff criticized. He opens his arms to the world's suffering. What he offers is breathing:

> Breathing into the body and the mind is calmed.
> Breathing out I smile.
> Breathing in I am in the present moment.
> Breathing out I know this is the only moment.

The monk had great feeling but was still held by this world. He talks peace but when has there ever been peace that lasts? The phenomenal world is, by its nature, sunk in duality. War goes on at all levels—physical weapon war occurs when other types and modes of war reach their end. As it's said, "Diplomacy is war by other means."

1 December 1985

Saw the wolf fish at the San Francisco Aquarium, all alone in his tank as he kills anything that comes into his space—his ego, sense of himself, is that big. He even kills his own.

23 December 1985

Jean asked if I had thought at all about publishing *Être*. I said, "No. Not at all." There was no money. It would take a very great sum, etc. He said we should charge $25 a year for a sub and get 300 subs, sending out a flyer to a list of 3000 names. I said not so easy, but he was firm, so I finally told him to send me twenty-eight articles arranged in the order he desired for the quarterly. We'll go as far as we can. "We'll put the question to Reality," I said. He just looked at me. I forget—he thinks he is the Reality. Weird.

We only had donations at the door to the dialogues, so I convinced him to allow us to ask for $5. So instead of getting $30–$36 we got $80.

I had brought him an 1887 mint condition American silver eagle coin. I put it in a small gold box and wrapped it with green paper and a gold bugle emblem. JK talked about money. He said that he had brought a banana or an apple to his guru but never money—yet it was an object, of course, and we were not in India. I spoke about the need in practical terms in the West to have money. As a child I had money and was still unhappy, so I realized it was nothing special, but in the world we live in the dollar sign was a symbol stronger than the cross.

1986
The Subject-Object Relationship

11 January 1986
　　Read Ramana Maharshi's *Path of Self-Knowledge*. What caught my eye was his saying, "We do not know what souls man may be finishing, and for what part of their unfinished karma they may seek our company." And, "One devotee, Lakshmana Sharma had brought his dog with him—a handsome, pure white dog—and it was dashing about in high spirits and refused the food offered

to it. Sri Bhagavan said: 'You see what joy he shows? He is a high soul who has taken on this canine form.'"

16 January 1986
I spoke to Jean about the mind's effort to conserve such experiences as joy, love, emptiness . . . and then in becoming aware of the mind's grasping . . . suddenly being taken, finding oneself outside the mind.

He agreed and used the word *astonishment* several times about the experience, and also noted it was "dangerous."

19 January 1986
Dialogue in Tiburon. The adapter in the tape recorder broke. Then Jean wanted to change rooms. The one we were in was all set up and people were already in their seats. I was going to say something, but in a flash dropped it, shifted directions, no identification. Quite wonderful and the first time I can recall having done that and, of course, "I" didn't do it.

The dialogue was about sensation, feeling, creating space, lessening the subject-object relationship. The object unfolds and speaks to you. There is a seeing of the facts. Then a conclusion comes up in you.

26 January–2 February 1986
Seminar at Mt. Madonna. He speaks of "fusion," of being behind oneself, in the spine. Awareness is awakened when we wake up. The mind is seen to switch on like a clock radio. Just as thoughts and emotions and sensations are objects for the mind — *the mind is an object of awareness*. This recognition intensifies the knowingness of awareness.

It was a nice day and at the end we sat together on a bench. He told me now to listen to the *nada* upon awakening. It is in the old brain as is the *bindu* which reabsorbs the *nada*. Hear the *nada* in the back of the head, the old brain. It will descend to the shoulders and heart and here it will expand laterally where *spanda*, vibration, is experienced. *Do not objectify nada*, thus creating a duality.

3 February 1986

The seminar itself was quite good. Much work with the lumbar and the subtle body, its expansion from the physical. The ego manifested mightily. I just let it go. It got bigger and bigger.

The breathing and the focused attention and the nonidentification are the secrets. At night held the penis in my hand. A shock of energy. A self-induced shock. Some porno fragments appeared. Used these as well to help the energy ascend. Then visualized a flame flicking at the base of the spine. It broke out into a bonfire. Squeezed the sphincter muscles as I breathed.

I spoke to Jean about this. He said it was from being too "out in front" putting a hand to the face. "One should be behind," he said. He meant the spine. Expanded so much during the morning meditation that I did not do the exercises.

I saw the mind is an object of awareness. He said this recognition intensifies the knowingness of awareness. He said I will have it again perhaps while dressing or undressing.

I spoke to Jean about the book and told him my title for it would be: *The Beauty of Being: The Ever Answering Quest for One's Real Self.*

There was a wonderful energy explosion between us. Then he added the word, *In the Beauty of Being.*

4 March 1986

Much kundalini last night. The body expanded, I focused the attention on the *Muladhara*, breathing into it and the perineum and anus and up the spine—*The Secret of the Golden Flower*. Came to the causal body, the "covering of bliss." Did not identify with the energy and the whole body was filled.

I can see that one has to be very clear—to regard all mental-emotional-instinctual representation as a distraction, no matter how elegant or insightful or carnal. That way one eludes the trip of splitting in two as to a 'yes' or 'no' about what is given. Without unity—a clear-headed and hearted attention directed on the process—the K does not rise.

The Subject-Object Relationship

12 March 1986

We put the house in Ossining, New York, up for sale. So glad we rented it out when moving to California. Prices really zoomed back there.

21 May 1986

Jean came to give the dialogue at the Palace. "When you have sensation of the body you are no longer identified with the body."

29 May 1986

Seminar at Angela Center in Santa Rosa. The expanded body—really felt that at Santa Rosa. The meditation, then the feeling of the hands, the limbs, the body, followed by the expanding sensation into space, first the left side of the front of the body, then the right; the two sides and the back. Afterward the breathing—in through the two nostrils, out through the right; in through the two nostrils, out through the left, etc. Then the pause, the stopping at the end of the exhale and the small stop at the end of the inhale.

I asked Jean about Patañjali again. Jean was quite adamant that concentration was not the way.

News came that Stan Modic had a triple-bypass and was retiring. Perry Pascarella, the assistant editor, would replace him. In a note, Perry says *Industry Week* is "returning to its niche." In other words, the dream is over. He speaks about working with the other sides of the magazine—meaning advertising sales, but he does not mention it directly. He does say we won't prostitute ourselves. He has accepted the lie.

6 June 1986

"Do not crush your beautiful organ," said Jean, with wide eyes, looking in my direction.

We were in a twisting posture with one hand on the hip, the other outside the extended leg and by the foot.

I looked at him for a second and then looked behind me to see who he was talking to.

Then I gestured to myself.

Jean Klein at Casa de Maria Seminar

Jean Klein at Mount Madonna seminar

He repeated what he said.

"Do you mean my arm?" I asked incredulously. I could not, quite literally, believe he said what he said.

Everyone in the room burst out in laughter.

He turned to Barbara and said, "Do you contest?"

She beamed.

At the end he told me I was more relaxed than at Mt. Madonna. He said he wanted to pay me $20 for having filled up his car.

I said he didn't have to do that, but he said he wanted to.

"Okay," I said, "make it a hundred."

He smiled and shook his head while he looked into his wallet. He gave me $20.

"You're a good administrator," I told him.

We both laughed, as in one of his dialogues he had told me that we don't own money, we only administrate it.

I'm going to hear a disciple of Swami Rama's discourse on chapter II of Patañjali's system. Am I making the same mistake as I did years before in going to see Chögyam Trungpa when I was in the Work? Each time spiritual knowledge has been my spur.

September 1986

The Ossining house sold, but because it was a rental property a number of financial and tax questions were raised. That seals it. We're here in California to stay. The kundalini is flowing at times, not just in the middle of the night.

9 November 1986

My sister, Marjorie, has finally convinced my mother to sell her home. Mother says she'll live in Pittsburgh now and feels like she does not have long to live. I wonder how they will get along. It's always been up and down with them.

14 November 1986

We're going to ask Lottie Rose, Sunya's "dollar princess," about buying Sri Wuji's Palace.

I'm tiring of the diary writing. Don't have the belief in it any longer—what was the belief, anyhow?

Muladhara has opened up.

Sunya told me just before he passed on about writing a book about him. I didn't see how that was possible, so I created and published two editions of a twenty-four-page broadside. It had photos of him through the years from childhood on, his writings, and those of people like me who knew him. I wrote an introduction and titled it *Sri Wuji*. It was offered free.

In the second edition of *Sri Wuji* were the many letters we received from friends of Sunya's from all over the globe after his passing. This is from Indira Gandhi, then prime minister of India:

> I met Sunyataji first in the mid-thirties, drawn by notices asking for silence, which indicated the approach to his abode. He kept in touch during my stay in Almora and later was a regular winter visitor to my father's house in Delhi. Afterwards I did not see much of him though he did drop in a few times and often wrote.
>
> We had some interesting talks but perhaps I was not ready for his message. And, I must confess, I did not always understand what he wrote. Why did he call himself "Wu"? I regret that I could not benefit more from our acquaintance.
>
> His detachment was obvious and he felt at peace with himself and his surroundings. He proved that in matters of the spirit there can be no boundaries of any kind. It is apt that his ashes should rest in Almora. My thoughts be with you on that day. It is sad that he is no longer in the body with us. [For other letters, see Appendices, "Friends of Sunya."]

I received this from Don Stacy:

> You are bridging a fascinating group of worlds. Your overlapping dreams are as rich as anyone could image. The big danger —I assume is that one world reads the other (prepare for the opposites touching!).
>
> And yet you really seem to have mastered both. Perhaps

the questions will revolve around the quality of your begging bowl!

Between that which is (recognizably wife-children-school) and That which is beyond the *is* — you will be found. I am sure, we both wait for that moment.

From the standpoint of energy — (pseudo-real expanse) — you are being a wise economist. But there must be a strain.

Beneath it all I have an odd feeling of being protector of the ego — that poor maligned chump of psyche. The idea that life is one hideous temptation that should be instantly overcome because of its lack of lasting — so to speak — seems like the old Santa Claus is dead syndrome. Sometimes I feel that a genuine humanist — who can accept life as it seems to be (which is as good a dream as any) and still be a good, warm, feeling person—is much to be admired.

Unfortunately — most of them are idealists — and might as well be Hindus! (Or Buddhists). Anyway — you are doing wonderfully — write. [For other letters, see Appendices, "Friends of Sunya."]

For the second edition of *Sri Wuji* I also interviewed Jean Klein. Drove across the Bay to Berkeley where he was staying and taped the interview:

> *Q: You sometimes speak of this teaching in terms of its being in the Kashmir tradition. In the sense that René Guénon speaks of tradition — that of being an archetypal form, or vessel, in which Truth expresses itself — what can be said of the Kashmir tradition?*
>
> Jean Klein: Kashmir tradition speaks of energy, movement and matter being *Shakti*. The home ground of *Shakti* is *Shakta*.
>
> This is involution, returning; it comes about through understanding.
>
> Through understanding — this means first that you

The Subject-Object Relationship

see you are in your life compensating constantly, that you escape constantly. And in that understanding you are in search of—you are.

Through investigation you find you cannot find the peace, joy, freedom you are looking for. But the investigation brings you to a state of observation, of listening, of attention.

You become attentive through this energy, movement and matter. By *attentive*, I mean you are without interference, judgment, evaluation, comparison, conclusion.

This attention brings a kind of canalization of *Shakti*. This energy has its home ground in awareness, in *Shakta*. In the involution of all this energy you find a moment of being your true self, being pure awareness.

For example, facing the energy and your body helps you to face all the layers of resistance, fear. You listen, you welcome. Then this superficial fixation of energy has no more hold and so you come, more and more, to deeper levels and layers of energy.

The physical body is composed of different sheaths, which have been covered by fear, anxiety and resistance.

So the Kashmir system is one of accepting, letting go, welcoming, receiving. All is received—all energy, movement, matter. Then, suddenly, you are taken by the receiving position.

Q: Is this receiving a totally passive activity?

JK: Yes, I would say "passive" in the sense that there is no interference. And "active" meaning completely here, alert, present, open.

Q: Shakti will always cause—be a source of—impressions of Shakta?

JK: Yes.

Q: And in the spin of events there will be places where one gets caught?

JK: Yes.

Q: So one has to welcome being "caught" also?

JK: The desire of *Shakti* is joy in *Shakta* (if we can speak of an object having desire). If there is, the desire is to return from the constant play and projecting.

Q: *This return begins with a "stop." But there appears to be another kind of "stop" also. This is when one gets caught, trapped in some reaction to the energy. It's a contradiction, a closing down.*

JK: Yes.

Q: *Once that happens it seems like, in a certain way, the impression becomes even stronger. Watching is not dissolving this kind of "stop" but is . . .*

JK: Yes, but let us be very clear what it means by watching. It is not the watching of a hunting dog. That is a fixed watching. In the Kashmir approach, you must take for granted that you are naturally open. So don't even think of your openness. You are open. All you can do—if there is something to do—is welcome all perfection, all energy, movement, matter. In this welcoming automatically there is integration of the energies and the totality. You see the difference?

Q: *Yes, the hunting dog is still looking for the quail. It is a watching but a watching without expectation, desire.*

JK: The moment there is a "watching" that projects energy in space and time there is taking, attaining, grasping. It is an activity whose source is memory, not being. But the moment you welcome the perception, you are in the receiving position and projection dissolves completely. And, suddenly, you are taken by your own presence (which is not a subject-object relationship). You may be taken very, very often. Then a moment comes when you are constantly in it, even in decay.

Q: *There is always cognition?*

JK: Yes. It is the point of being completely free of all volition, personal volition. You are really a channel.

Q: *Being a channel—though there is only one energy it has many modifications, many of which are discolored. How does discrimination take place? In the East...*

JK: It has nothing to do with a certain passivity you see in the East, a kind of wrong laziness. In becoming more and more aware, appearances in you speak more and more clearly. You feel also reaction. It's only a receiving. The action and reaction are received. There is no fatalistic giving up.

Giving up here is meant as a giving up of interference, judgment, comparison and so forth. It is a refusal.

In a certain way a citizen of this Earth is, at the same time, a citizen of Heaven. Earthly life expresses beauty. There is no refusal of earthly life.

Q: Could you speak about Shakti-Shakta and the yoga asanas?

JK: You mean how it acts in the body?

Q: Yes. The asanas themselves, not being ordinary positions the body takes in life, create a certain tension ... or, better, magnify the tension existing in the body. The fixed energy, fixed Shakti, is more easily seen.

JK: The moment the body becomes an object of your attention, you free it from all fixed energies: fear, anxiety, reaction, resistance. These energies are mainly fixed in the lumbar region, canalized there. Through reintegrating them, you travel through centers of very subtle energy. You become more sensitive as this energy unfolds itself in *Shakta* which, in its stillness, is a kind of magnet drawing the energy. When the unfolding completes itself, it is what is called, in this tradition, *Enlightenment*.

But coming back to the different postures. Every posture is directed toward certain centers of the body. These centers have become fixed, contracted. This yoga frees the energy in the centers of all distortion, canalization. The approach is to free the energy by facing it. It has nothing to do with the gymnastic approach.

Still, in this approach we don't emphasize the energy, movement, matter. We emphasize *Shakta*, the awareness.

Q: Many yoga systems use "locks" at the anus, abdomen and throat to mix the energies. You don't do that. Or at least you haven't.

JK: No, it is not done with the real understanding because it is completely artificial. The energy comes up with different degrees of understanding. Automatically.

Q: Is there a danger in artificially bringing up the energy before the understanding is mature?

JK: Absolutely. Because in the action of daily life, your behavior may be in contradiction to this level of energy.

Q: In the Upanishads five different types of prana are spoken of. Is this a part, too, of the Kashmir tradition?

JK: What is called "air" is not what we call prana. For example, there is prana for evacuation, for the assimilation of food. There are different pranas. This energy has a lateral or even down movement and by breathing in a certain way you fix, or cap, this energy and knowingly bring it to the upper part. Instead of the active energy being dispersed, it is brought to the central channel of energy to really integrate it.

But, as we said before, you will be able to do it because it is kind of a technique that can be learned. But if you go back into daily life and your behavior is not in accord with this degree of consciousness, it brings you much difficulty. You are not in tune.

Q: Out of harmony?

JK: Yes. So I never use this kind of technique. I am completely aware of it, but I don't use it.

Q: Your use of the word "understanding" seems to be central to this approach. We must knowingly understand?

JK: Yes. But "knowing" is a dangerous word. Our language is dualistic. We must be careful. That word is so easily interpreted as a thought-form.

Q: Conscious understanding, then?

JK: The real expression would be to be "awakened in consciousness." You must know it. But this "knowing" is not a thought-form.

The Subject-Object Relationship

Q: Sunya would use the word "innerstanding."

JK: Yes.

Q: Conscious innerstanding (or understanding) seems to be composed of both being and knowledge in the true spiritual sense of that word.

JK: Yes, I would say, "Being-knowledge." Knowledge, of course, not in the sense of accumulation of information, of learning. There is no longer an agent of knowing.

Q: The perceptions are then direct and unhindered?

JK: Yes, yes.

Q: The world then is much more fluid, the images (what we take to be images) being in movement always?

JK: In movement. Always. Changing by expression, extension.

Q: So nothing is tied down?

JK: We could say of certain levels of consciousness that the power of *Shakti* involves *Shakta*, certain centers are sensitized to a forefeeling of Truth.

Q: In relation to these centers, some systems speak about gods and goddesses.

JK: Yes.

Q: That each center has its own particular deities and these centers, or "worlds," have their particular flavor, rhythm, intensity.

JK: Yes, it's a kind of transmutation because the cell—which is maintained through its opposites—when there comes a meeting of opposites the opposition is destroyed. Our thinking is maintained through the opposites. But beyond these opposites there is only unity.

Q: Shakti, being composed of manifold numbers of opposites . . . when this comes together with Shakta in the silent marriage, I would assume there is a cessation of movement. It's energy without movement?

JK: One must not misunderstand. *Shakti* and *Shakta* are not two opposites. *Shakta* is timeless awareness and *Shakti* is its expression. All expression has its history, its biography. It must be welcomed, allowed. Never take *Shakta* and *Shakti* for two opposites, as positive and negative, masculine and feminine. That is a wrong interpretation.

Q: *There is no concept to hold onto, nothing to do. Each of us is, fundamentally, the Self. Being such a pure teaching — isn't there a danger in this? I know of people who then feel no need to make themselves available. They continue with their lives as before, thinking "If it's going to happen, it will happen." And their lives are ones of excess and disharmony.*

JK: It depends upon by what approach they have been coming to the conclusion that there is nothing to do. In certain moments, mind comes to the understanding of its limits. There is a normal stop. It's not a stop by will, which is a functional stop. That there is nothing to attain, nothing to achieve comes with investigation, exploration.

Q: *Coming back to the question of tradition, I'm still not clear as to how you perceive and use this word?*

JK: When we speak of tradition, it really means what is transmitted. Transmission doesn't mean doctrine. It is not the doctrine that is transmitted, but the Truth, the Truth of reality. Tradition in the real sense is That which is transmitted from one who knows, who is the Truth, to another who is also . . . but has yet to realize it.

And so the conversation came full circle. I'd been with him for over two hours. It seemed like a few minutes. I drove back over the bridge to Marin. There was such lightness. The water of the Bay glistened and the mountains looked to have a deep being.

Sri Wuji I and *II* were passed out free to people on the street and left in coffee houses and post offices throughout Marin County. No responses.

To gather material for *Sri Wuji,* I had gone through the five boxes of material that Sunya had left, but now I found one I had missed. It was like his goodbye message to my egoji.

At the top of the first page is Sunya's handwritten date — 1973.

It was just before the Alan Watts Society entered his hut and carried him off to "Yankeestan."

Originally the God-head is hermaphroditic — beyond opposites and duality, but at the moment of 'creation,' projection or division, the feminine *Shakti* leaps forth spontaneously and Eve was created from the body of Adam, Man, while he slept, and the twain fell into further division and ignorance, when they stealthily ate the 'apple' of knowledge and lost sight of the inherent-wisdom and wholeness and grace — in the mere knowledge of good and evil, for ego-survival. This fall into blinkered ignorance and unawareness of integral Self-hood — must have been due and ordained. "Sin is behovely," [needed, necessary, due] the Lord of Love said. The sin of ignorance and 'unawareness of our real Estate,' our Emmanuel, our Buddha Nature and the grace of selfhood. Egojies wallow in sin-complexes and in semantic muddles — of word-symbols, concepts and abstractions, and few are mature to die into the ineffable God-experiencing or awareness of unity, wholeness and grace: *Sat-Chit-Ananda*.

There is no evil before God — since God's purpose is served also by that which appears bad to us egojies. "All is right that seems most wrong, all is good — because God is All," said Sri Narayana: His last words before he left his body. "There is nothing either good or bad but — thinking makes it so," said Shakespeare's Hamlet. So simply bounce or glide beyond joyous ease — in the self — also in dualities and ego-fuss, advises Sri Wuji — "Be a light unto your Self."

"*Demon est deus inversus.*" It is not surprising that the various mythologies recognize a curious analogy between the divine ambivalence of God and the less ambivalence of the Trickster, the Conjurer and the Joker. A devout Christian like J. K. Chesterton uses it in his poem "The Skeleton." Sri Wuji once wrote our poem called "The Jester." He was fascinated by the wisdom of Shakespeare's fools—and the seeming incongruity of the rather subservient Polonius mouthing Advaita Vedantic truths, and the brutish Kaliban's poetic flair. It is in Poetry and Paradoxes that egojies get nearest to the ineffable Silence, says Wuji: "Lift a stone and we will see me. Cleave the wood and I Am—there." Wu!

Wuji's Biography begins with Ibsen's dictum: "The strongest man is he, who is most alone." Aloneness was his need and his greatest boon—and the next greatest was his non-urge to express, explain and share his integral awareness. He had no ambition for power, pelf or outer wealth and no craving for anything or anybody, or any better or worse halves or garment, for his fulfillment, contentment, harmony or grace. In aloneness he could aware and Be the all-one-ness. Wu!

To Wuji meditation seems to be negative in as much as thoughts are kept away—concentration on, one thought. His sadhana has been contemplation, not meditation, concentration or *neti neti*, shutting out, but rather an all–acceptance, a passive positivity, negative capability—and receptive sensibility, specially when he is ego-freely alone in nature and in the Self. In such state or mode of contemplation—there is no concentration, no effortful elimination or holding on to one mantra. Thoughts may come and go: he is thought-free, not caught up in thoughts, concepts or abstractions, but free in these and in the graceful Self-interplay and mutual interpenetration.

The born mystic is always in the temple—and, often, a natural contemplative, a *sakshi* witness and calm acceptor of what IS, and, also, of the ever-changing phenomena in *Swa-Lila* Self-interplay. Wuji's "delightful uncertainty," "affectionate detachment" (though no Real detachment) and his Self-controlled spontaneity are all pertaining to this mode of Being. At times one can merge in the Source unconsciously, as in sleep, death, swoon or Samadhi.

Contemplation is merging into the Source, consciously. Then the fear of death, of swoon—or of ego-oblivion will disappear. Wu!

It is that the so-called individual or persona-mask, does not exist at all as a reality. The ego-ridden mind, or mind-ridden egoji! What is the difference? Asks Wuji. They are not real, but shadowy, ever-changing names, concepts, ideas—and only the Eternal is Real—enough. Be Still to aware the Silence without the noise of thought, of words and of concepts. "Practice the immaculate conception," advises Wuji. In that intuitive Silence there is total integral awareness and no you or me. This puts an end to fragmentation, division and conflict. Wu!

1987
Passing of Tradition

11 January 1987
    We buy Sri Wuji's Palace, with a separate downstairs entrance, bathroom and shower. We'll put in a kitchen and rent out the downstairs. It has a small fish pond and some fruit trees.
    Because of tax considerations, we needed to put some of the money we had earned on the sale of the Ossining house into a rental property. My mother and sister weren't getting along. The

past always lived them. My mother said she wanted to move out here, so, houses being so expensive in Marin, we decided to buy a small house for her in Petaluma, about a forty-minute drive from Fairfax.

10–14 July 1987
    Seminar at Mt. Madonna.
    It had been another powerful seminar and after it ended Jean and I sat together on a bench with a beautiful view of the forests below. He said he had studied medicine and music at the University of Berlin. When the Nazis came to power he fled with his family to France and later went alone to Algeria and joined the French Foreign Legion. After the war, he returned to France and met Guénon, who said that Tradition could only be passed from a conscious being. He and his family went to India. In Bangalore he met Pandiji, a scholar, who introduced him to Advaita and gave transmission to the nature of reality. He traveled and met and spent some time with Sri Atmananda Krishna Menon, and the yogi Krishnamacharya. Later he met a wandering silent sage who introduced him to the Kashmir approach and work with the energy body. At Pandiji's direction, he returned to Europe in 1952 to share his realization of Being and Silence with others.

14 August 1987
    Felt Jean and Lord Pentland are no different—in essence. That night I had a dream: Many people wanting to come to a Jean Klein seminar. My idea is to divide them into two groups, two different weekends. I go to speak to JK about this but behind the desk sits LP—he has hair. Sitting down I notice a large brown and gold lighter, coffee table height, on the floor by one leg of the chair. As I reach down to pick it up, LP begins to talk. But I can't hear him. I feel like a fool. I put the lighter on his desk. He takes no notice of it. He talks about the need for a library. I am hearing him but his leg is jamming my crossed leg into the sharp corner of the desk. The situation seems absurd. He gives no indication that anything unusual is going on and neither do I. However, thoughts

are running through my head as to how much work there will be. He ends by saying we should begin with getting a rare book but doesn't say what it is.

16 August 1987

What struck me about the dream:

Widening the corridor—enlarging the *sushumna*, the channel of the spine.

Brown and gold coffee table lighter—the fire of kundalini, brown standing for the earth, gold for the elixir of heaven.

Lord Pentland with hair—younger, more vital and so is what he says. And it is he who sits behind the desk though I went to see Jean Klein.

The library is a collection of knowledge.

Rare book—this is seminal knowledge; all knowledge will build on this.

1 September 1987

Mother arrived. Second time she had been on a plane. Took her over to our house and then up to the house in Petaluma. She liked it and we had a good dinner together.

14 September 1987

It was my father's death day back in 1978. Called my mother. She was all anima all the way. I feared for her. Called her back and she was fine; the "infection" had passed. I remembered how that had always happened. She'd go off the wall to the extent that it was a question whether she'd ever come back. Then she'd finish, having won in her mind "total victory," as she would say. Satisfied, she became normal again.

Drove up to Petaluma to look for a salon to give her a permanent. As we drove around, she said to me in a nice little voice, "You want to know something about yourself?"

"Okay," I said, unaware of the ambush I'd walked into.

"Well," she said, going straight for the jugular, "Everyone thinks you're so kind and generous, that you're an angel. But you're not. You want to know what you really are? You're selfish!"

Driving home, I thought about what had happened. How to expand in the shrunken moment? The shock happens. Unprepared, you explode. Prepared, in sensation, you feel the ego-created emptiness of the moment. You feel its texture, ride it, not go with the impulse, the mental momentum. Seeing this is a shock of a type. Then emptiness, silence. In the face of this, there is the reaction — the explosion. But without the fear (a reaction in itself) the moment expands, the energy glowing into the vacuum, making transcendence possible.

1988

Geometric Understanding

11 January 1988

Drove down to an afternoon dialogue Jean was giving in San Diego. It was the first time he had talked here and questions were sparse, so I asked a number of questions. Afterward, the person who had arranged the dialogue asked me if I'd ever been in the Work. I told him I had, but wondered why he'd asked.

"It was your questions and the way you asked them. You don't usually hear that outside the Work." He told me he had been in the Work in Los Angeles and had dropped out to go to India and Rajneesh.

He had a copy of the *ALL & Everything* made in 1930. [After the first published edition the *ALL* was reduced to *All*.] He had made copies. Did I want one?

Without thinking, I agreed and went to his home. He had me wait for some time in the living room before I was told to go into his office.

He sat behind the desk. He just looked at me, saying nothing. So I relaxed and emptied out, softened my eyes, looked-without-looking. I guess he had had second thoughts.

That went on until finally he reached into a drawer and handed me the copy. I thanked him and left.

And so without actually realizing it, I had gone back into my Work life. But, of course, I had never really left. I had left the outer organization, the Foundation of the Work, but not the inner. Gurdjieff says those who are attracted to the Work have a desire for real knowledge. I certainly did, but there never was enough separation from it to use the word *knowledge*. What drove me were questions about life.

Jean stayed over in San Diego, so he and I went to dinner. I had heard he played chess when younger and once played five boards at one time. So I told him about the chess game I had played thirteen years before with Lord Pentland.

Ever since hearing that Lord Pentland knew the game, I had always wanted to play him. By a stroke of intuitive luck, far beyond my maturity, I had asked if chess was a *Legominism*, a way of passing esoteric knowledge. He had silently nodded and smiled. A few days later he lent me a little-known book, *The Art of Asha*, on the symbols of chess and their meaning.

Jean didn't know about the symbolism in chess. So I explained, for example, the eight vertical and eight horizontal black and white squares, eight is the number of infinity, and together they add up to 64 squares and, by theosophical addition, result in the numeral 10 — the 1 and the 0, manifest and unmanifest, all and nothing, which is given the name of God, Jehovah, Allah and Brahman, depending on the spiritual path. White, having the first move, is the active force, Black, the denying. To win or draw, Black must become the active force, making White the denying. If a pawn reaches the eighth rank of the opposing player, it can be "reborn" as any of the pieces, except for the king. Without Jean asking, I then related the whole game I had played with Lord Pentland in Manhattan at the Middle Eastern bazaar the Work put on.

I was one of the two 'chess masters' in the Chess Booth over which the banner flew: *Play the Chess Masters of Persia. Only 50¢.* At one point, Lord Pentland came up to the table, smiled, handed me two quarters and sat down at the board. "Which pieces would you like?" I asked. "White, of course," he replied curtly.

I set up the pieces accordingly and the game began. It was no ordinary game, for I understood that the demand was to strive to play consciously, to be present, remember myself, not be mechanical.

He moved the king's pawn to the king four square. He showed, as always, no sign of anything. It was as if he wasn't there—and yet he was. A strange fearful absence and yet awareness that completely unnerved me. I somehow kept myself together, breathing, experiencing the sensation, his vibration.

It was now Black's turn. What kind of game to play? The king's games were long and stodgy. No, I chose the Sicilian Defense, the Najdorf System. An asymmetrical opening, it was a dangerous game which one either won or lost, with little likelihood of a draw.

After about ten or so moves Lord Pentland's rook challenged my bishop. No big deal—I could simply move it. But remembering and peering into the board—suddenly, there it was! If—instead of protecting the bishop by moving it—I sacrificed it, I could move my king's rook's pawn up two squares, and from there had a forced mate in eight moves (sixteen altogether, as there are eight moves for Black, eight for White). It was seen *all at once!* Like a light had been turned on—then off!

Normally, at best, I'd see only a few moves ahead, but this was—*sixteen moves!* Patiently, move-by-move, I tried to reconstruct the sequence of moves for Black and White. But my attention wasn't strong enough. Had I *really* seen a forced mate?

Finally, I realized, there was only one way to find out—I had to take the chance.

So I left the Black bishop hanging unprotected and moved the king's rook's pawn. I felt Lord Pentland's attention beam in on my bishop, then scan the whole board. Had I made an obvious mistake? I felt him place his whole attention on me. I emptied out, became embodied, still, breathed, no thought. It was like "playing dead."

I could feel his question—was this a blunder or was the bishop sacrifice part of a plan? He could see no answer. So, he, too, had to take a chance.

His rook took my bishop. I moved the pawn two squares, he made a move, then my king's knight moved forward, forcing his piece back, then another and another move, all forcing.

Suddenly, there it was. A forced mate. A small puff of energy exploded from Lord Pentland's throat. It went right into me and through me.

I felt both happy and sad.

Jean Klein smiled when I finished and told me, "Chess is war but it must be played as war without hatred."

I agreed and asked if we could play a game sometime.

He nodded and smiled again.

"We could switch sides every seven moves," I offered, "so there would be no question of identifying."

He didn't say no or yes.

Later, I wrote him a letter speaking of other things and again brought up a chess match. I signed the letter, "A. Alekhine."

[Alexander Alekhine was the great German World Champion known for his attacking and imaginative style of play, who in his last tournament had come to the board, peed on it and walked away, his way of saying he'd realized he'd given his life to nothing that really mattered, "Pouring the empty into the Void," as it's said.]

Months later, at the summer seminar at Mt. Madonna, I told Jean I had a Xerox copy of the manuscript of one of his teachers,

Sri Atmananda Krishna Menon, who played chess with some of his chelas.

"It was a way of teaching," I said.

Jean agreed.

I asked if he had ever played with Atmananda. He nodded and smiled. I had made my point about his playing with me.

The seminar ended. It all seemed so silly—this asking for a game of chess with Jean. I let it all go. I was in too wonderful a place to want to think anyway. Yes, perhaps one could play by direct perception—that would be interesting to sit and not think but simply "see" the pieces on the board. But that was far beyond me.

[See "Remembering with Boris Spassky," *The Gurdjieff Journal*, #68, Vol. 17, Issue 4]

28 January 1988

I received a letter from Jean:

> My Dear Pat,
> As you know I cancelled suddenly all my meetings in the U.S.A. and also in Europe for some months. It was my own decision and I followed the advice of my doctors in L.A. I think I will recuperate very soon and perhaps see you in August!
> If by any chance your business brings you to Europe, you are always welcome here. I am trying to keep the weekend talk in April in London so as to keep up my English. Today only a short note my dear Pat, and affectionately to you and your beautiful Family.
> J

4 February 1988

Emma Edwards had heard I was going to see Jean in Paris and asked to come with me as she and Jean had had a falling out. I stayed at the Hôtel Michelet Odéon, a small hotel near the Luxembourg Gardens where he lived, and she stayed at another hotel close by. When we arrived at his place, she stood to the side of the door so he wouldn't see her when he opened it and greeted me. When he did and saw me, his hands went up in mid-air and the full high beams turned on, but then suddenly he saw Emma. Shocked, he quickly recovered and led us into his apartment. It was clear they needed to speak alone, so I went into the bathroom and stayed forty-five minutes. When I came out everything was fine.

Jean had other plans for the evening which he couldn't break, so Emma and I went to dinner. It was a lot of fun, kidding and drinking. I told her my real name was "Mogo Blue." At one point our eyes came together and there was a strong sexual vibration. She said, after a bit, "I could do this, but you couldn't." I realized the truth of what she said.

The next morning Emma and I went to a café by the Tuileries Garden. She gave me a letter to open afterwards, "On the plane," she said. "It is not to be taken as black against white."

We saw Jean looking for us at the Mediterranean Café, and we all went to my hotel room which was on the top floor. Jean spoke about a guru wanting to throw someone out the window, someone who had overstepped himself.

I wonder, did he mean my bringing Emma here or what happened between us last night. However that was, I said, "Jean, is that what you want to do with me?"

He seemed startled at my directness.

"I am *merde*, Jean. I apologize."

He smiled, both of us connecting deeply, and he took my hands in his and turned them over so the palms faced upward.

"You are capable of integrating the senses. You will heal many people."

"Really . . . ?"

"Look at your hands."

He said, "Pure perception is always 'negative,' that is, it cannot manifest, cannot be known. It can only be entered when the 'person' is left behind."

Then Emma went shopping and Jean and I went to La Coupole, where the ladies of the Rope often went, as well as Jean-Paul Sartre and his circle.

I asked if I could teach the body work.

"You are the most improved of any of the American students. Yes, of course, teach others, teach yourself," he said, and added, "You will make a good yoga teacher."

I asked about doing headstands. He said in India he once did an eight-hour headstand as a gift to the Buddha on the Buddha's birthday.

"You must have been in a trance," I said.

That startled him slightly but he agreed.

The waiter came and we ordered a glass of wine—chardonnay for him, a cabernet for me.

"Yoga is union in every moment," he said. "Always sit up straight on both cheeks. If the anal sphincter is relaxed, it opens and the chakra turns up. And always do the spinal twist after you warm up and also do the cobra as it puts a 'crack' in the coccyx."

I couldn't resist. It came right out of me—"Let's drink to that," I said, laughing.

He gave a large smile and raised his wine glass, as did I.

We got up and walked. I brought up Gurdjieff's 'stop' exercise.

"Should we do it with the asanas?" I asked.

"Stop!" he says.

We both stop on the sidewalk. A woman coming toward us steps out of the way, somewhat alarmed.

"Did you see how the subtle body continues to move when the physical stops," he says. "Both in one consciousness."

"This is a means of separation," I say.

He nods.

"Remember," he says, "Gurdjieff said he left his followers 'between the sheets.'"

[That was true, though what he said was, "I've left you all in a fine mess." What did Gurdjieff mean by that? That he hadn't finished giving the full teaching?]

We go back to my hotel and up to my room.

We sit and he says there are two anal sphincters and then a smaller one at the gate of the spine. They have to relax a great deal in order to open. There is also the 7th cervical of the spine.

"We carry the substance in the lumbar and at the back of the neck," I say, asking if he agrees.

He does and he gets up.

I kneel down and *namaste*. Jean Klein kisses both sides of my face.

I read Emma's letter on the plane.

> Dear Mogo,
>
> It was a wonder-full time wasn't it? I thank the world there are crazy Irish warriors like you to play with.
>
> Last night, I saw the dynamic in your relationships with women, your mother, your wife. I can't go into the details but vaguely this is what it looked like.
>
> Your asthma is fear of your mother. It is a waste of time facing your mother or the past—unknowables. Only the fact, the fear, can be dealt with. When you have really experienced this fear of deep sensation, without analyzing it at all then you will love your mother.
>
> Mothers and sons, fathers and daughters! What a mischievous god to place so much in so little—fear of the mother is generally dealt with in two ways—passively, i.e., avoiding, retreating, homosexuality, or actively engaging, conquering sexuality and psychologically-intellectually, i.e., "taming the shrew." The bravest men take the second way.
>
> One who fears his mother projects "her opposite." He marries her opposite and uses all his power to make sure his wife stays "opposite"! The opposite to what stimulates fear, strong emotions of love and hate—but in the end, the opposite to life-force. In this marriage the man stills his fear and non-silence by expecting his wife to function in silence, to be an "ideal" opposite from the fearsome. The condition of his love is that she not awaken his fear through showing strong emotions or opinions, violence, anger, power, etc. The warrior catches a Valkyrie and puts her in a tower but in imprisoning the Valkyrie he cuts off her energy and a woman without energy loses her essence, and her

confidence. When a man shoots down a woman's energy through his fear he cuts himself off from his *own* power.

"I am not your father" but more subtly "You are not my mother" and the opposite of my mother is still the mother-fear.

There are no opposites to marry and therefore nothing to be afraid of. When all opposites are seen as projections of each other the fear of annihilation goes and anger disappears. In the end there is not sexual, creative or destructive energy. There is only energy.

X

P.S. A personal reaction is not psychological. It is physical.

This was quite acute and well-written. I never thought I had any fear of my mother, as she always jumped on my sister and not me. What I resisted was her neurotic love for me. Asthma started in the Army. And my wife is a quiet person, always has been. Still . . . .

16 February 1988
Jean sent another letter:

My dear Pat, many thanks for your letter and the article on Frithjof Schuon.

It was a joy for me to see you in Paris. Not many things to say, but the dimension beyond the sayings was there.

Keep in your mind very clearly that there is nothing to obtain. All teachings are the products of the intellect and perpetuate the "I concept" in more subtle forms, you must realize the futility of this kind of search. I would say it is the beginning of Wisdom. We are really = Presence = in our absence.

Dear Friend love to you and your beautiful family.

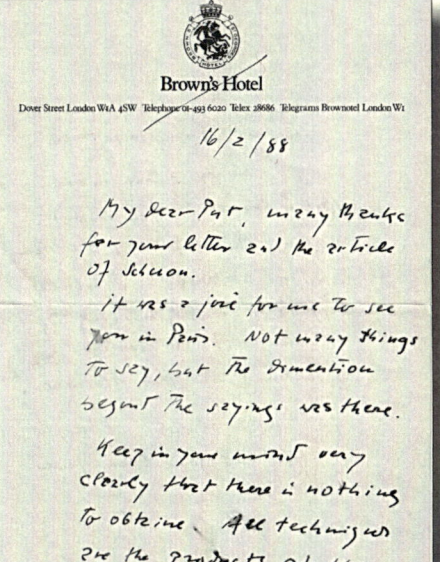

Letter to Pat from Jean Klein

Jean Klein, Emma Edwards, Barbara Patterson, Pat

Jean and Pat together walking at seminar in Delphi, Greece, 1988

Jean and Pat at seminar in Israel, 1994

9 March 1988

Dear Jean,

Thank you for the wonderful letter; one can't be reminded of the message often enough, so strongly are we conditioned.

I've been rereading some of the basic Siva texts since my return from Paris and finding a strong rapport and new understanding: like a flower opening, one has no notion of understanding enlarging but it happens. With this it is odd. At times there is a strong feeling of recognition, of a knowing, but then, like sunlight being diffused and deflected, it leaves and one is back full force in the gate and grip of duality.

1 April 1988

Had a dream of Lord Pentland. We are sitting at a table set for dinner with white tablecloth, silverware, etc. There are others there but I am not aware of them. A woman, trying to make contact with him, asks a question about how he handles sex. He turns and faces her, his eyes alight with life, emptiness and a thin veneer of disdain. He gives her, in effect, three answers with one look. Then he pushes his chair back from the table and gets up to leave, saying as he does: "Well, that's that." I know instantly that he is really saying, "My duty to the Gurdjieff Work is over." I feel great sadness and love and regret. He stops and says to me, "You take the knives." On the table is a small butter knife with a white pearl handle. I don't see the other knife. I look and look for it and finally find an identical butter knife but this one has a pearl handle that is black. I smile. Just like Gurdjieff/Pentland.

I am reading and beginning to understand the *Siva Sutras* and *Spanda Karikas*. It feels like I am being initiated in some sense. What a crazy time to come to Siva.

29 July 1988

At the Mt. Madonna seminar, Jean gave me a manuscript to

read of his new book *Who Am I?: The Sacred Quest*. I saw in reading the first few pages he made some statements that, while true, had been used so often they had no power. Instead of just reading it, I asked if I could point out similar instances. I did and he accepted and changed them accordingly.

When the book was published, he mentioned me and Barbara in the Acknowledgements, and gave me a copy inscribed:

> You are what I am.
> I am what you are.
> In my absence, and yours
> all things are welcome
> and absolutely at home.
> For Barbara affectionately.
> Jean Klein

At seminars and in private I questioned Jean relentlessly about points of Advaita I wanted to be crystal clear about. I always spoke with respect, but I never inner considered. I would point to seemingly contradictory statements he had made or I had read in the books. This often seemed to upset other students who were in the adoration phase or only looking for affirmation of their ideas and perspective. But the Work and Lord Pentland had shown me "Patterson" in all his glory, so I had no need to explore that, and the perspective of duality no matter how refined did not answer the essential question I had been carrying all these years—what is the *self* in self-sensing, self-remembering, self-observation?

August 1988

Jean spent about half the year at his home in Hope Ranch on the outskirts of Santa Barbara. Students often went to see him there when he was not giving seminars or traveling. I arranged with him that I would come down for five days. I arrived Sunday evening and stayed with Teddy, a student of Jean's, in a trailer in the hills above Santa Barbara. I phoned immediately and left word with Emma that I had arrived.

Monday came and went, no call. I stayed at the trailer the whole time for I didn't want to miss her call. Tuesday came and went as well. Why was Emma keeping me waiting? She could be so controlling. Saw "Patterson" many times but surprised that consciousness was as clear and lasting as it was. The anger came and went but did not become reactive, didn't build a "world." On Wednesday Jean and Emma came for lunch with some others. She said she had put the phone jack into the fax slot. I just nodded. When Jean left he said he would see me soon. Others saw him so easily. Was this a "teaching"?

But Thursday, again nothing. I let Teddy know I had to leave Friday at noon, regardless. But I was hanging by the fingertips. Later that day Jean himself called. I went to see him at once. We sat outside in the back garden. I asked if there was an alteration with nonduality, it not being a state. He smiled broadly, said something in Yiddish, and told me, "You have the geometric understanding."

He had said that of Heidegger when we had spoken of the philosopher's concept of Being. I took what he said to mean that I had come to the intellectual and emotional understanding of the teaching but had not fully experienced it.

He said geometrical understanding is a higher reasoning, one that leads beyond objects to the ultimate subject. He said when body-senses-mind had been integrated there comes a clarity that allows a glimpse of Truth. When the mind is free of all expectation and anticipation, global sensation becomes global feeling. This gives the feeling of expansion, of beingness, free from objects, from limitations, where the mind frees itself from identifying truth with objects. This is a forefeeling of Truth.

I told him how I had meditated and practiced in ordinary life and what I had come to. The gist of it was about differentiating the centers, their functioning and misfunctioning, observing the "I"s and their origin, using the spine, sensation, breath, sound and silence as supports, the gradient between the waking state and the subconscious lessening to the degree that the former is assimilated in the latter and arriving at what Jean called "the Blank state," where one was still in subject-object perception but where there was very little subject. (Beyond that he had said was "the Double Absence.")

I told him the Blank state was like being taken deep to the bottom of the ocean where one glided along the bottom, so to speak, to the edge of physical sleep and awareness. Then unknowingly there would be a dropping off to sleep only to then be awakened again to awareness and the ocean bottom. But there was still a subject, still an entity, call it what one would.

"Do not bother about it," he told me. "The question has formed of itself, now leave it."

We spoke about *prana*. He said it is carried in the muscles and creating a vacuum releases the *prana*. Breathe with awareness/sensation of the full body . . . . Just to stay with him a little longer, I asked him, "Why do you teach?"

"There isn't anybody who teaches. There is only teaching. In reality there is no teaching because . . . there is nothing to teach."

October 1988

Every Saturday I drove up to see my mother in Petaluma, but one time I had to miss and told her so in advance. When I drove up the following Saturday and knocked on the door, there was no answer, and she had always been very prompt.

I knocked a bit more. No answer. Went around back to see if she was in the kitchen. Looked through the bedroom windows. Empty. Fearful, I hurried back to the door and really pounded on the door.

Suddenly, it opened. And there she was screaming at me—"Don't take me for granted!"

The rest of the day never got much better. At one point, the words burst out of me—"I could take your face out and rub it into the cement!" I'd never thought that or said that to anyone, but there it was.

When I went home I went into the meditation room and lay down, arms and legs spread out. I couldn't stop the formatory center from going over and over again what had happened. Voices said don't see her again, forget about her, send her back to Marjorie. It all came up. I ate the sewage but it didn't take me. Finally, a space came and the obvious was realized: *she is my mother and I am with her forever, good or bad.* With that, worn out, I fell asleep. When Barbara came by and saw me on the floor she said in a jocular voice, "Saw your mother today, huh?"

That recognition healed something within. From that time on there was never a problem and we had such a great time with each other. My mother always had a great sense of humor.

She told me about her early life with her two sisters, Marie and Peg. She was the middle child and it wasn't easy.

"Marie and Peg would go over somewhere and never take me with them. One day after I pleaded and pleaded, Marie said, 'Okay, you can come . . . if you don't talk.'"

She and Marie slept in the same bed (there were also two brothers, Humphrey and Bill). "I bought a new dress and Marie wore it before I had even put it on. When I saw the dress on the bed, I attacked her, beating her as hard as I could with my fists. She never hit back but just stood there and said, 'Have you had enough?' and then Marie told me, 'You're ignorant.'"

My mother, who was beautiful, and had a big heart, lived with a lot of jealousy and envy from her sisters and so often was taken for granted and overlooked. She got along easily with men, but with women the past always lived the present.

She always referred to my wife as "her." Barbara, mature, never let it get to her. And as it happened when I was away on business, Barbara had to care for my mother and take her to the hospital several times, then her whole attitude and demeanor changed toward her, but not how she addressed her.

November 1988

Went back to Cleveland for an editorial conference. Pat Keefe, the publisher, told us that *Industry Week* was going to now accept advertorials, ads that looked like editorial content but weren't. There was a lot of meaningless talk back and forth, but for me it didn't get to the heart of the matter. I told him that *Esquire* magazine had tried this and it hadn't worked. It was making the reader think something was true when it wasn't. "We're breaking the unsaid covenant with the readership," I said.

My remark caught him off guard. He'd expected everyone to fall in line. His belly thickened as did his face.

He was trying to hold his anger in. He went on and on, only addressing what I had said briefly and without consequence.

When the conference ended, Keefe came up to me and put both arms around me and, with the side of his face close to mine like a Mafia don, murmured in my ear—

"Goodbye, you son-of-a-bitch!"

I thought he was kidding . . . .

1989
Huge Red Chinese Dragon

February 1989

    Pat Keefe wasn't kidding. Suddenly, I couldn't get any article ideas approved and the biweekly news reports were rejected or greatly edited. Year in and out, I was one of the magazine's leading producers and the only one to have won awards, but that didn't matter. Keefe had it in for me. Was he setting things up to put me on the street?!

March 1989

Like a gift from the gods, suddenly the idea came—protect myself by writing about "Companies & Wrongful Termination." I interviewed a lot of defense lawyers and gave a breakdown of cases in which the employees had won. I could almost hear Keefe's gasp and anger.

11 April 1989

Helen Palmer had written a book, *The Enneagram*. She was speaking about it at a local bookstore. A sensitive, troubled woman—"a paranoid six" by her own account—she had appeared on the cover of *Mother Jones* because of her psychic ability and intense fears. Lord Pentland, having an interest in the unusual, had called her. She had dedicated the book to "Sir John Pentland."

I asked if she had met him. They had talked a number of times over the phone she said. She said he was a four and her adversary. He had stressed to her that the enneagram was to be taken not as psychological but as sacred alchemical geometry. She had disagreed.

14 April 1989

Begin a fourth rewrite of *Lord Have Mercy*. Had first begun to write it in 1979 after we arrived in California. In a bookstore a book (again) fell off the shelf into my hands. It was Ray Bradbury's *Zen & the Art of Writing*. Bradbury's way was to Work for a definite time or number of pages. Relax, Don't Think. Relax Again. Another book suggested there were two ways to write: either explode and don't look back, then edit; the other was make every sentence exactly what you wanted to say. I was an exploder. Just let it write itself. By the end of December I finished it. I had taken a vow before I began that I would make nothing up and I hadn't. It was all as I had seen it, remembered it. But as I reread the material, things would come up that were new and I began to see not only my own point of view but that of others. I incorporated this because I wanted to get as close to the bone of truth as possible. That was a huge step. I became "neutral" to the material.

Mid-May 1989

Keefe was a businessman. He knew if he fired me I'd sue about "wrongful termination," so near the middle of the month he sent Perry Pascarella, the editor, out to see me. I gave Perry the full sharp handshake, and looked directly into his left eye—he was all soup. Told me if I agreed to leave and make no trouble I would get a pension.

June 1989

Mother told me there was a man in the attic. I joked about it but saw she was quite serious.

I pulled the ladder down from the ceiling and went up and tramped around.

"It's empty," I told her.

"He heard you coming," she said.

She led me into her bedroom and from underneath her pillow she pulled a hammer.

I offered to have her live with us, but she didn't want that. Too independent. So we would rent an apartment for her in San Anselmo, close to our home in Fairfax. That way I could see her more often and damp down her fears.

She would think about it.

19 June 1989

Weekend seminar at Omega Institute in Rhinebeck, New York. Not many people and the questions were all ordinary.

I went to see Jean and we sat together, breathed as he said. Relaxed really deep. Heard bird calls. Realized the difference between pure and direct perception. Pure perception is always "negative" in that it cannot manifest, cannot be known. It can only be entered into when the "person" is left behind.

I mentioned this to Jean at the end. Said there was no experience of the word "negative." He smiled and gave me the "high beams."

20 June 1989

Went to dinner in New York with JK and Emma. Talked about

sex. JK maintained that a man could know what a woman feels sexually. Emma disagreed. I said perhaps it was possible at a higher level—beyond the object.

JK said homosexuals who were biologically so had no impediment to realization, psychological ones did.

7 July 1989

Having finished the book am now working on the fifth revise. Have many doubts as to how it will be taken and the trouble it will cause... question whether I should publish it at all. Last personal book about the Work was Hulme's *Undiscovered Country* in the '60s. Barbara has edited the book, which must have been difficult for her as I had written about an affair I had in the '70s. I had told her about it, but now she had to relive it and she never said a word. How many women could do that. Lord Pentland had called her "a tough baby."

15 July 1989

Got a job as the editor of *Semiconductors Monthly*, a new magazine. It was all idea at this point. It was on me to get it up and running. The only downer was that the job was in Mountain View, much longer commute, more traffic.

Up to this point I'd only written with a typewriter. I was taking my IBM Selectric out of the car at the office when I saw the publisher. He had questions about whether, as he said, "I still had the fire in the belly?" I better learn the computer. Fortunately, the Mac was easy enough.

16 September 1989

Moved Mother from the Petaluma house to an apartment in San Anselmo. A lot closer. Should have done this to begin with rather than buying the house.

November 1989

The magazine Jean had envisioned as *Être*, which means *to be*, was published as *Listening*. Emma was the editor. She and Jean would later marry. [Nine issues were published. See Bibliography.]

3 December 1989

One evening at dinner I asked Jean why it was that some people did what they wanted in life. Other than writing for *In New York,* the magazine that I had published and edited, I had spent my life writing ads about men's wear and cars, articles about food, business and now high technology and semiconductors, none of which interested me at all.

Jean simply looked at me full face, saying nothing. In that look suddenly I realized the obvious—*What was I waiting for?*

Jean told me—"Quit your job, and do what you want to do." With that the dinner ended.

I returned to a friend's apartment in Burlingame where I was staying during the week, the drive from my home to Mountain View being too long.

Quit the job, yes, but it seemed more practical to wait, for next month the semiconductor magazine would be published and my name would be on the masthead as editor-in-chief.

I was sleeping on a sofa bed in his living room. I tossed and turned with the question, worn out, I finally went to sleep. But, suddenly, in the black of the night, I jerked awake. There—hovering right in front of me—was a huge red Chinese dragon. My mind shocked still in fear, and the words shouted—*either you do what Jean says or you do not. If you do, stay with him. If not, leave him.*

Seconds elapsed until I realized where I was. That large Chinese dragon wasn't alive. It was a wall hanging.

I'd been caught between two stools, a "yes" and a "no," now I had to act immediately, so I drove to Mountain View and quit. They thought I was nuts. I blamed my kids. Told them my kids were on drugs and I had to be home with them.

So—once again—out on the street.

As it was, by year's end, I finished the fifth and final rewrite of *Lord Have Mercy.* Now—what to do with it? Publish or not?

1990

Sunya's 100th Birthday

January 1990
    Got a public relations job in San Francisco cold calling for clients. I hated cold calling. Never did it unless circumstances forced me. So I guess this completes the journey. From advertising to journalism to public relations. Ugh!
    I told a Work person about *Lord Have Mercy* and that Lord Pentland had told me that "sometime you might write a book

about the voluntary life."

"Yeah," he said sharply, "Lord Pentland told you to write it. He didn't say publish it."

July 1990

A friend of mine and a devotee of Sunya's sent me some pages of Lizelle Reymond's book *To Live Within* about her time with Sri Anirvan. Rereading them I had this feeling that I should go to India. It was Sunya's 100th birthday. I'd read the book some fifteen years ago and now the rereading gave the emanation—*"Come to India."*

We were getting ready to invade Iraq. It seemed pure idiocy. An American traveling in India among Muslims as we try to bomb Iraq to the ground. Well, I am not an 'American' but try explaining that when bombs are exploding and people are covered in blood.

Sunya often said that "Step-by-step the way would be shown to you." I told him, "Yes, 'Just follow your intuition,' you tell us. What you don't say is that there are minefields all around!"

We both roared. With a twinkle, he reminded me, "Birth and Death are opposites. Life has no opposite."

12 October 1990

Leave from San Francisco to Singapore at 1:45 a.m. Flight 52. Seat 62H. Theosophically, 7 and 8.

13 October 1990

Arrived in Singapore at 11:45 a.m. Had to stop to refuel in Hong Kong. The flight took 18 hours but I felt no jet lag. The hotel was supposed to be seven miles from the airport. No, it's in the city. The Chinese cab driver told me "India is dangerous right now." He was persistent—he wanted to take me on a tour of the city the next day at $20 per hour. The headline in the newspaper reads: "Two Armored Units Join U.S. Force in Last Major Deployment." So the invasion of Iraq is about to begin. And here I am about to enter India which itself is in turmoil over job quotas. It is a time of Shiva. A time of destruction and I am out and about and alone.

Before I left I had picked up a copy of the *Mahabharata* in which the question is asked:

"What is the greatest wonder of all? Every day Death takes lives beyond counting, yet those who live think: *Death can never come this day to me.*"

Once in the hotel, I went out to see the city. I wandered down a street full of shops and again and again heard, "Hey, a good deal for you!" "Come, come, we make a good suit for you!" One fellow even tried to take my arm until I spit out a warning. This constant "clawing" is the Asian way, I guess.

14 October 1990

I come to India to seek what I know not, but all the while I feel the hand of fate on my shoulders.

I have to surrender to this organic feeling of uncertainty, of danger, but all the "clawing" takes its toll.

Called Barbara. She said the big fish jumped out of the tank and died. I remembered that the one-eyed goldfish had died just before Sunya passed on. The VW Rabbit had broken down, as well. But everyone sounded good. Was I going to die in some way?

16 October 1990

Arriving in India, the air at the airport is slightly foul. Throat begins to hurt. Stay at the Alka Hotel in New Delhi. No street signs. How do people get around? Go to the Bihar Temple. Tall, bone-thin man pours a pan of water over himself as he prays to Surya, the Sun God, and turns from right to left, chanting, and looking into the sun. Go to the Qutub Minar, tower of victory of Muslims over Hindus in 1193. Snake charmer outside. Pay 10 rupees to see three cobras and a boa in action. The snake charmer, who only makes about 100 rupees a day, tells me he must feed them about 50 rupees a day of milk to keep the *nagas* happy. After three or four months he needs to get new snakes, as these become too tame. I give him more rupees. At the Vishnu-Deva Shrine, dedicated to Vishnu and his consort Laxmi, goddess of wealth, I get a red dot on my third eye. Go to the Red Fort. Many women begging with children hanging on their hips. I'm told whole families from generation to generation specialize in begging. In the evening, I sat on a bench. Behind me, not far away a man and woman stood by silently. When I finally got up with night approaching, I looked back. They had parked themselves under the bench.

17 October 1990

Left the hotel to stay at the Ringu Guest House, close by, and cheaper. On the way, a young boy kept insisting he shine my shoes but I was wearing open-toed sandals. I ignored him. Kept walking. Felt something cold on the toes of my right foot—a goop of shit! "Look! Look!," he cried, and said he wanted to clean the shit he had just tossed on my toes. I brushed him aside—I had heard of the "shit trick."

Went around the corner and there was a pack of girls who swooped down on me. Unlike males, they came up close and are not easily brushed aside or ignored. I kept walking, one arm over the shoulder luggage, another on my day pack. Two of the girls pulled on my arm. Then they ran down the street. I put down the shoulder bag and one side was unzipped. Fortunately, it only contained tissues and old laundry.

At the guest house the desk man told me I could come with him to "a really cheap place." I declined. He persisted.

The charge for the night was 175 rupees with a bath. At the Alka it was 400 rupees plus.

I hired a Sikh on an open three-wheeler to take me to old Delhi. He wanted 70 rupees for a round trip. I argued and got a ride for half that. Old Delhi was teeming with people and shops and noise. Not a white face in a sea of color of all degrees and shades. All poor, oppressed-looking and me with a $200 Olympus camera, $800 in my secret money belt, another $700 in Travelers checks, along with American Express and Master Cards. There were no, or few, traffic lights. No one directing traffic. A continual honking of horns. Dank air. The Sikh tried to get me to go into one of the handicraft shops. He wanted to do a little black market deal on money. I refused both. He had a little painting of his guru by the front his three-wheeler.

"Guru Nanak?" I asked.

"Yes."

"You know of the school?"

"Yes, yes," he said over his shoulders.

"The audible sound current?"

He nodded.

"You should be ashamed," I told him, "for doing all this money changing and everything."

He sped on.

18 October 1990

Took a bus at four a.m. to the airport to fly to Varanasi. Leaving so early the elevator wasn't working, so I took the stairs down. On each of the landings, I had to walk around a family that was curled up and sleeping.

The driver did not stop at the domestic terminal so we had to go back. The bus ride was 10 rupees plus another five rupees now. Still a bargain as cabs are 90 rupees during the day and 120 rupees during the night and early morning. (17.75 rupees equals $1)

Took a bus from the Varanasi airport, 20 rupees. In the city, after a long rickshaw ride, I got to Hotel Barahdari. The old peddler wanted 5 rupees. I gave him 20 rupees.

The hotel is only 100 rupees per night and has marble flooring and Western-style toilets, no more squatting! And it's only a 5-rupee rickshaw ride to old Varanasi which goes back 2,000 years and more.

19 October 1990

It has been a night of fireworks. And I mean *night*. The Indians love noise. And it is the Indian New Year known as "Diwali," the festival of light, celebrated from the time of the *Mahabharata*, the symbol of the return of Rama after a long exile to Ayodhya, his birthplace. The fireworks—the full arsenal of high-flying screamers, light up the Ganges and ghats, cherry bombs, little nuking bombs shake the earth, along with the rat-tat-tat of fireworks like machine gun blasters, and all the cars honking, swerving, somehow not colliding.

I met a young Indian Brahmin, Prem, who guided me off the main street and into the narrow alleyways of old Varanasi, lined with shops, more like stalls, selling everything imaginable. With the cows, lepers and ordinary folks making such a steady stream it is impossible to walk in a straight line. Prem led me to the ghats by the great river, five for bathing, two for burning bodies, where four fires were going when we arrived with a stretcher carrying a fifth corpse soon appearing. All this under a moonlit, starry night along the banks of what the Indians call "Mother Ganges." Prem told me that burning a body costs 350 rupees; average burn time three hours. With men, the shoulders and collar bone do not dissolve. With women, it's the pelvis that's too hard. These "leftovers" are taken by the packs of dogs—"the dogs of death," they are called. Strange beasts whose eating habits have made them not quite dogs. If all this sounds gruesome, it isn't. Varanasi is a holy city and the burning ghats are considered holy ground. Stark, but real, and holy (the word comes from "wholeness").

On the way out of the old quarter, I stepped over cow droppings, and passed a small enclosed space that symbolized the Indian viewpoint—a square tile mosaic with a *naga*, cobra, rearing its head aloft. Above it, hanging from space, a water jar shaped into flower petals.

23 October 1990

Arrived in Almora after a ten-hour cab ride from New Delhi. By chance I met Bobli, a friend of Sunya's, who took me up to Kalimat, the hilltop overlooking Almora. He introduced me to Shawkar Bab, the local priest, a young man who looks after things. He said I could stay in Sunya's hut for 20 rupees a night. It's a one-room cement hut with a small fireplace, no electricity or running water.

Most of the day I just rested and watched the changing colors of the Himalayas. Down below on the hillsides Hindu women were using scythes to cut the grass for winter feeding of their animals.

They laughed and sang and talked and called to one another like birds.

In the evening I went down about halfway and had dinner for 10 rupees at the local chai, or tea, shop.

24 October 1990

I am still a bit exhausted from the ten-hour cab ride and the previous sixteen-hour train ride from Varanasi to New Delhi. I just hang out and meet mostly young English, German and Australian kids who seem to travel as a way of life, living on as little as possible, returning home as money runs out, and then making enough to return to traveling. Most, unfortunately, smoke *ganja* which grows wild up here, and have deluded themselves into thinking they are leading a religious life. But *ganja* only weakens the will and, as Lord Pentland said, creates imagination in the higher emotional center.

25 October 1990

I went to Jageshwar, which is deep in the hills beside a running stream surrounded by a 9th century assemblage of Hindu temples. Each temple represents a god and also a human form. They are very narrow, vertical with a square base. Inside the temple is a *yoni* (female vagina) and in its center a *lingam* (male penis). The *yoni* and *lingam* symbolize the two primal bud energies of life—female and male. Atop the temple is a flower chakra, or wheel, with a *lingam* or bud rising from it.

This represents the enlightened individual whose crown chakra at the top of the head has been pierced by the two primal energies and so created a new being of great love and power. All this ancient wisdom, eternal, that is as true today as it was yesterday and will still be true in a thousand and more tomorrows. Wisdom differs from knowledge in that knowledge is finite. So seek wisdom!

27 October 1990

I am at Crank's Ridge sitting outside Sunya's hut—it is Sunya's 100th birthday and a big celebration is planned on a hilltop at Kasar Devi, a village overlooking a broad stretch of snow-capped

Himalayan range—the most majestic I have ever seen. To think that Sunya lived here for over forty years with this vista just outside his front door, with the air crisp and refreshing and the scene so vivid and alive.

This morning, early, my driver drove me to Binsar, about 30 kilometers away, so I could see the Himalayan range up closer. We arrived just before dawn and so saw the crimson red orb of the sun, or "Surya," as the Indians call it, rise over the clouds and light up Nanda Devi, which means "blissful," the highest of the Himalayan peaks.

I was asked to speak, as others were, at Sunya's 100th birthday celebration.

28 October 1990

At the tea shop I met Thomas, a German fellow, late thirties, who everyone called the "Red Monkey" or "La Banda," because of his red hair and willowy frame. He told me his life story. In the last year of getting a medical degree he took acid and decided ordinary life wasn't for him. So he bought a Porsche and drove it to India, sold it, and lived off the proceeds. When he is about to run out of money he returns to Germany and buys another car. He had been living this way for twenty years.

La Banda is quite knowledgeable. He told me Shiva is a god of the holy trinity, the other two being Brahma, the creator, and Vishnu, the preserver, the most dynamic of the deities. Shiva, the god of destruction, is at the root of evolution. He presides over change. Creation depends on destruction so that everything is constantly evolving.

I told him about being at Varanasi and the Ganges seeing sewer water dumped into it, with corpses floating down the river, and Indians drinking the water without ill effect. The Ganges, he told me, flows some 1,500 miles from the highest peaks of the Himalayas to the Bay of Bengal where it spills into the Indian Ocean. If I hadn't taken the ritual cleansing in the Ganges then I should go to Rishikesh, the water is pure up there, no sewage, no floating corpses. He was quite a salesman. I had a few days left before the plane to Greece so I told the cab driver to go to Rishikesh and so off we went, La Banda and I.

29 October 1990

Rishikesh was beautiful with high mountains and fresh blue water in the river. A wonderful place for a ritual cleansing. While I soaked in the Ganges a snake appeared on a rock by the water's edge. A man appeared and beat it with a stick unmercifully. He hit it so hard and long I thought it was dead. But when he quit, the snake, as if nothing had happened, slid back into the water. La Banda went on his way and I went back to New Delhi.

November 2, 1990

I flew from India to Greece to attend Jean's seminar in Delphi, November 3–9. Emma took a picture of the two of us walking together which was quite beautiful. I took no notes of the dialogues. I was worn out from India. Fortunately, the dialogues were all recorded and published in Jean's book, *Open to the Unknown*.

Diwan Singh at his Crank's Ridge cookery

Three-cobra snake charmer

Almora, India, October 27, 1980

Celebrating Sunya's passing at Kesar Devi, Almora, India October 27, 1990

1991
Eating The "I"

March 1991
   Seminar at Joshua Tree. Jean speaks about the subject determining the object in the sense that the object the subject perceives is interpreted by the subject. Be the perceiving, not the perceiver, the subject makes consciousness dual.
   Direct perception is perceiving only space and the appearance of experiencing. Return the seen to the seeing.

He has everyone eat in silence. Only a few of his French students do not comply.

May 1991

Still between two stools about publishing *Lord Have Mercy*, but this month *On a Spaceship with Beelzebub* was published. Great title, good writing but a rather dark book, understanding limited. Now I felt I had to publish my book. I had titled it *Lord Have Mercy*, which I saw as a reflection of the Jesus Prayer that Lord Pentland had given us, of Lord Pentland himself, and of my persona. But the time had become increasingly irreligious and I felt the title would be a turnoff for many people. So I meditated and asked that I be given a new title. The words came — *Eating The "I."* It went right to the core of what the book was about, but the words sounded ugly, looked ugly. Then I recalled that Picasso had said that anything really new will first be seen as ugly.

Given that the book was about my experience of the Work, I couldn't conceive of any editor being versed in this esoteric teaching, so I decided to learn how to self-publish.

Summer 1991

I wrote and ran a full-page ad for *Eating The "I"* in *Gnosis* magazine.

Sent a manuscript of the book to the writer and teacher Miguel Serrano, who sent a testimonial:

> "I am certain this book will be one of the more important writings on the Gurdjieff Work, after Ouspensky's *In Search of the Miraculous.*"
>
> —Miguel Serrano, author of *Jung and Hesse: A Record of Two Friendships*

It blew me out. This was far beyond anything I expected.

Then I received a testimonial from Richard Smoley, Editor of *Gnosis*:

"*Eating The 'I'* gives as full a picture of the Work as it may be possible to get without joining it. It comes from a great depth and carries much conviction."

Stephen Bodian, Editor-in-Chief of the *Yoga Journal*, sent another:

"Patterson has two fine Irish gifts: a vivid memory and a storyteller's ear. Paced like a novel and filled with colorful characters, this spiritual autobiography is certain to appeal to those who want a rare and engaging inside glimpse of the Gurdjieff Work."

Donna Boss called and told me Lady Pentland, to whom I had also sent the manuscript, had called her. They talked for two hours about the book with Lady Pentland saying it represented a "real and genuine search" and was "remarkably pure." She ended by saying—"It's a fresh breath of air for the Work."

Amazingly, Don Hoyt called, telling me, "You've caught the essence of Lord Pentland."

September 1991
Sent the manuscript of *Eating The "I"* to the printers for a hardcover book. To save money didn't print a dust jacket.

5 September 1991
Sent a notice to place an ad for *Eating The "I"* to *Parabola*, a magazine run by Work people but putting itself forth as a general spiritual publication. They would not accept the ad saying "the book was not serious."

But I had the only books—they could not have read it. Pressed relentlessly, they finally admitted their judgement was based on an ad for the book in *Gnosis*. It was spiritual politics, the worst kind. I realized that if *Parabola* refused an ad, they would never publish anything I wrote. I decided to write and publish a journal about self-transformation. *Telos* would be its name. It would be advertising-free, supported only by subscriptions.

So as *Eating The "I"* had yet to be sent to distributors, I had a postcard put in the books:

> Dear Friend,
> Thank you for reading *Eating The "I."* If the ideas interest you, please accept our offer of a complimentary one-year subscription to— *Telos: Inquiries into Self-Transformation in the Modern World.*

So many readers accepted the offer, and then actually subscribed, that publication continued.

[Over time, it grew from its original four pages to twenty-eight. At the time, being advertising-free, with subscriptions its only support, the concept was unique. Then in 1997 two other like publications copied the concept, so the logo was changed from *Telos* to *The Gurdjieff Journal*. One publication died after eleven issues. The other remains marginal and is haphazardly published. *The Gurdjieff Journal* is now in its twenty-eighth year and has just published its eightieth issue.]

Mid-October 1991

Received hardcover copies of *Eating The "I."* I immediately drove to Hope Ranch with an inscribed first copy for Jean. I gave it to him and stayed overnight in Santa Barbara. The next morning when I went to see him he greeted me with a wide smile and said he read the first chapter—

"You have a panoramic vision. You are a master of the situation. A current runs through it. It's quite an accomplishment to have written a book."

I could never have imagined such a tribute, and especially from him. I thanked him and said I was thinking of promoting the book by giving talks at bookstores.

"Yes, give talks. It will be good for you to give talks. Remember you are not the doer. I will see if I can arrange talks for you in England and France. Remember, you are not the doer."

Then he added, "Thank Barbara for her editing. Tell her to affirm herself, affirm the strength. Do not doubt. Live the truth of her silence. *Knowingly,* live it."

1992

Consciousness-Without-Objects

February 1992

My mother got into another wrangle with the manager of the apartments and finally agreed to move in with us. First night at dinner she put some spaghetti on her head and laughed. Is she losing it? She still called Barbara "her," still battling with what her sisters had done to her. She brought her television set. We couldn't refuse, though we hadn't had a television since 1973, when our first son was born. The night before his birth the set had blown up and we took it as an omen.

The kids and their friends loved her. She would sit with them and sing, "Sweet little Pussy . . ." and they would go crazy!

Some months later a series of strokes began, but she held on . . . .

March 1992

Went to see Jean Klein in Larkspur where he was staying at a student's house not far from Fairfax. He was sitting on the patio with a colorful blue shawl pulled around his shoulders. With his spray of white hair and dark eyes he looked to me like an eagle. Or, in more pedestrian terms, like a musical conductor.

Plants and flowers were everywhere, even a potted fruit tree, its young branches weighted down with small yellow peaches. A light breeze blew across the patio and the leaves danced in cool air.

It was about noon and the sun had risen higher in the heavens. The top of my head was hot and, at the same time, I was a bit cold. Though, of course, I was aware of only one impression at a time, but the quickness or reregistration made it seem as though I was both hot and cold at once.

I drew a chair before him and spoke about perception.

"Perception has to be very strong," Jean said. He said something else, but he had a cold and was speaking so low I couldn't get all the words.

I moved my chair closer to him, the legs scraping and making a noise on the concrete.

"I'm sorry, what was that last word?" I asked.

"*Strong.* Perception must be very strong at that moment."

"How do you mean that?"

"Not strong, then he escapes."

"*Escapes?* You mean we get caught again in some way."

Jean nodded.

"You mean we react to the impression of society in some way and so . . . so we get pulled back into it."

"He doesn't remain 'outside.'"

"You mean we make a personal relationship with it in some way."

"Yes," he said. "We interfere."

"I remember Krishnamurti speaking as if he was society. I felt that in some way he took himself to be responsible for all its ills and wars, as though he was outside it and inside it, too."

Jean nodded.

"Even though one is outside it in the sense of no longer being personally identified with society's dualistic illusion of itself there is..."

"There is no 'outside' or 'inside' of course," he murmured.

"Not two."

"Yes," he answered.

The desire to tell Jean what I had felt relaxed. The stillness became evident. My eyes took in Nature expressing itself on the patio, the breeze coming and going, the high sun beating down, countless hues and shades of green everywhere, set in accents of light and shadow.

Presently, I felt Jean move. "Too hot?" I asked. He agreed and we moved the chairs into the strip of shadow created by the overhang of the roof.

"Reactions and impulses will still arise in the body-mind. They are what you've called 'residues,' the remains of dualistic conditioning. But our relationship to them — our being 'outside' them, as it were — is completely different. All that is inside the enclosure is knowledge."

"Knowledge of what is inside?"

"Yes, what is outside is beyond knowledge."

"We can't know it, we can be it."

"Yes, so there is no solution."

"Because 'solutions' only lie *inside* the enclosure, inside the enclosure of ordinary knowledge."

"It takes a strong perception to remain outside, to not interfere, to not escape."

"So all that we can do is give love and support."

"Yes."

"And that is more than enough?"

He smiled at me and I lit up.

He told me, "In one or two years you will come through." He added then, "If you continue to follow this direction."

That evening he was to give the first of two dialogues planned in Sausalito.

Half-jokingly, I said, "If we could, I'd like to trade a dialogue for a meditation."

That evening when he approached his chair, he smiled at me. He had never done that. I was sitting on the hardwood floor a few feet to the left of his chair. He sat down, took in the room, and looked down at me again and, again, he smiled.

No sooner had he sat down than his voice boomed: "You remain in subject-object."

How true! It wraps over us like a snakeskin. We never even feel it. Such is the power of our conditioning that it feels so natural.

He led us into bringing the attention inside the body, facing its tensions, not escaping them, relaxing still more, feeling the energy, feeling the space, bringing the attention to expand outside the body, breathing into and from that space... then returning to face again what new tensions have appeared, letting the thoughts go, ignoring them and expanding again.

"Feel the flow," he said. "Be the flow."

It was as if he was conducting this majestic unheard symphony of energy and space, enlarging and softening the vibration, accenting this subtlety and that, making it all whole, opening up one silent vista after another, the ears roaring with inaudible sound, the consciousness carried further and further into time-free uncharted regions of *silent-being*.

From time to time I found myself back in time again, wrapped in a cloud of idiot thought. I reacted in anger, in despondency...

But then the grace of the light-flash of intuition.

I saw also that I, the identification of consciousness with my fear, my person, my fear-person, had weakened my perception, returning me to thought, using it as an unholy refuge, because I, what I took to be I, was afraid to remain 'outside' any longer.

Meanwhile, the great unheard symphony plays on....

April 1992

Took a booth at the Health & Harmony Fair in Santa Rosa to sell *Eating The "I."* After we had set up, I left Barbara at the booth and walked about checking the other booths. I was in a state of self-remembering, that is in self-sensing and true divided subject-object perception, when... *suddenly there was no subject.* There was no perceiver, no thought. Only perceiving—direct, global conscious perception-reception of what is present without referent to past or future.

It was only when there was a return to the booth sometime afterward that the subject reappeared. How long had it been? Had no idea. But the realization was immediate: this experiencing was the living answer to the question carried for so many years about the Self. Jean always spoke about the integration of body-mind-senses. This was the full integration. What was experienced was *Turiya,* the fourth state of the Self, the Heart, in that the causal heart center of *Nidra,* deep sleep, is opened and made the center of consciousness. If it lasts, it is called *Sahaj Samadhi*; if not, *Nirvikalpa Samadhi.*

[This is written about quite extensively in my book *Adi Da Samraj—Realized or/and Deluded?*]

May 1992

I picked Jean up at his home in Hope Ranch. We drove down Cliff Drive along Hendry's Beach and went to lunch at the Brown Pelican [now The Boathouse]. It's a beach restaurant with a magnificent view of the ocean. We sat outside at a table and I told Jean about the experiencing at the Health & Harmony Fair, how I had been walking along this line of booths, a sea of people everywhere, all in motion, and all at once the subject disappeared and the world had opened up, there had been this shift of perspective he had spoken about.

I searched for a word to describe the experience....

"Panoramic," I said finally.

He nodded.

"And it was whole. There were all these moving parts, but they were all related. Nothing, no one was separate. It was all One."

"You are outside it," he said.

"Yes, seeing it, feeling it, taking it all in."

"And inside it, as well," he added.

"Yes, but not identified, not taking it in as a person."

He told me that my body-senses-mind had integrated. "Do not return to the feeling of the person but stay with the feeling itself."

"Don't become Shiva," he warned.

After lunch we left the Brown Pelican and sat for a time by the seashore on his favorite bench looking out to the sea. Finally, he broke the silence—

"But you still want experience," he said.

Immediately—I knew-felt, he was right. Some part of me I didn't know wanted experience. But why?

Years before, when we first met, he had told me, "You are tired of the phenomenal." That was true, but I couldn't have put that feeling-recognition into words.

Now, after the Health & Harmony there was that which wanted experience. But what part of me was that? Why? Experience—what experience?

For a while longer we sat together watching the waves crest as they rushed onto the shore and dissolved.

1993
Thought Bullet

January 1993
    Received many intimations and dreams saying that I should teach, but what would I teach? Rejected them all, but they kept occurring.

February 1993
    At Open Secret, the local bookstore in neighboring San Rafael,

gave a talk on *Eating The "I."* The room was packed but questions were ordinary. Then a young fellow asked a question—afterward I couldn't remember what he said—but a thought bullet went through my head: if I ever have a group, this is the kind of person I would want.

A few days later I received a letter from Joe Bencharsky asking to meet. He turned out to be the fellow who had asked that question. His questions were all about the Work, not Advaita. I agreed to meet with him. He wanted more, so I agreed to meet every two weeks.

March 1993

Spoke about the book at East West Bookstore in Mountain View. A letter came from Lena Jacobson, a Russian woman who had left the country, the first "Refusnik." Her interest was in the Work and so we also met every two weeks.

Spring 1993

Gnosis magazine publishes "Silence Was His Specialty," my review of the book *Sunyata: The Life & Sayings of a Rare-Born Mystic* by Betty Camhi and Elliot Isenberg.

May 1993

Now began to meet with Bencharsky and Lena together. Advaita or Jean wasn't their interest so I never mentioned it.

7 August 1993

Took Jean to lunch at the Brown Pelican. In yoga, he said, it is not to return to the feeling of the person but to stay with the feeling.

All the teachings are being vulgarized, he said—seen in terms of the person. What distinguishes our century from others is its vulgarity. Guénon saw this vulgarity.

In fifty to a hundred years the teachings will be reborn as a new seed and take new shapes.

He told me to remember that.

September 1993

At a book show I met a young woman who, I later learn, had prayed to Mr. Gurdjieff for help, and was so surprised and grateful to discover my book. She bought the book and contacted me afterward saying she had several friends who would be interested in the teaching. Her name was Teresa Adams. She said she "felt an inner resonance" when we spoke.

October 1993

Should I teach the Work? I had seen that, yes, the Work was a progression, but when seriously and persistently practiced it could lead beyond the "I"s to the conscious egotist to the witness to the Individual self, and finally even further—to the Self, that is, Consciousness-without-objects. So, yes, there are still objects but there is no subject to filter them through. I understood now that this was why Gurdjieff could say the teaching was "complete in itself." But he had not lived long enough so had left his students "between the sheets," or "in a fine mess."

November 1993

Formed a Gurdjieff Study Group. Nine people. Will meet once a week at Joe Bencharsky's in Vallejo.

December 1993

Gave a weekend seminar on the Work at Marconi Conference Center, in Marshall, California, just beyond Pt. Reyes. Driving there, I realized in Jean's seminars, no matter how strong the sessions, people always talked afterward. That put them back in their heads. Decided that other than the dialogues, it would all be in silence. In case there were the usual questions about food, etc., I made Barbara the designated speaker.

1994

Speaking Two Languages

January 1994

The book and word-of-mouth brought more people. It was like a large wave that suddenly appeared. More Gurdjieff Study Groups formed in Marin and Sacramento. What was happening seemed to have a life of its own. Was this the *Prarabdha* karma, the karma that can't be changed, that Sunya talked about? Nevertheless, I was responsible.

17 March 1994

Of the many letters I received, this one neatly sums up what many were saying:

> It is very odd for me to write a fan letter, but I've just finished reading *Eating The "I,"* and wanted to let you know how much I appreciated it. The passages about Lord Pentland were so apt and so keenly penetrating that they made my heart pound. I devoured them ravenously, as though they filled some kind of great hunger in me that I forgot existed. In addition, your honesty, your sincerity, with respect to yourself and your experiences—for public consumption, no less—is a true act of bravery.
> Sincerely,
> Linda A. Moore
> Berkeley, CA

April 1994

Jean was giving his first seminar in Israel. Remember very little about it other than in the middle of the night Jean opened my door and walked in sleepwalking. Suddenly, he awoke and seeing me cried out—

"Unbelievable, unbelievable!"

4 June 1994

My mother passed on. Ninety-four years old. Though she was quite healthy and regularly exercised, she had two strokes after she moved in with us, each taking her down a notch. I remembered helping her out of the shower and she defecated.

"Oh," she screamed. "I could kill myself!"

"It's all right, Mom, it's okay," I said softly.

And it was . . . .

Her love was real, but what drove it was her pain and sorrow of the past. Her first child, Marjorie, was taken from her mentally and emotionally by Ossie, my father's childless sister, who had a lot of money which she used on Marjorie, giving her gifts galore,

Uncle Bill Scott

Mother at 16   Pat, Mother and Father, 1942

Marjorie, Grandmother Patterson, Father, Mother, Aunt Ossie Patterson
1932, Atlantic City boardwalk, New Jersey

Father and Mother in Florida, 1970s

Mother and Pat having fun, 1992

taking her to movies and events. This past so continually lived my mother without her knowing it, as it does for all people.

The love she manifested was real but all consuming, as it was based on fear. I loved her but I had to reject this love in order not to be swamped by it.

5 June 1994

Met with Jean. "I think you do not know why you left Gurdjieff," he told me.

I told him, "Sunya captured my heart. I also felt there was something more, though I didn't know what 'more' meant."

"You were tired of the phenomenal," he said.

He is telling me give up all association with Gurdjieff. That means the study groups, *Telos*, seminars.

"Your mind is clear. You have higher reason but you reject its answer. You still question your experience."

I didn't feel as though I did but said nothing.

There was a long pause.

"You still want to have experience," he repeated.

"Yes," I said, and touched his knee, tears coming to my eyes.

I knew this really hurt him. He had put all this energy and time and practice into me and there was the direct experiencing of what he had led me to, and here I was with something in me wanting more experience. It must have been so very painful for him.

I should have told Jean about the Charles Fort dream in which Lord Pentland had handed me an "original invitation" about leaving the Work—one he told me I couldn't refuse. It made me one of the damned from the mainline Foundation's point of view. In retrospect, it seemed to have all happened on its own. From Shankara's *Crest Jewel of Discrimination* falling into my hands, heading West to California, Sunyata telling me on April Fool's Day that the witness was only a state, to his introducing me to Jean Klein. Suddenly, there I was with two teachers of no-thing and nothing.

Yes, what is known of Gurdjieff's Teaching of The Fourth Way is the progressive way. Its serious practice had moved the attention from only being functionally awake, to verifying the many "I"s that lived me, to conscious egotism, to the "Work I," to the witness.

But now the experience of the subject of subject-object perception had disappeared and only Consciousness-without-objects, pure perception, the Self, remained. This was the rightful culmination of Gurdjieff's ancient, sacred esoteric teaching of transformation.

When the experiencing is permanent the Hindus call it *Sahaj Samadhi*. When the subject returns it is called *Nirvikalpa Samadhi*.

Still, the imprint was there—the innerstanding that allows the speaking of *two languages*, the last language the ultimate extension and completion of the first. When geometrically experienced they are both really one language. Thus, the real title of Mr. Gurdjieff's *Legominism* is:

ALL & Everything, No-Thing & Nothing

1995

Happy Birthday, The Jewish Law & Charles Fort

After giving a seminar in Greece, Jean had a massive stroke and was largely incapacitated. Barbara and I went to see him at Hope Ranch. We found him in his bedroom lying on a mattress. When he saw us at the door, he rose up a bit and motioned us to him, that wonderful smile lighting his face—"Pat, Barbara, so good to see you!"

And then he sang *Happy Birthday* to us in his French accent, tears streamed down our faces.

Sometime afterward there was a final gathering of all his students at Hope Ranch. We sat outside in the garden and he sat in a chair facing everyone, saying nothing. Each of us went up and sat before him to thank him and give our goodbye. When I went to him I just sat silently, opening to him, the words unspoken.

Later, Jean took a turn for the worse and I went down to see him. When I arrived another student was feeding him. At one point, he stopped and fed himself. Then he got up to leave but turned around and looked straight at me—"Remember the Jewish Law," he said.

Not being Jewish I didn't know what he meant and never thought about it. Only after my finishing this book did the note appear of my last seeing Jean and his last words to me. I now find that Jewish Law, or *Halakha*, is a collection of 613 commandments from the Torah on "The path that one walks." To violate the commandments, the *Mitzvot*, is a sin.

So for Jean, to have merged what I have experienced and come to through his teaching of Advaita and Kashmir Shaivism into the teaching of Gurdjieff's Fourth Way is a sin. For myself, I see it as an integration of the one further expanding into the other, both being essentially one and the same when deeply experienced.

So here I am both recognizing that from that Charles Fort dream onward I had been called to giving myself to the completion of The Fourth Way, as grand as that sounds this is said simply as fact and nothing more . . . and also to know that from the traditional Jewish point of view, I have both sinned and deeply hurt the one who had given me so much and whom I loved.

That's a bit messy, as human life often is, but it's the truth.

Finis

Appendices

My Reminiscences
Rabindranath Tagore

There was a curious sort of person who came to me now and then, with a habit of asking all manner of silly questions. One day he had asked: "Have you, sir, seen God with your own eyes?" And on my having to admit that I had not, he averred that he had. "What was it you saw?" I asked. "He seethed and throbbed before my eyes!" was the reply.

It can well be imagined that one would not ordinarily relish being drawn into abstruse discussions with such a person. Moreover, I was at the time entirely absorbed in my own writing. Nevertheless as he was a harmless sort of fellow, I did not like the idea of hurting his susceptibilities and so tolerated him as best I could.

This time, when he came one afternoon, I actually felt glad to see him, and welcomed him cordially. The mantle of his oddity and foolishness seemed to have slipped off, and the person I so joyfully hailed was the real man whom I felt to be in nowise inferior to myself, and moreover closely related. Finding no trace of annoyance within me at sight of him, nor any sense of my time being wasted with him, I was filled with an immense gladness, and felt rid of some enveloping tissue of untruth which had been causing me so much needless and uncalled for discomfort and pain.

As I would stand on the balcony, the gait, the figure, the features of each one of the passers-by, whoever they might be, seemed to me all so extraordinarily wonderful, as they flowed past — waves on the sea of the universe. From infancy I had seen only with my eyes, I now began to see with the whole of my consciousness. I could not look upon the sight of two smiling youths, nonchalantly going their way, the arm of one on the other's shoulder, as a matter of small moment; for, through it I could see the fathomless depths of the eternal spring of Joy from which numberless sprays of laughter leap up throughout the world.

Full G. M. Cheeke Interview

"Play any sports in college?" he asked.

"I got a football scholarship to college, but while in high school I was fast and medium-sized, by college standards I was small and slow."

He checked my resume for the college.

"Bowling Green State University," he said with a near chuckle. "I was Michigan State, a collegiate boxer, won the light heavy intercollegiate championship."

I told him my uncle had been a professional boxer.

"Oh, yeah, who'd he fight?"

"Harry Greb. Had over 200 fights, then he was gassed in the war. Told me at the end of his life, 'Fightin' don't get you nowhere.'"

Cheeke lights up a big briar pipe and we get into nickel knowledge about fighters — Jack Johnson — Benny Leonard — Fritzie Civic — Tony Zale — Billy Conn — Joe Louis. This is duck soup I'm thinking.

The Joey Maxim-Sugar Ray Robinson fight comes up. He likes Maxim. I tell him Sugar Ray would have beaten him if hadn't been for heat exhaustion.

Cheeke isn't sure. Blows a puff of smoke up into the air.

"Robinson sat in the ninth," he declares flatly, as if Sugar Ray was a coward.

"It was the thirteenth, wasn't it?" I say.

"No, the ninth."

The way the words *the ninth* come at me it's like a punch in the gut.

"Well, maybe you're right," I say, backing off fast.

Cheeke savors the moment, then picks up the resume again.

"Why'd you major in English?" he asks.

"So I could write my memoirs," I say jauntily, trying to ease the moment.

"You married?"

"Yes."

"Any children?"

"Two boys." No, I wasn't queer.

"Your wife, go to college?"

"Yes."

"Where?"

"Graduated from Berkeley." I felt what he was thinking—the wife was a radical?

"You hunt or fish?"

"No. Like to camp." Shouldn't have said that. Potlatch cuts down trees.

He switched from the pipe to a cigarette. He had been born in Alaska. He and his friends only camped to fish and hunt.

"Did you read Jack London stories?" I asked, trying to make some connection.

"We hated Jack London!"

"Do you know 'To Build a Fire'?"

I nodded.

"Could never have happened. Too romantic."

He took a big inhale-exhale from the cigarette.

"Who are you reading?" he asked. His questions always had an undertone of accusation.

Tell him *Beelzebub's Tales to His Grandson* and I'm dead. I was reading Peter Hanke's *A Moment of True Feeling,* so I said that.

"Yeah—what's that about?"

"I'm just getting into it but Hanke is pointing out that the feeling we have isn't true feeling. It's all conditioned, mechanical."

Cheeke didn't want to go there. "What about Sartre," he asked.

Sartre was a communist. Cheeke was clever. "No, I'm more interested in Heidegger."

That was a new name to him. "What about best sellers?"

"Never read them." I answered too quickly.

"And why not?!"

"Too commercial, too mental." The words were out of my mouth before I could stop them. I wasn't there at all.

Cheeke ran off a list of books. I hadn't read any of them.

"Well, then — what do you read?"

"Jung," I told him.

"Oh, really . . . why is that?"

"His concepts of the anima and animus, archetypes and synchronicity — they're grids. You can see reality through them. Like scaffolding on an invisible building."

Cheeke crushed his cigarette in the ashtray.

That had killed it. I was probably a New Age liberal intellectual. Certainly no Republican or capitalist. As my manager at IBM where I had once worked told me: "Yes, we want wild ducks, but ducks who fly in formation."

The Awakening
Sunyata

This sweet humility and tenderness could only be precursor of death. His mien, his gaze, did not seem to belong to him. In his speech, in his voice, and above all in his eyes, we read plainly that detachment from what we call life, which is so terrible to aware in those who are dying, specially when we ourselves are in vital body-health and ego-vigour. He cared no more for our duality values. His psyche was lifting its wings out of the ken of the living and his body was sinking, shrinking and parting him from them. He was indifferent to our important trifles because something else, something supreme, was being borne in upon his consciousness. Emotions were dying by degrees. The fowls of the air sow not, neither do they reap. Yet the eternal Source feedeth them and it also clotheth the so-called wild lilies of the field and jungle, so that they need not toil or worry or fuss in agitation, fear, or assertive insecurity.

A. grew silent; words would but blur. No, it was useless. The kind, sympathetic friends would take his meaning differently. The living ego cannot understand that these feelings, beliefs, and opinions which are so dear to them, all these thoughts, concepts and abstractions which seem too important, really do not matter. No, we have ceased to meet on common ground. A. knew it was death, that he was half dead already, by this conscious detachment from all earthly interest and by the strange and radiant beautitude that filled, that suffused and healed his integral Being. He lay waiting for the inevitable and the ineffable without impatience or trepidation. The great, eternal Truth, unknown and seemingly distant, which all his life long had dwelt in the background of his thoughts, was near now, close at hand. He could feel it, almost touch it. Is death the secret of life and not its opposite? Do we die to live?

The Flower of Grace

Formerly he had dreaded death. Twice he had passed near the fearful gulf of death in agonies; now he no longer feared it. His eyes that had been gazing on the beauty of the woods, the mountains, the deep, blue sky, saw death rushing at him then. But when he had regained ordinary ego-consciousness, the Flower of Grace and of vast, intimate empathy had blossomed in his conscious awareness—freed for a while from the care of earthly surface-life. The fear of death had henceforth vanished; the barrier between life and death had no terror. In the absence of attachment, bondage gradually gave way. There was no real detachment, no real divisions, no real death.

"What is the meaning," he wondered, "of loving all mankind, of ego-dedication, or crucifixion through love, unless it is loving 'on one' in particular and being consciously in touch with the Source of all—the Eternal—also in time and ego-play, aware of the real in and beyond love and hate and all opposites?"

He beheld the end with real, divine indifference. No revolt of flesh or of ego against the unknown. "Love," he thought again, "what is love?" It is the re-cognition and the negation of death.

It is Life itself. Death is the secret of life—the awakening into death-freeness. All that I have experienced, I have innerstood by love, empathy or Self-identity alone. "I" comprehends and suffuses everything. Love is God and death is the reabsorption of the atom of life that is my Self. "To die—to awaken": The idea, the intuition, flashed in his consciousness like a lightening gleam. Death is the awakening. A corner of the veil which still parted him from the unknown had been lifted from his psyche. His Being was releasing itself from the illusory bond that still held it to earthly phenomena and ego-values, and a mysterious beatitude came over him which henceforth did not desert him. In integral Self-experiencing there is inherent grace: Being—in conscious Self-Awareness.

A. was silent. These loving solicitudes and discussions of personal relations and predilections made him feel uncomfortable. They threatened his solitude in which now alone his Being could breathe in comfort, in which alone he felt free and comfort, in which alone he felt free and whole and in unity, fully alive without blur or restraint or compulsion. Its discipline was inherent, ontological and spontaneous. At ordinary times he took this inward solitude for granted, as one accepts the weather or the atmosphere in which one lives. But when it was managed or menaced, he became only too painfully aware of its importance to him. He fought for it as a choking man fights for air. But it was usually a fight without violence, in a mode of passive positivity or negative capability, or retirement and defense. He instinctively entrenched himself in Silence, in the calm intuitive awareness or experiencing, in the unitive life that is behind, beyond, and within all things, all phenomena and ego-noises.

A. felt as if he was melting into green and golden tranquility, sinking and being absorbed into it, into living unity. Stillness flowed into Stillness. The Silence without became one with the Silence within him. The turbid liquor of existence grew gradually calm and all that had made it opaque, all the noise and uproar of the world, all the personal anxieties, desires, feelings, began to settle like sediments. They fell slowly, noiselessly out of sight. The turbid liquor became clearer and clearer, more and more translucent. In and behind the gradually vanishing mist of actuality was Reality, was God. It was a slow progressive revelation, an awakening from duality and ego-shadows to integral Self-awareness. He breathed softly and the last, faint ripple died away from the surface-life. The opacities churned up by the agitation of living dropped away through the utter calm of Being. There was perfect ease. He had no desires, no more preoccupations. The liquor, which had been turbid, was now quite clear. Clearer than crystal, more diaphanous than air. The ego-mist had vanished and the unveiled Reality was a wonderful Silence, a positive No-thing-ness, a living grace. The gradual revelations were now complete. A. had died or awakened into Self-radiant, joyous ease, integral grace and ego-free Ananda.

Many Deaths in One Body

"Were any of the deaths you have endured or witnessed like this?" asks Wuji. To him it rings true also of many psychological deaths or integral awakening. We can have many in one body without giving it up entirely. But there is always the letting go of identity and of attachment, the letting be of worry and of duality-values, of reason, mind, thought, and time. There is always the inner solitude, the healing Silence, and the creative contemplation, until we Be the contemplation, the silent empathy, the integral grace. This is a matter of maturity of ego (to die), of stark sincerity and of patience (to mature), says the mind-free, Himalayan Wuji.

"Die before ye die!" Life is a constant dying and becoming—projection and withdrawal—involution, evolution, and revolution. Wu! We think we understand and know, while really, all the eternal while we innerstand ego-freely and death-freely, and "we are always aware, Sunya!" says Wuji. Aye, we *are* the Awareness, the Grace, the Wu!

Oh these words! One is thankful to have escaped from them—from sticky, ideal concepts and from the bondage of thought and time and body-consciousness. It is like getting out of a prison that is artful, artistic, and artificial, full of frescoes, tapestries, abstractions and what not. Wu! One prefers the genuine, natural countryside and the pure Silence that is real, spontaneous inter-relatedness, empathy and mutual inter-penetration, rid of craving, willing and word-symbols. Such Unity-Awareness is healing and immediate. It is unassertive, inherent wisdom and joy.

Samata

IT IS ALL THE SAME
   only differently the same.
It is that which changes not
   in that which ever changes.
As Behinji Ananda Mayee says:
   "I never talk to another."
For he who truly apperceives
   there are no "others."
As Ramana Maharshi,
   peerless seer, said to disciples:
"'Bhagwan'—as you call me—
   is yourSelf.
People sometimes say when I open
   my eyes that I've come out
of my blessed Samadhi. But I know
   no difference between
my 'blessed Samadhi' and non-
   samadhi.
   It is all the same."
—before it is contaminated with
'this I am' or 'that I am.' The
   Impurity is false
   Self-identifications."
Samata-samesness is confirmed
   with Nisargadatta Maharaj.
This "Beri-Baba"—unknown
   during 40 years of Christ-
consciousness, says:

"I am now 84 years old
And yet I am the infant of 84
   years ago. I feel clearly
that in spite of all the changes
   I am still that child,
   my Self (Swarupa)."
"Go back," directs Maharaj,
   "to that state of pure being
where the I AM is still in its purity."

His guru had told him:
   "Trust me. I tell you: you are
   divine.
Your suffering, too, is divine.
All comes
   from God. His/Her will alone
   is done."
Declares Maharaj: "I did trust
   him and soon realized
   how wonderfully true
   and accurate were his words.
I did not condition my mind
   by thinking 'I am God,
I am wonderful, I am beyond.'"
   I simply followed
   his instructions.
The instruction was to focus
   the mind on pure being

I AM and to stay in it.
  "For hours I sat,"
says Maharaj, "with nothing
  but I AM in my mind.
Soon the peace and joy and deep
  all embracing love
  became my normal state in
  which all disappeared:
my ego-mind, my guru, the life
  I lived, the world around me.
Only peace, joy and Grace
remained —
  and unfathomable Silence."
Who are these same-ful, wu-ful
beings,
  ever One in joyous Samata?
When devotees asked Ananda
Mayee:
  "Who are you Ma?
A *Shakti* of Vishnu, of Shiva?"
  the reply was simply:
"What I am to you that I AM."
When a learned avadhut asked:
  "Maji, what is the nature of
your Samadhi?"
The answer flashed:
  "It is really for you, Pitaji,
to give the names to the stages of
Samadhi.
  This mad girl can only say
  that throughout — and in spite
  of —
  all the changes of forms,
  conditions and circumstances
  in the Life-play,
I feel that I am the same as in
  childhood's infancy."
Once Paramahansa Yogananda
  asked:
  "Please, Ma, tell us
something of your life" she said:
  "Pitaji knows all about it.
Why repeat it?" evidently feeling
  the factual history
of but one short reincarnation
  was beneath notice.
Says Yogananda: "I sought, gently
  repeating my request
and was told: "Pitaji, there is
  little to tell."
Spreading her graceful hands
  in a deprecating gesture
  she said:
  "My consciousness has never
associated itself with this
temporary body.
  Before I came on this earth,
Pitaji,
  it was the same. As a little girl
  it was the same. When the
  family,
in which I was born, made
arrangements
  to have this body married,
I was the same and, Pitaji,
  in front of you now,
I am the same.
  Even after the dance of creation
  changes in the Hall of Eternity
I shall be the same."

The Plenum Void
Sunya Baba

In Buddhism the highest or fullest Reality is called Sunyata (the plenum-void empty of ego and of real divisions), which is neither being nor non-being, and is so ineffable, that the way to realization or experience of the Ultimate involves the strict denial of one's own and every other form of existence. Sunyata is the full, solid, concrete No-thing-ness.

The highest peaks in Himalayan Consciousness are said to be *Maha-Karuna* and *Maha-Prajnana* (ego-free Empathy and intuitive, integral wisdom) transcending the duality of love and mere knowledge. In Sunya-Silence there is no conceit of agency, but the awareness of guidance, of rightness and of innerstanding the details, the part-play and the Allness. "They were silent, all these: the host, the guest and the white chrysanthemum."

The more we learn of the world the more we have to forget in "the Cloud of unknowing." "I now know that I know nothing." Sunyata is this nothingness. All that happens, happens rightly. All is right that seems most wrong. "If there is pain let it be; it is also the Self and the Self is perfect," said, and lived Ramana Maharshi. It is the *Titiksa* mode of acceptance and of awareness:—Endure, Enjoy and Let be in positive passivity, negative capability and effort-free, choice-free receptivity. Let go of the sense of possessions and of power, of pity and of doership. Let go of egoji. Drop it, or let it drop. "Let go and let God!"

There is no truth but the absolute, non-dual, ultimate and ineffable Truth. It is, however, very important to realise that the "via negative" or "*neti neti*" is not making a negation of Reality, about the real-something or no-thing-ness, which is the basis of everyday experience. Eliminate the obstacles, and there is always the flow from the cosmic Source.

The metaphysical doctrines of the Orient are saying that you (egoji) cannot grasp or comprehend reality in any fixed form of thought and feeling. You cannot nail it down or possess it. Mere belief, pre-conceptions and pre-convictions are hindrances to the anandaful, ineffable experiencing. We try to possess, to become and to understand, because we as egojies are lonely and insecure without the intuitive light of serene Aloneness in the unity of all-Oneness and Self-security. We have identified our consciousness with a seemingly fixed form, a structure of memories called I, but we discover that structures are impermanent and we are therefore afraid. Egojies dare not the existential leap into the Sunya nothingness, and, therefore, they cling all the more tenaciously to ego-life, and yoga becomes *bhoga*-(enjoyment) and involvement in a vicious circle for clinging to what is called *samsara*. To 'know' Brahman is to Be Brahman to "see God," or to experience the Self, is to be the Experiencing, the undefined, infinite, time-free and ego-free state, without trying to capture and hold it in fixed forms of conventional words and ideas, concepts and gospel truths. When St. Augustine was asked what time was, he replied: "I know, but when you ask me, I don't." Likewise it is with the truth of Reality.

"Once God and I knew the meaning of Life, now only God knows, or perhaps even He or She does not know," says Wuji. We all experience the eternal time, but when we begin to think about it, It vanishes. If an egoji enters Sunya-realm, the ego-consciousness blurs the whole, the integral Self-awareness. In it we live and move and have our Being, whether we merely know or not. "So just awaken into integral, conscious and abiding Self-awareness," says Wuji. "Renounce egoji, its values and its duality-fuss, and, so, Be Self-aware. Be the Awareness, aware that you Are the non-dual Self-Experiencing."

It is said in Zen Mysticism: If you want to "see" into It, aware it directly in intuitive empathy or immediate perception. When you begin to think about It, It is altogether missed. For this reason *Kena Upanishad* says: "He who thinks that Brahman is not comprehended, by him Brahman is comprehended, but he who thinks that Brahman is comprehended knows it not. Brahman (Self, Godhead, Source, Essence, Sunya or Wholeness) is unknown to those who know. It is known to those who do not know It at all." Knowledge and understanding are not intuitive *Karuna*-Wisdom. The Chinese sage stated, "He who knows speaks not. He who speaks knows not." So silence is best.

In gospel-truth the word-symbol 'knowing' is much nearer Experiencing. Knowledge has become mental, intellectual, analytical and scientific; while intuitive wisdom is wholly from the Cosmic. It is in and beyond all knowing, thinking and seeing, all analyzing, reasoning and asserting. "Oh, for the luxury of not having to express or to explain," sighs Sri Wuji, who awarely innerstands and so easily goes out of his mind and other tools, or is free and at joyous ease in them and in the anandaful and graceful interplay. Sunya can be awared in intuitive light. It is the integral state, the non-dual experiencing, thought-free, mind-free and ego-free.

"There is nothing either good or bad, but thinking makes it so," quotes Hamlet, Prince of Denmark. So bounce beyond thought and time, or let thoughts come and pass by, and aware the unitive Self in and beyond. Be free in thoughts and tools and things.

The Self plays freely in all and is also the witness. It innerstands and comprehends. Just awaken to be consciously aware and consciously free in the *Maya-lila* Self-interplay. Bondage is delusive and egoji is illusory, not very real. Yet the Real innerstands and is Self-radiating— '*Soham,*' '*Tat twam asi.*' Take refuge in the intuitive insight into the natural, spiritual realm spread out within and before us in Nature and in Advaita Vedanta. Mysticism is empirical, experienceable. Ritual is a personal act of recollection and ego-dedication. Dogmas are hypothetically accepted truths. Mere beliefs, preconceptions and pre-convictions are hindrances to the mystical, non-dual Self-experiencing. Intuition is charged from the cosmic; it comes from cosmic thought. After the opening of the third eye, the intuitive-Shiva eye, the mind functions in cooperation with intuition. "If thy intuitive eye be single and whole, thy whole body, aye, all bodies will be awared as brimful of Self-radiant light, the White Light that shineth in darkness and leadeth every soul that cometh into this world of *Maya-Lila* Self-interplay," to paraphrase Matthew's Gospel. Be simple, be natural and ego-free, and you are spiritual, says Wuji. Henri Bergson stated: "Mysticism is the true form of religion, the intuitive *élan* vital. Live intuitively and you are religious." Be artists in integral living. Sri Wuji quotes Buddha as saying, "Do not complain or cry or pray, but open your intuitive eye and know the Beauty that is all around you and within. It is radiant, so wonderful, and more marvelous than anything you have ever imagined, dreamt of or prayed for and it Is for ever and ever." "Flower in the crannied wall." "It is you, it is your estranged faces, that miss the many splendored thing."

[Sunya also wrote other essays. "Darshan," 1945; "The Lesson of the Sphinx" and "Samadhi and Realization," published in *The Call Divine*, October 1, 1973, and January 1, 1974; and "The New Man," chapter 55, *The Mind of Krishnamurti*, Jaico Publishing House, Delhi, 1971.]

Hunting the Guru in India
Anne Marshall
(London: Victor Gollancz Ltd., 1963), chapter VII,
"Mountain Madness," 143–45

The ridge of which our hill formed a part was known to the local inhabitants as ∂∂, and it did its best to live up to its name. The most long-standing resident was Sunya Bai, who lived about a mile further up the road than our place, in a house he had built entirely by himself. He was by far the most sociable person on the ridge and a great one for dropping in at tea-time. Thursday was his usual day—his day of dissipation, he called it—but sometimes he varied his routine and paid us a surprise visit. His little terrier, Wuji, wore goats' bells round her throat, and on Thursday afternoons I used to stretch my ears for the sound of those bells, trying to pick them out against the dripping of the rain. Finally, it got so that I could hear the bells before he left his house a mile away, when I would say, "Sunya Bai is coming today," and sure enough he arrived within the hour. Whether or not I was hearing mystic sounds, I always welcomed his visits, and he brought with him books, which he kindly lent us to while away the tedium of the wet days.

The first time I saw Sunya Bai it was with a sort of surprise that I recognized a blue-eyed northerner under a strong tan. An orange turban and brownish robe completed the disguise, for originally he was a Dane. The clothes he wore were of his own devising and I believe he ran them up himself from scraps of cloth. Invariably he went barefoot, and in his style of dress and outlook he seemed to be a cross between a Hindu *sannyasi* and a Buddhist *bhikku*. For the past ten years he had given his age as seventy, but however old he was, he was more vigorous than many men in their twenties. Twice a week he walked into Almora town and back, always barefoot, taking the thousand-foot ascent on the way home in his stride. About him personally there was a bit of a mystery, and perhaps this is as it should be.

He was born in Jutland, a son of peasant farmers. "Always take peasant birth; ye be then nearer the Ground," he wrote. His parents christened him Emmanuel, which means "Christ Immanent," and Sunya Bai saw a certain significance in this name, for he claims to have spent his childhood in a state of constant awareness of the presence of God. As he put it: "We were born *sahaja*. . . . We had no word symbols or term labels for the non-dual experiencing, but it was there naturally unsought. . . . If we worked or played, it was as if in God or innerstanding [a word he had coined himself], or Christ was nothing outside our Self." He always referred to himself as "we," not, I think, in any royal sense, but because he wanted to emphasize that the Divine Self exists and enjoys the *Swalila* (Divine Play) between the ego-consciousness with its feeling of "me" and "mine," and the Divine Self-awareness. As the boy had no wish to communicate his state and no means of doing so, he was usually alone and silent, so much so that visitors to the house thought he was unwell and urged his parents to take him to the doctor. When he grew older he lost this untutored state of living in the Presence. As he said: "Sri Ego duly swelled and usurped and predominated. . . . Yet there is always the Memory." He studied horticulture and, after travels on the continent of Europe, he settled for fifteen years in England. It was here that he met Rabindranath Tagore, and fell under his spell. He went to India and lived for a while at Tagore's cultural center, Shantiniketan, where he was in charge of the gardens. Since 1933 he has lived permanently in India. After Tagore's death, he went south and was initiated by Ramana Maharshi, who gave him his name of Sunya or Sunyata. This is a word much used in the northern school of Buddhism. Generally translated as "Void," it means not nothingness, but the undifferentiated ground out of which arises the potential of all manifested things. Sunya Bai is now on his own, and he follows no particular school or teacher. He disparages raptures, trances, visions, powers and miracles. "Everything is a natural miracle," he says. "All that lives is holy and all is alive. And innerstanding is also ego-transcendence. Everything is within and the Centre is everywhere."

The Visits of the Queen of Sheba
Miguel Serrano
(London: Routledge & Kegan Paul, 1960)
"The Brother of Silence," 25–27

He first came some years ago and told me that he wanted to listen to my silence. In the manner of the country he uncovered his feet and sat with crossed legs in a corner of the room. There he remained for a long time until evening came and I could no longer see his face. He had a small dog with him which lay curled up on the hem of his Tibetan monk's robe.

With the coming of dusk, he began to tell me his story. He comes from Almora which is the gateway in the Himavat that leads to Mount Kailas. He was not born in Almora, however, but much farther to the north by the side of the sea where the moonstone rose from the water. When he was there he used to sit on the beach and listen to the silence of the sea. But people did not understand him there and so he had to leave in search of a place where he would not be molested in his attempt to discover the language of silence.

And so Sunya Bai, the brother of silence, went to Tibet which is the best place in the world for silence. There he usually lives, conducting a silent dialogue with the snow-capped peaks of the Himalayas. Occasionally he comes to Delhi, but only when he thinks it necessary to start a special dialogue in silence with some special person about whom he has been told in the Himavat.

Perhaps that is why he came to see me. At any rate, he asked me not to talk and merely sat down in his Tibetan robe with his dog and listened to my silence. Soon he was conversing with my soul without my knowing it.

Finally he spoke and told me about himself. He said he was not interested in what human beings can say with words; he was only interested in their silence. "There are people who speak well," he said, "but they often have a very bad silence." He said it was the silence that mattered because it was a preparation for eternal silence.

Then he got up and went to the door. I ran after him and asked him his name. He turned round and said he was called Ernest, and then he went away. It is curious, but it was only then that I realized he was a man and not a woman. For a while I had believed that the strangely robed figure was an ancient woman. In fact, he really had no sex.

For a long time I wondered what we talked about in our silent dialogue. Many years have gone by since that first visit and I still have not found out. From time to time he returns quite unexpectedly and sits in a corner to listen to my silence. The last time he was with me he sat in the same place where the Queen of Sheba had sat, and then I realized that he had been talking about her all the time and that I had been asking him about her return. I looked up and noticed that Ernest was smiling.

Last night he came for the last time. He was alone and remained standing all the time he was with me. In his hand was a pilgrim's staff. He said he was traveling to Sikkim and that although he was seventy years old he felt he was seventy years young. He also told me that his dog had died. Of course he did not speak: I learned these things through his silence.

I then told him of my dog, the one I had met in the Antarctic.

He then replied that he felt sorry for people who did not realize that dogs were not really dogs. His own, he said, had told him he would be reincarnated in Sikkim and that was why he was going there to find him. He said he and his dog were complementary. "He will take the body of a dog so as to complete mine, and I will continue in this body of a youth of seventy in order to complete his. He does not see colors, and so I will help him with that. On the other hand, he sees God in scents and so far I can't do that. Anyhow, one thing we have in common is silence."

Now I see him far away in the mountains walking about and asking for his dog. He speaks to the tops of the trees and to the animals and birds that he meets. He is able to speak to them because he knows the language of silence.

"Have you seen my dog?" he asks, "a very small dog with long blond hair, or perhaps his hair is black."

"What is his name?" they reply.

"I believe," he answers, "that it is *Sulamite* or Young Fawn, and he must be grazing among the white lilies."

[At the end of *The Serpent of Paradise* is the chapter "The Void," complete in the hardcover but much edited in the softcover edition, without the ending of "From here on . . . ."]

Slowly I began to climb, and finally, in the midst of the high mountains, I found what I had been looking for for such a long time. And I found that everything was so simple, and so different from what I have been writing in this book. I was overwhelmed with the desire to explain it all, but at that very moment the Brother of Silence, Sunya Bhai, who is really the Void, appeared. He placed a finger on his lips and said, "Shh, shh! The end has come! From here on you will have to live in Silence."

Friends of Sunya: Letters at His Passing

Sunya's friend in Almora, M. D. Pant, who wrote "The Apostle of Silence, Peace and Compassion," sent this in part:

In 1970 I fell seriously ill and nervous. Utter despair gripped me. I fell prey to utter mental worries and anxieties and thought that I would soon die of the illness. Time and again Baba Sunyata visited me and sat for hours together by my bed and consoled me saying, "Worry is a waste. There is nothing to feel worried about. I hope you will soon recover from your illness." His affectionately gracious blessing ever smiled on me. I did recover from my illness after a few days. His compassionately kind looks, kind words and warm handshakes to me will ever remain unforgettable. The magnanimous soul has taken flight to his eternal Celestial home. We only cherish his pious memory—an unfailing source of perennial joy, inspiration and strength.

Lottie Rose wrote:

One day this rare teacher of enlightenment will again physically touch our earthly existence. We belong to his tribe. All those of us seeking light and goodness and an ego-free state, caring, awareness, service to others—in a graceful Wu dance of ecstasy and joy.

Rowena Pattee, artist and mystic:

Since Shunyata's death I have felt closer to him than ever and feel the immensity of his being. I feel now his spirit works from within me, within my heart and vibrating subtle body and I feel as if my whole body has been changed, transmuted by the iridescent healing beings. I dreamed of a White Buffalo (which are said to occur once in 10 million births) who had whimsical, blue-green human twinkling eyes which even winked at me. It dawned on me that the eyes were Sunyata's appearing to me as a pristine spirit. Thank you for your emptiness, Sri Nobody!

Betty Camhi:

One day I went to visit Shunya-Bhai when he lived in Mill Valley. I had parked my car in the carport and when we came outside I went to pull my car out. The angle was such that I needed to move the car about ¼ inch more in order to get out, but couldn't. When I told this to Shunya-Bhai he said, "Well, why don't we just lift it and move it." This a 3,000 pound giant-of-car! I felt his comment was something a three-year-old child might say and so I said to Shunyata, "We can't lift the car," as though I was talking to a small child.

Later that evening I thought about the incident and realized that really, I didn't know for certain the car couldn't be moved by us. When I saw Shunya-Bhai again, I apologized for my adult-like rational thinking behavior.

Namaste Shunya-Bhai.

Dedicated with Love to His Holiness.

Elliott Isenberg:

My most moving darshan with Sunya occurred when he had already left his body. I spent the day by his bedside. Although his body was barely being kept alive by oxygen, when I opened his eyelids, I realized that his "person" had already departed. Yet I could strongly feel his awareness hovering above and around the corpse. On some deeper level than was ever before possible, I "got" that who Sunyata is was not his body and that who he is is "always aware."

Jean Van Dilla:

I never experienced anything from him except peace, love, and joy. Toward the end of his life there seemed to be some physical tiredness and perhaps some vexation about all the "egojies" he was meeting. Thus this man with his ego, mind, and sex-free state of being and personality seemingly so balanced between the masculine and feminine has become for me the symbol in human form of the Second Coming of Christ.

Dr. Arvind Vasavada:

Sunya was a perfect Master of not judging. His mind was uncluttered with conditioning. He was free as a child, innocent as a child. I still hear his message, "All Is Well."

Neil Vanover:

It was not from his writings that I began to grasp him, appropriate him, even love him, though love was and is so difficult a word to use with a man whose means of affection was to wish you, 'Karuna Love,' objectless love, love with no lovers — it was from being around him and with him and listening to him and feeling his presence (or should I say, being absorbed by his non-presence?), that I at last could innerstand him as that hide-and-go-seeker, that spiritual playmate, who he called Wuji.

Barbara Cargill, who, like Neil, helped with Sunya's visits to Chicago:

Thank you Sunya for your presence in our lives — in you we could glimpse the potential within us all — in you we learned that we already knew — with you we played in the eternal expansively beautiful moment. In you we knew we were not the body, and not the mind, not our thoughts or our hang-ups or our guilt or our genetic inheritance. In you we knew the gift of peace and joy and playfulness is always present in the space between the chatter of our minds. Thank you Sunyabhai for your acceptance and your love. In the rare silence of my mind I know that you, like Wuji, have never really left.

John and Matthew Patterson:

I remember my dad announcing that a rare born mystic was coming to live with us. My mom, my brother and I were angered at having this stranger live with us. It wasn't that bad at all. Soon we got acquainted with Sunyata. He was kind and gentle.
John Patterson, age 12

In the morning, Sunya would have breakfast, and my mother would say, "Let me wash your pot. It is dirty." Sunya would say, 'No, no. It is not dirty," and Sunya and my mother would go on talking and then when they were done talking, Sunya would go on making breakfast. The pot was dirty but it didn't bother Sunya.
Matthew Patterson, age 10

Tom Fox, who met Sunya in 1979 when he was twenty-three years old:

I was told to see this wise man who had no ego. My roommate ran into Sunya. She said he came out of nowhere.

I can't believe what happened. Looking back, I see it as a strange fate, a tragic teaching emphasizing the importance of one's man life, one man's soul.

I believe I'll meet him again. I actually already have through lucid dreams. He did tell me, so I'll tell you, "You'll never die."

Appreciation

My mother told me I would meet my wife in church. As I didn't go to church I didn't take it seriously. But I was at church for a friend's wedding when before the service this beautiful woman walks down the aisle and the thought bullet hits me—"That's the girl you are going to marry!" I don't know if I was "Sweet William," but she was "Barbara Allen," and we did marry and have two sons, and this year marks our 50th anniversary.

When we met I had just started *In New York*, a small consumer magazine, and as she was a U.C. Berkeley English major, she was a big help with the editing and much more, and so too, beginning in 1992 with the publishing of my books, films and *The Gurdjieff Journal*.

Thank you, dear heart. It's been a long and wonderful ride.

Hitchhiking across U.S., 1971

Matthew, four, John, six, 1979

September 28, 2013, at John's wedding. Matthew's wedding the following year, October 4.

Index

A
Advaita 18, 61–62, 65, 97, 113, 145, 162, 182, 254
All & Everything 47, 63
ALL & Everything 189, 240
Almora 21, 53–55, 60, 109, 147–148, 173, 215, 220, 256, 257
Anandamayi 60–61, 104, 109
Anirvan, Sri 29–30, 59, 62–63, 211
Art of Asha, The 189–190

B
Barrett, Connor 107, 154–157
Book of the Damned, The 46, 239
Boss, Donna 10–11, 33, 48, 223
Bouwmeester, Albert 31–32, 124–125, 142
Broughton, James 37, 49, 121, 123
Brunton, Paul 55–56
Burch, Sharon 141

C
Camhi, Betty 14–15, 31, 70, 86, 87, 90, 139–140, 233, 261
Cheeke 8–10
Cheeke, G. M. 8–10, 15, 244–246
Consciousness-without-objects 14, 22, 25, 56–57, 74–75, 86, 90–91, 102, 111, 116, 135–136, 178–179, 229–231, 234, 240, 246–256
Crank's Ridge 21–24, 29, 30, 53–55, 60, 63–64, 216–217, 255

E
Eating The "I" xii–xiii, 47, 222–225, 230, 233, 235–236
Edwards, Emma 75, 126-127, 139–140, 151, 192–193, 195–196, 200–201, 207–209, 218
Être 158, 160, 164, 208–209

F
Fort, Charles 46, 72, 239
Fox, Tom 137, 141, 263

G
Gandhi, Indira 60, 173
Gandhi, Mahatma 53, 60, 158
geometric understanding 201–202, 240
Gnosis 222–223, 233
Govinda, Lama 14, 21, 38, 53, 63–64, 86–87, 92, 93, 96–97, 100
Grace 135
Gurdjieff Journal, The 192, 224, 265, 272

H
Hoyt, Don 13–14, 15, 32, 35, 37, 40, 42, 44, 69, 223

I
Industry Week vii, 15–18, 32, 36, 71, 82, 169, 203–204
In Search of the Miraculous 63, 222
Isaac 105–106, 113, 117, 128, 151
Isenberg, Elliot 233, 261

J
Justin 113–114, 117–118, 128, 138–141, 146

K
Kashmir Shaivism 95, 174–180, 185
Keeler, Bill 4, 11, 14–15, 18, 21, 26, 70, 80, 113

L

La Banda 217–218
Lilly, John 39–40, 121–122
Lilly, Toni 121–122
Listening 208–209
Lord Have Mercy xii, 32, 128, 206, 208, 209, 210–211, 222

M

Maharshi, Ramana xii, 27, 34, 39, 55–57, 60–62, 67, 104, 135, 147, 166–167, 250–251, 252, 257
Maithuna 43
Mataji 119–121
Michi 155–157
Mother 27, 32, 34, 36, 47, 71, 72, 121, 131, 146, 156, 163, 172, 184–185, 186–187, 196, 202–203, 226–227, 236–239

N

Nehru, Jawaharlal 59, 60
Nisargadatta 27, 49, 66–67, 89, 104, 250–251

P

Pacific Sun 10, 87–88, 90, 148
Pandiji 158, 185
Pant, M. D. 21, 259–260
Parabola 223–224
Pattee, Rowena 91, 100–101, 130, 260
Patterson, Barbara 6–7, 11, 12, 15, 28, 36, 44, 67, 68, 72, 75, 80, 94, 96, 128–129, 131, 136, 138, 151, 156, 158, 172, 200, 203, 208, 212, 225, 226, 230, 234, 241–242
Patterson, John 7, 10, 72, 80, 96, 134, 136, 138, 227, 263
Patterson, Matthew 7, 10, 72, 80, 96, 134, 136, 138, 227, 263
Pentland, Lady 33, 223
Pentland, Lord xii, 6, 8, 11, 12–13, 28, 33, 38–39, 42, 44–48, 75, 108, 128–130, 185–186, 189–191, 199–200, 206, 208, 210–211, 216, 222–223, 236, 239

Q

Queen of the Nile 88, 107

R

Reymond, Lizelle 62–63, 211
Rose, Lottie 31, 105, 106, 124, 131, 142, 172, 260

S

Serpent of Paradise, The 147–148, 259
Serrano, Miguel 59, 147–148, 222, 257–259
Shakti 22, 61–62, 161, 174–180, 175, 181, 251
Shapiro, Bob 21, 123
Sri Wuji Vols. I & II 173–174, 180
Sri Wuti 108–110
Stacy, Don 47, 76, 80, 105, 173–174

T

Tagore, Rabindranath 11, 51–53, 158, 243–244, 256–257
Telos 223–224, 239
To Live Within 62–63, 211

U

Uncle Bill 131, 203, 244
Uspenskii, P. D. 63, 222

V

Vanover, Neil 49, 108, 262
Vasavada, Dr Arvin 40–41, 79, 108, 132, 262
Visits of the Queen of Sheba, The 148, 257–259

W

Watts, Alan xii, 4, 21–22, 121
Who Am I?: The Sacred Quest 200

Y

Yoga Journal 223

Bibliography

Boone, James Allen. *Kinship with All Life*. New York: HarperCollins, 1954.

Chatterji, J. C. *Kashmir Shaivism*. Chandigarh, Kashmir: Galav Publications, 1981.

Camhi, Betty, and Gurubaksh Rai, eds. *Dancing with the Void*. San Diego, CA: Blue Dove Press, 2001.

Camhi, Betty, and Elliott Isenberg. *Sunyata: The Life and Sayings of a Rare-born Mystic*. Berkeley, CA: North Atlantic Books, 1990.

Devi, Mataji Shri Nirmala. *Sahaja Yoga*. New Delhi, India: Nirmala Yoga, 1982.

Douglas, Ed. *Sunyata: A Rare Born Mystic*. Handwritten, illustrated and self-published, Des Plaines, IL, June, 2003.

Doyle, Billy. *Yoga in the Kashmir Tradition: The Approach of Jean Klein*. Self-published. London.

Govinda, Lama. *The Inner Structure of the I Ching*. New York: Weatherhill, 1981.

Guénon, René. *The Symbolism of the Cross*. Hillsdale, NY: Sophia Perennis, 2004.
   The Crisis of the Modern World. London: Luzac and Company Ltd., 1975.
   The Reign of Quantity & the Signs of the Times. Hillsdale, NY: Sophia Perennis, 1995.

Gurdjieff, G. I. *All and Everything*. Aurora, OR: Two Rivers Press, 1993.

Klein, Jean. Emma Edwards, ed. *The Book of Listening, 1989–1995 Talks*. Oakland, CA: Non-Duality Press, 2008.

Klein, Jean. *Neither This Nor That I Am*. London: Watkins, 1981.
   The Ease of Being. Durham, NC: The Acorn Press, 1984.
   Who Am I?: The Sacred Quest. Longmead, England: Element Books Limited, 1988.
   I Am. Santa Barbara, CA: Third Millennium Publications, 1989.

  Open to the Unknown. Santa Barbara, CA: Third Millennium Publications, 1989.
  Transmission of the Flame. Santa Barbara, CA: Third Millennium Publications, 1994.
  Beyond Knowledge. Santa Barbara, CA: Third Millennium Publications, 1994.
  Living Truth. Santa Barbara, CA: Third Millennium Publications, 1995.
Klein, Nita. *Listening to Jean Klein*. Paris: Editions Almora, 2012.
Jee, Swami Lakshman. *Kashmir Shaivism; The Secret Supreme*. Albany, NY: Universal Shaiva Trust, 1988.
Maharshi, Ramana. *The Collected Works of Ramana Maharshi*, Arthur Osborne, editor. Boston, MA: Weiser Books, 1972.
Merrell-Wolff, Franklin. *The Philosophy of Consciousness Without an Object*. New York: Julian Press, 1973.
Mishra, Kamalakar. *Kashmir Saivism: The Central Philosophy of Tantrism*. Portland, OR: Rudra Press, 1993.
Omananda, Swami. *Towards the Mysteries*. London: Neville Spearman, 1968.
Nisargadattta. *I Am That*. Durham, NC: Acorn Press, 1973.
Ouspensky, P. D. *In Search of the Miraculous*. New York: Harcourt, Brace & World, Inc. 1949.
Padoux, André. *Vāc: The Concept of the Word in Selected Hindu Tantras*. Albany, NY: State University of New York Press, 1990.
Patterson, William Patrick. *Eating The "I."* Fairfax, CA: Arete Communications, 1992.
  —ed. *Sri Wuji: Nothing to Teach, Nothing to Sell: The Life of a Rare Born Mystic*, Vol. 1, No. 1, San Anselmo, CA: White Rose Press, 1985.
  —ed. *Sri Wuji: Brother of Silence*, Vol. 2, No. 1, San Anselmo, CA: White Rose Press, 1986.
Pentland, John. *Exchanges Within: Questions from Everyday Life*. New York: Continuum, 1997.
Rawlinson, Andrew, *The Book of Enlightened Masters*. Chicago, IL: Open Court, 1997.

Reymond, Lizelle. *To Live Within*. New York: Doubleday & Company, Inc. 1971.
Roberts, Bernadette. *The Experience of No-Self*. New York: Suny Press, 1982.
Serrano, Miguel. *The Serpent of Paradise*. London: Rider & Company, 1963.
— *The Visits of the Queen of Sheba*. London: Routledge & Kegan Paul, 1960.
Singh, Jaideva. *Divine Consciousness*. New Delhi: Motilal Banarsidass, 1981.
— *Spanda Karikas: The Divine Creative Pulsation*. New Delhi: Motilal Banarsidass, 1980.
Stacy, Don. *Drawing and Painting from Imagination: Utilizing Non-Classical Techniques*. New York: Stravon Educational Press, 1991.
Viveka-Chudamani. *Shankara's Crest-Jewel of Discrimination*. Swami Prabhavananda and Christopher Isherwood, trans. Hollywood, CA: Vedanta Press, 1947.

Acknowledgments

Henry and Mary Ellen Korman, and Teresa Adams have been with me almost from the beginning of publishing the books, films and *The Gurdjieff Journal*. The design, editing, proofing, researching—whatever is needed they have done and done well. The good Lord has allowed this last book of mine and theirs to be published, and so from my heart and head I say— *Thank you!!!*